March 2001.

FILE COPY

THE HOUSE OF HERVEY

A History of Tainted Talent

By the same author

Elgar: The Man
Denton Welch: The Making of a Writer
The Honours System
Acting as Friends: The Story of the Samaritans
Eddy: The Life of Edward Sackville-West
Michael Ramsey: A Portrait
Windsor Castle: Past and Present
Exploring Oxford
The Church of England: A Portrait
The Queen Behind the Throne
The King Who Never Was: The Story of Frederick, Prince of Wales
Mervyn Stockwood: A Lonely Life
Bedford School: A History

Sutton Pocket Biographies

Scott of the Antarctic
George IV

Edited

The Journals of Denton Welch
The Collected Short Writings of Denton Welch

THE HOUSE OF HERVEY

A History of Tainted Talent

Michael De-la-Noy

CONSTABLE • LONDON

Constable Publishers
3 The Lanchesters
162 Fulham Palace Road
London W6 9ER
www.constablerobinson.com

First published in the UK by Constable,
an imprint of Constable & Robinson Ltd 2001

A copy of the British Library Cataloguing in
Publication data is available from the British Library

ISBN 1–84119–309–7

Printed and bound in the EU

For
Anne and Nicolas Stacey
With much love

CONTENTS

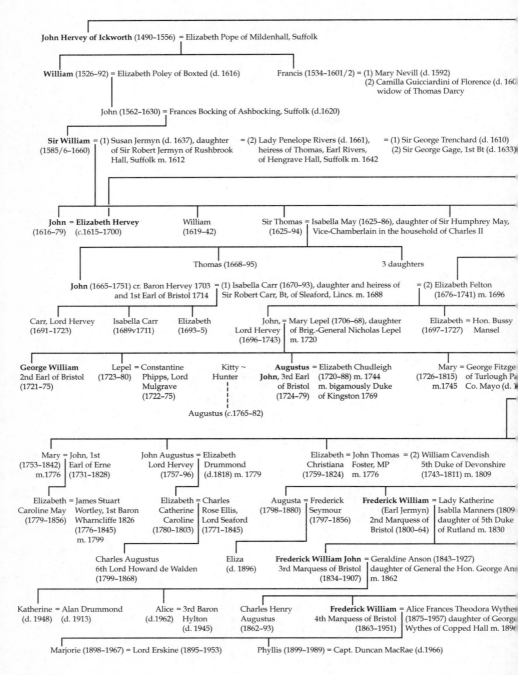

John Hervey of Thurleigh (d. 1475) = Joan Niernuyt (d. 1474)

Herveys of Thurleigh

John Hervey of Ickworth (1490–1556) = Elizabeth Pope of Mildenhall, Suffolk

William (1526–92) = Elizabeth Poley of Boxted (d. 1616)

Francis (1534–1601/2) = (1) Mary Nevill (d. 1592)
(2) Camilla Guicciardini of Florence (d. 160[...])
widow of Thomas Darcy

John (1562–1630) = Frances Bocking of Ashbocking, Suffolk (d.1620)

Sir William = (1) Susan Jermyn (d. 1637), daughter = (2) Lady Penelope Rivers (d. 1661), = (1) Sir George Trenchard (d. 1610)
(1585/6–1660)   of Sir Robert Jermyn of Rushbrook   heiress of Thomas, Earl Rivers,   (2) Sir George Gage, 1st Bt (d. 1633)
Hall, Suffolk m. 1612   of Hengrave Hall, Suffolk m. 1642

John = Elizabeth Hervey   William   Sir Thomas = Isabella May (1625–86), daughter of Sir Humphrey May,
(1616–79)   (c.1615–1700)   (1619–42)   (1625–94)   Vice-Chamberlain in the household of Charles II

Thomas (1668–95)   3 daughters

John (1665–1751) cr. Baron Hervey 1703 = (1) Isabella Carr (1670–93), daughter and heiress of = (2) Elizabeth Felton
and 1st Earl of Bristol 1714   Sir Robert Carr, Bt, of Sleaford, Lincs. m. 1688   (1676–1741) m. 1696

Carr, Lord Hervey   Isabella Carr   Elizabeth   John, = Mary Lepel (1706–68), daughter   Elizabeth = Hon. Bussy
(1691–1723)   (1689 v 1711)   (1693–5)   Lord Hervey   of Brig.-General Nicholas Lepel   (1697–1727)   Mansel
(1696–1743)   m. 1720

George William   Lepel = Constantine   Kitty ~   Augustus = Elizabeth Chudleigh   Mary = George Fitzge[...]
2nd Earl of Bristol   (1723–80)   Phipps, Lord   Hunter   John, 3rd Earl   (1720–88) m. 1744   (1726–1815)   of Turlough P[...]
(1721–75)   Mulgrave   of Bristol   m. bigamously Duke   m.1745   Co. Mayo (d. [...]
(1722–75)   (1724–79)   of Kingston 1769

Augustus (c.1765–82)

Mary = John, 1st   John Augustus = Elizabeth   Elizabeth = John Thomas = (2) William Cavendish
(1753–1842)   Earl of Erne   Lord Hervey   Drummond   Christiana   Foster, MP   5th Duke of Devonshire
m.1776   (1731–1828)   (1757–96)   (d.1818) m. 1779   (1759–1824)   m. 1776   (1743–1811) m. 1809

Elizabeth = James Stuart   Elizabeth = Charles   Augusta = Frederick   Frederick William = Lady Katherine
Caroline May   Wortley, 1st Baron   Catherine   Rose Ellis,   (1798–1880)   Seymour   (Earl Jermyn)   Isablla Manners (1809[...]
(1779–1856)   Wharncliffe 1826   Caroline   Lord Seaford   (1797–1856)   2nd Marquess of   daughter of 5th Duke
(1776–1845)   (1780–1803)   (1771–1845)   Bristol (1800–64)   of Rutland m. 1830
m. 1799

Charles Augustus   Eliza   Frederick William John = Geraldine Anson (1843–1927)
6th Lord Howard de Walden   (d. 1896)   3rd Marquess of Bristol   daughter of General the Hon. George An[...]
(1799–1868)   (1834–1907)   m. 1862

Katherine = Alan Drummond   Alice = 3rd Baron   Charles Henry   Frederick William = Alice Frances Theodora Wythe[...]
(d. 1948)   (d. 1913)   (d.1962)   Hylton   Augustus   4th Marquess of Bristol   (1875–1957) daughter of Georg[...]
(d. 1945)   (1862–93)   (1863–1951)   Wythes of Copped Hall m. 189[...]

Marjorie (1898–1967) = Lord Erskine (1895–1953)   Phyllis (1899–1989) = Capt. Duncan MacRae (d.1966)

Owners of Ickworth House are in **bold**

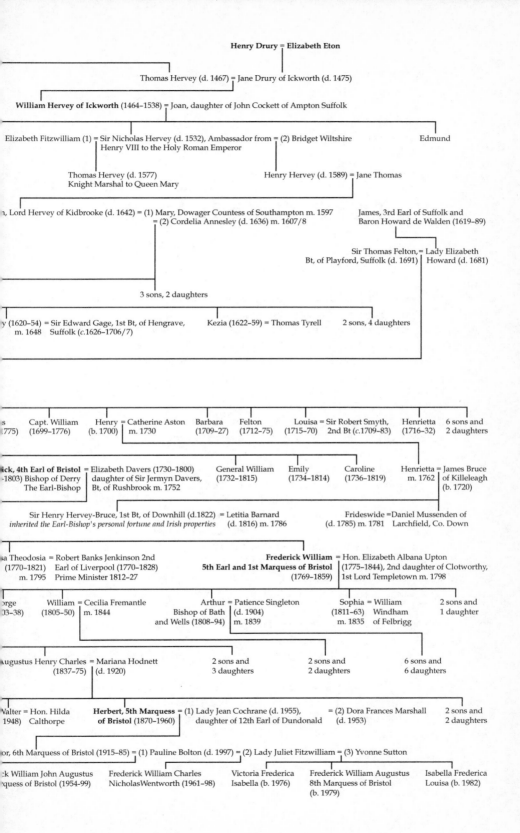

Henry Drury = **Elizabeth Eton**

Thomas Hervey (d. 1467) = Jane Drury of Ickworth (d. 1475)

William Hervey of Ickworth (1464–1538) = Joan, daughter of John Cockett of Ampton Suffolk

Elizabeth Fitzwilliam (1) = Sir Nicholas Hervey (d. 1532), Ambassador from = (2) Bridget Wiltshire   Edmund
Henry VIII to the Holy Roman Emperor

Thomas Hervey (d. 1577)   Henry Hervey (d. 1589) = Jane Thomas
Knight Marshal to Queen Mary

n, Lord Hervey of Kidbrooke (d. 1642) = (1) Mary, Dowager Countess of Southampton m. 1597   James, 3rd Earl of Suffolk and
= (2) Cordelia Annesley (d. 1636) m. 1607/8   Baron Howard de Walden (1619–89)

Sir Thomas Felton, = Lady Elizabeth
Bt, of Playford, Suffolk (d. 1691) | Howard (d. 1681)

3 sons, 2 daughters

y (1620–54) = Sir Edward Gage, 1st Bt, of Hengrave,   Kezia (1622–59) = Thomas Tyrell   2 sons, 4 daughters
m. 1648   Suffolk (c.1626–1706/7)

s   Capt. William   Henry = Catherine Aston   Barbara   Felton   Louisa = Sir Robert Smyth,   Henrietta   6 sons and
775)   (1699–1776)   (b. 1700) | m. 1730   (1709–27)   (1712–75)   (1715–70)   2nd Bt (c.1709–83)   (1716–32)   2 daughters

ick, 4th Earl of Bristol = Elizabeth Davers (1730–1800)   General William   Emily   Caroline   Henrietta = James Bruce
-1803) Bishop of Derry | daughter of Sir Jermyn Davers,   (1732–1815)   (1734–1814)   (1736–1819)   m. 1762 | of Killeleagh
The Earl-Bishop | Bt, of Rushbrook m. 1752   (b. 1720)

Sir Henry Hervey-Bruce, 1st Bt, of Downhill (d.1822) = Letitia Barnard   Frideswide = Daniel Mussenden of
inherited the Earl-Bishop's personal fortune and Irish properties   (d. 1816) m. 1786   (d. 1785) m. 1781   Larchfield, Co. Down

sa Theodosia = Robert Banks Jenkinson 2nd   **Frederick William** = Hon. Elizabeth Albana Upton
(1770–1821)   Earl of Liverpool (1770–1828)   **5th Earl and 1st Marquess of Bristol**   (1775–1844), 2nd daughter of Clotworthy,
m. 1795   Prime Minister 1812–27   (1769–1859)   1st Lord Templetown m. 1798

orge   William = Cecilia Fremantle   Arthur = Patience Singleton   Sophia = William   2 sons and
03–38)   (1805–50) | m. 1844   Bishop of Bath | (d. 1904)   (1811–63)   Windham   1 daughter
and Wells (1808–94) | m. 1839   m. 1835   of Felbrigg

ugustus Henry Charles = Mariana Hodnett   2 sons and   2 sons and   6 sons and
(1837–75) | (d. 1920)   3 daughters   2 daughters   6 daughters

Valter = Hon. Hilda   **Herbert, 5th Marquess** = (1) Lady Jean Cochrane (d. 1955),   = (2) Dora Frances Marshall   2 sons and
1948)   Calthorpe   **of Bristol (1870–1960)** | daughter of 12th Earl of Dundonald   (d. 1953)   2 daughters

or, 6th Marquess of Bristol (1915–85) = (1) Pauline Bolton (d. 1997) = (2) Lady Juliet Fitzwilliam = (3) Yvonne Sutton

:k William John Augustus   Frederick William Charles   Victoria Frederica   Frederick William Augustus   Isabella Frederica
rquess of Bristol (1954–99)   Nicholas Wentworth (1961–98)   Isabella (b. 1976)   8th Marquess of Bristol   Louisa (b. 1982)
    (b. 1979)

LIST OF ILLUSTRATIONS

AUTHOR'S NOTE

With so many characters bearing the same title (and so many the same Christian name; Johns, Williams, Augustuses and Fredericks abound in the Hervey family) there is an inevitable danger of confusion, but I have tried wherever possible to make it clear to which Lord Bristol or Lord Hervey I am referring. In any instance where the bearer of the courtesy title Lord Hervey is mentioned it may be taken that he is the eldest son of the current earl of Bristol (once the Herveys became marquesses the senior courtesy title became Earl Jermyn), and if no obvious connection exists between father and son then 'Lord Hervey' relates to *the* Lord Hervey of Ickworth, second son of the 1st earl of Bristol, father of the 2nd, 3rd and 4th earls, and author of the *Memoirs* of the reign of George II.

Quite deliberately, the narrative is not strictly chronological, for events in the lives of various members of the Hervey family overlap, and to have attempted, for example, to entwine the story of Lady Elizabeth Foster with that of her father the Earl-Bishop would have meant too many interruptions to the main thrust of each one's tale. Hence a character who has apparently died in one chapter may briefly reappear in another, but only because the narrative has of necessity slipped back in time.

Yvonne, Marchioness of Bristol, third wife and the widow of the 6th marquess and mother of the 8th, has kindly responded to a number of queries. The cooperation and hospitality extended by Lady Juliet Tadgell, at one time the second wife of the 6th marquess of Bristol and mother of the late Lord Nicholas Hervey, has been exceptionally generous. I am also immensely grateful to Mr George Lambton, a half-brother of the 7th marquess of Bristol, for his encouragement and help.

For personal memories, assistance with research and the loan of photographs I am also heavily indebted to the following: Mr David Adshead, Historic Buildings Representative at the National Trust; Mr Sebastian Beaumont; Mr Richard Bland, the archivist at Clifton College; Miss Jean Cook, the librarian at Tonbridge School; Mr Brian Cronan; Mr Donald Foreman, Secretary-General of the Monarchist League; Miss Rita Gibbs, the archivist at Harrow School; Mr Robert Harrison, archives officer at the House of Lords; Mrs Penelope Hatfield, the archivist at Eton College Library; Mr Richard Hill, Projects Manager for East Anglia at the National Trust; Miss Marianne MacDonald; Mr Tom Mayberry, assistant county archivist at Somerset County Council; Mr Peter Meadows, under-librarian at Cambridge University Library; Miss Holly Seager of the British Library; and Dr P J Thwaites, curator at the Royal Military Academy Sandhurst.

PRELUDE

'The man had become an exhibition. He sat in his stately dining room beneath his family portraits and he could not eat. He could hardly speak. An all-consuming misery underpinned his drug habit.' These were the observations of Jessica Berens, a visitor to Ickworth House in Suffolk, home of the Hervey family for six generations; she recorded them when, on 12 January 1999, she came to write an obituary for The *Independent* of Frederick William John Augustus Hervey,[1] 7th Marquess of Bristol, Hereditary High Steward of the Liberty of St Edmund, patron of thirty livings, Old Harrovian, Earl of Bristol, Earl Jermyn and Baron Hervey of Ickworth. 'At various times in his life,' Miss Berens recorded, in a summing-up both stark and sympathetic, 'he was estimated to be worth between £1 million and £30 million but, in the end, he was just a junkie – scabrous, pathetic, helpless, desperate – in and out of court, almost penniless, usually friendless.'

The Marquess himself believed he suffered from an hereditary depressive illness. When he was thirty-five, seeking scapegoats for his own disorientated behaviour and speaking four years after succeeding his father in 1985, he recalled that both his parents suffered from manic depression, which was in fact a very considerable distortion of the truth. He described his own affliction as making him feel as though he was 'in a sort of grey, rainy late afternoon' when 'nothing in the house has any features at all.'[2] By the time of his squalid death at the age of 44 an inveterate addiction to heroin and cocaine had reduced the shrewd mind of potentially one of the twentieth century's most original and talented businessmen to that of any homeless vagrant. His health was ruined, along with his dignity; his fortune squandered; his ancestral home and its priceless contents lost for ever to his heirs.

What had brought John Hervey, 7th Marquess of Bristol, in the eyes of many sober and hardworking modern men and women an all too disgraceful advertisement for a depraved and degenerate aristocracy, to such a catastrophic end? Were his problems, as he seemed to believe himself, hereditary and therefore beyond his control? Or were they in part environmental? If one considers the conduct of his father (in John's opinion 'semi-mad'), conduct which resulted in the thirteen-year-old heir to the Hervey titles being made a ward of court, the most probable explanation is six of one and half a dozen of the other. That many of John's ancestors were eccentric would be putting it politely; many were vicious too, promiscuous, bisexual, politically ambitious and often exceedingly clever. In this respect, John Bristol's background was not dissimilar to that of many landed and titled families. Although one seldom associates the Sackville-Wests of Knole with unbridled licentiousness or financial wrong-doing, one of the most talented twentieth-century members of that ancient family, Vita Sackville-West, felt moved to comment to her cousin Edward, when writing a history of the family,[3] 'They were a rotten lot, and nearly all stark staring mad. You and I have got a jolly sort of heredity to fight against.'[4]

We are all to some extent the victims, or at any rate products, of our heredity, so that environmental factors (the behaviour of one's parents, for instance) are often the result of inherited genetic traits, but it does seem clear that 'well-bred' families are more prone to wild and often irresponsible behaviour than are those of more plebeian stock. Perhaps they are simply faced with greater temptation, for wealth often brings with it the dubious luxury of leisure. Many a headstrong prank carried out by a thoughtless scion of a noble family has been the consequence of an inflated sense of his own importance allied to the lack of any sense of obligation towards others or a need to earn respect; until quite recent times respect from those they deemed their social inferiors was regarded by the aristocracy as a right of birth. The squire who seduces the servant girl, the drunken peer who horsewhips his stableboys are staple characters in racy romantic novels based on the swashbuckling world of Olde England. It takes some measure of maturity to shake off the trappings of privilege when suddenly egalitarianism is insisted upon in a society still so dominated by honours and snobbery as Britain's. The fact that individual members of many ennobled families have succeeded in so doing is greatly to their credit; that others have so far failed is not very surprising. Few have failed so spectacularly as the 7th Marquess of Bristol.

1

'THE MOST MAGNIFICENT ENTRY'

The land around Horringer, three miles south-west of the cathedral city of Bury St Edmunds, was home territory to the Hervey family long before they achieved either fame or notoriety. Ickworth Hall, the manor house outside Horringer, was acquired by a fifteenth-century ancestor, Thomas Hervey, when he married Jane Drury, whose property it was, and it was the rich Suffolk farming land that supplied the family with much of their wealth for generations to come. The town of Bury St Edmunds too (it was not until 1914 that Bury became a cathedral city for the newly constituted see of St Edmundsbury and Ipswich) provided the family with lines of communication to Westminster and the court, for it was in the Hervey family's pockets that the parliamentary seats for the borough of Bury St Edmunds were neatly tucked.

By the time John Hervey was born, on 27 August 1665, whose creation in 1703 as a baron and advancement eleven years later to an earldom would ensure the family's future social status, the estates had passed through a succession of William and

John Herveys, the 1st Lord Hervey's grandfather, William, receiving a knighthood, as did his father, Sir Thomas Hervey, MP. They could also boast minor but not unimpressive connections with the seat of government. John Hervey's maternal grandfather, Sir Humphrey May, had been vice-chamberlain to Charles II, and an uncle, John Hervey, had served as Treasurer to Queen Catherine, Charles II's wife. He was also MP for Hythe, and as a member of the Royal Household he was expected to vote in parliament according to the wishes of the king.

But Bishop Burnet tells us he one day failed in this duty, and was rebuked by the king. When, the following day, John Hervey voted in accordance with the king's wishes Charles said to him, 'You were not against me today.' 'No, Sir,' Hervey replied, 'I was against my conscience today.'[1]

There have been other families by the name of Hervey and one cannot be certain from which of these, if any, the Herveys of Suffolk were descended. Suffice to say it has always been an unusual name, and can be traced back at least to the eleventh century, when a Hervey or Hervacus served as bishop of Bangor and later as the first bishop of Ely. He was said to exhibit few spiritual qualities but a great gift for graft.

Not surprisingly, the John Hervey we need to concentrate upon, the future Earl, attended the excellent Bury Grammar School, and it was equally natural that he should have progressed to nearby Cambridge, where he was entered at Clare Hall. Having failed to take a degree, his academic nakedness was suitably covered up when the university conferred on him an honorary doctorate of law two years after his elevation to the peerage. At forty a contemporary described him as 'a great sportsman, lover of Horse-matches and ... a handsome man in his Person, fair complexion, middle stature.'[2] He was also musical and well read, astute and ambitious, and not averse, in 1688 when he was twenty-three, to securing financial independence from his father by marrying Isabella Carr, the only surviving child of a Lincolnshire landowner, baronet and Chancellor of the Duchy of Lancaster, Sir Robert Carr.[3] The following year a daughter was born, and in 1691 a son whom they named Carr after his wealthy grandfather.

In 1692 John Hervey was appointed a youthful deputy-lieutenant for Suffolk, and two years later he was returned to parliament in the Whig interest as a member for Bury St Edmunds. At a time when the sovereign was wildly partisan in favour of one political party or another (a situation that persisted well into the reign of Queen Victoria) it could be something of a gamble deciding which party to support, for vast swaths of patronage resided with the crown. If the monarch chose a Whig administration, there was little to be gained by being a Tory. On the other hand, in the eighteenth century the party political system was still in its infancy, and the historian Sir Lewis Namier has estimated that probably fewer than half the members of the House of Commons thought and acted in party terms.[4] The government tended to consist of those MPs who were prepared to support the sovereign's policies; the opposition were those who opposed the monarch.

In fact, however, John Hervey's genuine political convictions coincided with eighteenth-century Whiggery, which broadly speaking sought to limit the authority of the crown while increasing that of parliament. Since 1689, England had enjoyed the unique experiment of being ruled jointly by two monarchs, William III and Mary II, and as it was Mary who effectively reigned while her taciturn husband ruled, it mattered very little at this time which party English politicians supported, for William tended to favour his own Dutch countrymen anyway. It was to prove Hervey's good luck that the initial preference for

[7]

the Tories of William's sister-in-law Queen Anne, who came to the throne in 1702, was not to prove implacable, and that the Hanoverians, from the moment of their landing in 1714, were greatly enamoured of the Whigs.

It can be a great oversimplification to equate eighteenth-century Tories with the twenty-first-century Conservative Party, or eighteenth-century Whigs with twentieth-century Liberals (whose party was not even founded until 1828), especially when one bears in mind that both George I and George II were Whigs, or at any rate chose Whigs for their ministers. They did so simply because they felt more confident of support from the Whigs than the Tories, whose opposition to the Hanoverian succession throughout the reign of Queen Anne had hastened their eclipse. Neither monarch had a liberal sentiment in his body as we would understand such sentiments today. It is true that Dissension and Whiggery tended to run hand in hand, but those Whigs like John Hervey who did the bidding of George I were profoundly conservative in outlook and temperament. Unlike the Tories, who were hopelessly divided in their loyalties, the Whigs had supported the Hanoverian succession almost unanimously, and when Queen Anne died they were bound to reap their reward. Most of the wealthiest peers were Whigs; peers were almost invariably given ministerial office (Sir Robert Walpole, England's first prime minister, was to be an extraordinary exception); by and large it was Whigs who ran the country's commerce and banking; and although Tories formed a majority in the country for perhaps the first half of the eighteenth century, the Whigs were regarded as forming some kind of establishment party.

In 1693, after a mere five years of marriage, John Hervey's wife Isabella died giving birth to a second girl. Two years later he married again, alighting once more upon an heiress, Elizabeth

Felton, whose father, Thomas Felton, was a polished courtier and the heir to a baronetcy. Elizabeth's mother, Lady Elizabeth Howard before her marriage, was equally well connected; her father was Earl of Suffolk. John Hervey was by now well on his way to serious prosperity, and by the time he had inherited his father's estate a year after making his second marriage he was worth £2,000 a year.

It has been suggested that John Hervey married a second time 'for the purpose, among others, of begetting sons,'[5] which would have been a reasonable attitude for him to take, bearing in mind the high level of infant mortality and the fact that by his first marriage he had only one son, Carr, still only four years old. But he could never have imagined that eleven of Elizabeth's children would survive into adulthood. In April 1696, Elizabeth, not surprised to find herself already some three months pregnant, told her husband, 'our young unknown frind is as well as can be, considering his uneasy habitasion.' The 'young frind', their first child and oldest son, was to turn out a semi-invalid and a master of invective, bisexual, witty, brave and a brilliant recorder of the court of George II – in every way a worthy forerunner of a bevy of Herveys, many of whose exploits it would be difficult for a novelist to conjure up.

From the moment of his birth, John Hervey junior enjoyed the ministrations of a doting father. He was born on 15 October 1696 in a rented house in Jermyn Street, London, after Elizabeth had endured a seventeen-hour 'painful perillous' labour. But clearly he seemed healthy enough at the time, for instead of being whisked straight to the font as sickly infants often were, ten days elapsed before he was baptized, at the parish church of St James's, Piccadilly. As an auspicious start to his life, one of his godmothers was a duchess. Less in keeping with his future ill-health and effeminacy was his father's decision to call him Jack

– for Jack somehow betokens a strapping country lad. If Jack's decidedly ambiguous development was a disappointment to his father, he never for one recorded instance showed it, nor ever doubted the abilities of his first-born son by his second wife.

In 1697 Elizabeth gave birth to a girl, named after herself, and the following year the family moved from Jermyn Street to 6 St James's Square, renting it initially from the widow of John's uncle and namesake John Hervey, who had acquired the property in 1677. On the death of his aunt Elizabeth in 1700 John Hervey purchased the house, insuring it for £5,000, which gives some idea of the imposing style in which the future Lord Hervey felt it important that he should live. No. 6 St James's Square was to remain the family's London home until 1955, and could not have been more conveniently situated for the Houses of Parliament.

It was the Upper House of Parliament that John Hervey was eager to enter, and by 1702 his thoughts were turning towards the construction of a country seat suitable for a peer. In theory he already possessed one, Ickworth Hall, a fairly substantial Tudor manor house standing just to the east of Ickworth Church on the site of an earlier house dating from the thirteenth century. Unfortunately Ickworth Hall had been allowed to fall into a state of disrepair, a succession of tenants having, by 1700, 'suffered the seat of the family to run into such ruine and decay that daily the tiles, sometimes by loads, fall off the Mansion-house, whereby the timber-roofs have lain so exposed to the sun and rain that they being rotten fall down, and have destroyed the planchard floors, which now in some places lie upon one another.'

John Hervey reckoned that any attempt to try to restore the old Hall to a habitable state was too much of a daunting task, so he turned his attention instead to renovating and extending a farmhouse, Ickworth Lodge, about half a mile away, and until 1828 the Lodge remained the Hervey family's Suffolk residence. Determined to supervise the work himself, John travelled to Suffolk in the spring of 1702, taking the five-year-old Jack with him. The work must have been swiftly undertaken for by the autumn both parents, twenty servants and seven children (Isabella and Carr from Hervey's first marriage; Jack; Elizabeth; Thomas, born in 1698; William, who arrived a year later; and Henry, born in 1701) were installed.

Soon the farm was stocked with cattle and sheep, but it was another four years before Hervey was able to reintroduce deer to a thirteenth-century deer park that had long since disappeared. This involved rehousing tenants in the village of Horringer and planting new protective groves. By 1731 the architect Thomas Robinson was exclaiming that the park at Ickworth was 'by much the finest park I ever yet saw, being about 1,200 acres and above 25,000 pounds of exceeding fine timber.' The Lodge, on the other hand, Sir Thomas thought 'so very bad a habitation that I am astonished how so large a family have so long made a shift in it.' For a brief moment John Hervey had considered more grandiose plans, perhaps having heard rumours of a peerage; he discussed with John Vanbrugh the possibility of the newly fashionable architect designing a country seat to replace Ickworth Lodge. It is more than likely that Sir John explained that buildings on the scale of Castle Howard in Yorkshire, begun by him in 1700, did not come cheaply, and that he tended to think only on the very grandest scale. Indeed, in 1705, in collaboration with Nicholas Hawksmoor, he was to furnish the Duke of Marlborough with Blenheim Palace. On mature reflection, Hervey decided to make do with his farmhouse, which became an E-shaped building with an eight-bay central block flanked by projecting wings, the whole edifice being decorated with mock battlements.

In 1702, the year that saw the start of renovations on the farmhouse, William III died and Queen Anne, younger daughter of James II and the last member of the House of Stuart to reign, came to the throne. In the words of her biographer Edward Gregg, 'After her first parliament was prorogued on 27 February 1703 the queen had overcome her reluctance to create new peers in order to give the Tories a working majority in the House of Lords.'[6] The Marquess of Normanby became Duke of Buckinghamshire (a title now extinct) and a Tory earldom and three Tory baronies were created. Writing to Hervey on 9 May 1702 his wife had remarked, 'We mett last night at Court, which was full of nothing but Sey[mours], it was the sadest drawing room that ever was seen.' Queen Anne's drawing rooms were renowned for their dullness at the best of times; what is interesting is that even before Hervey had pulled off his longed-for peerage, his wife was being received at court, despite her being a Whig. Her reference to Seymours was to Francis Seymour-Conway, one of the Tories ennobled the following year.

Fortunately the influential Duchess of Marlborough, until her falling out with the Queen her most intimate friend, was a friend also of Hervey's father-in-law, now Sir Thomas Felton, to whom she had promised to do what she could for Hervey. As Sarah Marlborough was herself a Whig she saw it as both a duty and a pleasure to press upon the Queen the desirability of evening up numbers somewhat by appointing a Whig peer in addition to four Tories. Who more suitable than John Hervey? Once Sarah had enrolled the cooperation of her husband besides that of Lord Godolphin, Anne's newly appointed Lord Treasurer and confidential adviser, it was game, set and match. In her memoirs, written when she was an old lady, the Duchess was able to record, 'Mr Hervey had laid aside all hopes of the peerage, and was therefore surprised to the last degree when a message came to him from the duke of Marlborough that he must come on such a day by the back stairs to kiss the Queen's hand on being made a peer.'

It was as Lord Hervey of Ickworth that John Hervey was introduced into the House of Lords on 22 June 1703, having chosen as his motto, doubtless bearing in mind his obligations to the Duchess, *Je n'oublierai jamais* – I shall never forget. Five years later his father-in-law received his own reward, being appointed Comptroller of the Queen's Household, a post worth £1,200 a year. When he died a few months later it was not surprising that Jack (since 1703 the Hon John Hervey), now an attractive twelve-year-old, accompanied his father behind the hearse on its melancholy trudge from London into Suffolk, for Sir Thomas Felton had bequeathed to his eldest grandson his entire estate save for his art collection – and that went to Jack's father.

But even without such a windfall to celebrate it is perfectly conceivable that Jack would have been the favoured son to represent his siblings at his grandfather's funeral. Both his parents were for some reason – perhaps because of his engaging personality and cherubic looks – devoted to him. He was seldom out of their company. His half-brother Carr had inherited an estate from his short-lived mother, and to Aswarby Jack had gone on a six-week visit in 1705 with his parents and four brothers and sisters. But the following year he was at Aswarby alone with his parents and, aged just nine, he was the same year invited to dine at Chatsworth. This was merely a preliminary to visits to the Archbishop of York and the Earl of Carlisle, now comfortably ensconced at Castle Howard. Such an itinerary would not have been countenanced by Lord and Lady Hervey had they not believed that Jack would behave with decorum and also benefit from meeting such influential magnates and from viewing such a wealth of paintings, china, furniture and architecture; and it was a striking feature of Jack Hervey's later career at the court of George II that although not himself endowed with great wealth or a glorious house he took regal magnificence in his stride.

Jack was a quick-witted and precocious child. He mastered French when very young, largely thanks to the ministrations of a Huguenot tutor; another Frenchman, who doubtless conversed in French, taught him dancing. And yet a third Frenchman was engaged by Lord Hervey as chaplain. By the age of twelve Jack was fluent, a fact his father found hard to believe, casting unwarranted aspersions on a letter in French his son sent him from Newmarket. It was entirely his own work, Jack assured Lady Hervey, but Lord Hervey was not so sure. 'I wish the orthography, as well as the sense of it, were all his own,' he commented to his wife.

It may have been because Jack's academic abilities had outstripped the level of education Bury Grammar School could offer that in January 1712, when he was fifteen, he was dispatched to London in charge of three younger brothers and entrusted with the school fees for all four of them. Their destination was Westminster, refounded by Queen Elizabeth in 1560 and now thriving under the benign influence of a scholarly headmaster, Dr Robert Freind. The Hervey boys were spared the worst rigours of eighteenth-century public school boarding, for they were lodged, together with other sons of the nobility, in a house adjoining the school, in the care of a dame who acted as matron. But in common with all public school boys at the time, their curriculum consisted solely of a diet of the classics, for it was a working knowledge of Homer and Virgil that would ensure entrance to one or other of the English universities.

For all his foppish conduct in later life (he is said to have been the first person to take a daily bath) there is early evidence that Jack Hervey never lacked courage. His father owned a racing stable at Newmarket, and one of Jack's boyhood delights was to ride on the course whenever he could. To his mother's consternation, in 1713 Jack announced his determination to race a colt called Union, and only a promise to his wife to make sure the boy did not risk life and limb prevented Lord Hervey from allowing Jack to have his own way. Jack's 'working brain coynd & urgd a hundred Jesuitisms in order to evade your request to me at parting,' Lady Hervey was informed. But 'no part of his persuasion,' she would have been relieved to discover, '(which did not want for rhetorick neither) could ever shake ye firm resolves I had taken to gratify your (give me leave to call it) weakness for this once, since it tends to nothing but effeminacy, the very worst of education.' And he went on to warn his wife that Jack's 'age, strength & stature is now at such a crisis that you must determine to be content to see him live a shrimp or risque something to inable him to commence man. I'm of council for ye latter.'

We shall never know whether Jack would have come to harm had he been allowed, as his father would have wished, to ride the frisky Union, but to 'ye mortification ... to us both,' Hervey reported to his wife, the colt romped home with another rider on its back to beat the Duke of Rutland's colt and to win a purse of £500. Jack loved Newmarket, was unsparing in his advice to his father's jockeys, and kept careful accounts of his bets. But a few months after Union's triumph Lord Hervey decided to close down his stable, and with an eye to the main chance – for by now the accession of the Elector of Hanover to the English throne was becoming daily more of a certainty (Queen Anne had lost eighteen children and for many years had been in appallingly bad health) – he had the brainwave of offering some of his horses to Georg Ludwig, the Elector. While enjoying the traditional Grand Tour (not so called until 1760 but in vogue since the middle of the seventeenth century) Hervey's eldest son, Carr, now twenty-two, just happened to be in Hanover, and Lord Hervey's plan was to send Jack to Hanover with the horses if Carr reported back that they had been accepted. Unfortunately, Jack's exploration of Hanover had to be put on ice, for the Elector declined the equine gift. This threw Hervey into something of a panic, and he told Carr to remind the Elector that he had always been 'a most constant, zealous promoter in every measure that originally introduced or could since any way strengthen ye security of [the Hanoverian] succession; whereon everything that's precious to a free, Protestant people entirely depends.'

The eventual accession of the House of Hanover had been assured by the Act of Settlement of 1701, passed while John Hervey was an MP for Bury, and as a staunch Whig he would undoubtedly have been averse to the throne descending to Prince James, the exiled Catholic son of James II known to history as the Old Pretender. But there had always remained strong sympathy in England for the Stuart cause, there was no guarantee the Hanoverian succession would prove a smooth fait accompli, and Hervey was anxious to ingratiate himself with the future King George from whom, once Queen Anne was dead, he hoped he might receive more valuable patronage.

There was never any doubt to which university or college Jack's steps would be directed. In November 1713, shortly after his seventeenth birthday, he was accompanied by both his parents to Cambridge, where he was enrolled in his father's old college, Clare Hall, one of the very few Cambridge colleges at that time with any sort of reputation for learning. It contained a reasonable library and a tutor, Richard Laughton, who could actually speak French. Initially, Jack came under the tutelage also of a Fellow of Clare since 1704, the Reverend Thomas Seaton, but without even giving notice Seaton abandoned his undergraduates in July 1714. Jack's father saw this as a personal affront, and in a fury he wrote to Seaton to complain of his 'abrupt departure from my service, joyned to a small signification (it seems) you have been of to my son, either in his studies or other attendance on him.'

It was not only Jack's academic progress that worried Lord Hervey. He became a fusspot too with regard to his son's social and moral development. 'Example is so infectious,' he wrote to him, 'that our first and chiefest care should be to find out & frequent men of ye most sober & virtuous conversation, since we insensibly fall into ye imitation of ye manners of ye company we consort with, and gradually become ye very men whose images at first frighted us.' (John Hervey belonged to the last generation, as did Queen Anne, almost habitually to use the word ye; his children would not have dreamed of doing so.) Lord Hervey might have been truly frightened had he realized what progressive influences were alive in Cambridge at the time, for in addition to his continued study of Greek and Latin, Jack was immersing himself in unorthodox religious ideas and in the dangerous study of science – science being held to be the very antithesis of religion. Philosophy, history and even algebra were also on Jack's syllabus.

Queen Anne died, aged forty-nine, on 1 August 1714. The news reached Herrenhausen, principal home of the Electors of Hanover, on 5 August, and with domestic and political matters to attend to it was not until the last day of August that Georg Ludwig, a great-grandson of James I and Elector of Hanover since 1698, accompanied by his son and heir Georg August, the Electoral

Prince and later George II, began his leisurely journey (he lingered in The Hague for a fortnight) to take possession of the English crown. He was accompanied by two of his grotesque German mistresses and eighteen cooks, and did not enter his new capital until 18 September, landing that day at Greenwich. Among those who had scrambled to the south bank of the Thames to welcome England's new Hanoverian sovereign was Lord Hervey. That evening a jubilant Hervey wrote in his diary, 'King George & ye Prince of Wales arrived at Greenwich about 6 in ye evening; where I had ye honour to kiss both their hands.'[7]

Hervey was a little previous in dubbing the Electoral Prince Prince of Wales; it was not until his second day in residence at St James's Palace, at a meeting of the Privy Council, that the King invested his 'most dear son, a prince whose eminent filial piety hath always endeared him to us,' as Prince of Wales. Someone else quick off the mark was Carr Hervey, who within a week of the arrival of the Hanoverians sent what has been described as an obsequious letter, in French, to the new Prince of Wales asking for a position in his Household.[8] He became a Groom of the Bedchamber. The reason Carr wrote to the Prince in French was quite simply because the King spoke no English, the Prince at this time very little, and Carr spoke no German. It has always been alleged that Walpole discussed business with George I in Latin. A lack of the English language did not mean, however, that King George was ignorant of English political affairs. He had been primed by his private secretary, Jean de Robethon, a Huguenot refugee formerly in the employ of William III, and many of the presentations of total strangers such as Lord Hervey had been effected at Greenwich by the Earl of Dorset, a Gentleman of the Bedchamber, rewarded in 1720 with a dukedom. It came as no surprise to anyone, least of all himself, that Viscount Bolingbroke, an ardent Jacobite whom

Queen Anne had dismissed as Lord Treasurer as she lay dying, was not received, and neither were all but a handful of Tories – for with plenty of time to ponder future plans before he even succeeded to the throne, King George had already decided to dispense almost all his favours among the Whigs.[9] George actually hated the Tories, for he believed that by the terms of the Peace of Utrecht, negotiated in 1713, they had deserted Hanover, and throughout his reign he was gratified to find the Tories seemingly condemned to permanent opposition. In 1715, 217 Tories were returned to parliament against 341 Whigs; the situation seven years later was 178 Tories to 379 Whigs.

It had been at the Queen's House in Greenwich, the elegant residence commissioned from Inigo Jones by James I and completed for the wife of Charles I, that Lord Hervey first paid court to his new sovereign, and the scene of the King's arrival was to be commemorated by Sir James Thornhill in a painted ceiling at the hospital. On a visit to Hanover in 1719 Thornhill took the opportunity of sketching the King's nine-year-old grandson, Prince Frederick, who had been abandoned by his parents at Herrenhausen, so that he could include his likeness in the work; Prince Frederick and Jack Hervey were to become, for a short time, very close friends. And it was to St James's Palace, the metropolitan home of the sovereign since a fire in 1698 had destroyed most of the Palace of Westminster, that John Hervey hurried ahead of the King in order to witness his arrival. It was, he thought, the 'most magnificent entry that ever was seen,' King George and the Electoral Prince being seated in a glass coach, the King occasionally condescending to bow but not to smile, the Prince having been told to smile but not to bow. They both unbent somewhat two days later when the *Weekly Journal* reported that 'His Majesty and the Prince were graciously pleased to expose themselves for some time at the windows of their palace to satisfy the impatient curiosity of the King's loving subjects.'

There was no queen consort to share in these junketings, King George having divorced his wife, Sophia Dorothea of Lüneburg-Celle, in 1694 on the grounds of her adultery with a reckless Swedish nobleman. Nor was there as yet a Princess of Wales to be quizzed, for Caroline of Brandenburg-Ansbach, destined to become a generous and confidential friend to Jack, was still on her way to England. She eventually landed at Margate on 15 October accompanied by her daughters Anne and Amelia, with just five days to spare before the coronation, 'at which solemnity,' Lord Hervey noted in his diary, 'I walked in ye procession as Earle of Bristol.'[10] As his earldom was gazetted just twenty-four hours before the coronation, he presumably had to borrow the appropriate robes and coronet.

Clearly Hervey's protestations of loyalty had paid off, but there is no evidence to suggest that the King really had a clue who he was. It was customary for peerages to be created and knighthoods bestowed to celebrate a coronation, and no doubt Hervey's parliamentary colleagues thought his unshakable Whig credentials, so valuable at what was still an uncertain time for those who wished to uphold the Act of Settlement, deserved recognition by an advance in the peerage; hence his name was duly recommended to the King. There had been a previous earldom of Bristol, created in 1622 by James I for John Digby, who had held his newly created barony for only four years. James had taken a fancy to Digby when he was a young man, appointed him a gentleman of the privy chamber, and knighted him in 1607 when he was twenty-seven – an honour for which Digby may well have had to pay, and not only by sleeping with the King, whose homosexuality was notorious.

Between 1605 and 1609 an average of 74 knighthoods were sold every year, the King receiving £60 for every ceremony. Within four months of inheriting the throne of England on the death of Elizabeth, King James had created 906 knights; one morning, while staying at Belvoir Castle, he dubbed 46 knights before breakfast. To mark his coronation, another 432 new knights emerged from the woodwork. As an honour, Digby's knighthood was virtually worthless. After protracted discussions in Madrid, where he was first sent as ambassador in 1611, it was John Digby who eventually negotiated the marriage of the future Charles I. In 1616 he became vice-chamberlain to the Household and a privy counsellor and was granted an estate at Sherborne, but unfortunately Digby made a sworn enemy of the 1st Duke of Buckingham, with whom Charles I was as besotted as his father had been, and in 1626, and again in 1642, he was imprisoned in the Tower. He was finally sent into exile and died in Paris in 1653.

The 2nd Earl of Bristol, George Digby, who lived from 1612 to 1677, appeared at the bar of the House of Commons as a boy with a petition from his father. He was a brilliant scholar but unstable, became involved in a brawl at court and, like his father, was sent to prison. In 1641 he was called to the House of Lords in his father's courtesy title of Baron Digby, dared to make a speech against the attainting of Charles I's scapegoat the Earl of Strafford, fled to Holland and was himself impeached for high treason. Yet he fought with great courage for the King at Edgehill and was appointed a secretary of state. In 1653 he was given the Garter by Charles II, took part in the war of the Fronde, disgraced himself by becoming a Roman Catholic, and finally returned to live and die in the former Chelsea home of Sir Thomas More. When his son John, the 3rd Lord Bristol, died in 1698 the earldom became extinct.[11]

2

———•—•—•———

MAMA'S TEARS AND FEARS

Why the defunct Bristol title was revived for John Hervey is a bit of a mystery. There were no family connections with the previous holders of the peerage or the Avon port, but the ancient city of Bristol (the diocese of Bristol had been established in 1542), along with London and Westminster, was considered one of the most prestigious parliamentary areas. It has been suggested that Hervey wanted to flatter King George by replacing a previous Tory earl of Bristol with one who was a Whig, but this seems a little far-fetched; if it is true, as Jack Hervey's biographer alleges, that Hervey was offered a choice of eleven extinct titles, the chances seem to be that he simply alighted on one that took his fancy.[1] John's new peerage made no difference at this stage to Jack's status but his half-brother Carr now assumed Lord Bristol's courtesy title and became Lord Hervey while his sisters were now Lady Elizabeth Hervey, Lady Ann Hervey and Lady Barbara Hervey. Louisa and Henrietta were not born until 1715 and 1716 respectively. It is perhaps worth recalling Lady Bristol's amazing series of pregnancies. Having married at nineteen, she endured her last pregnancy when she was thirty-nine, and between those ages she bore twenty children. Beginning in 1696 with Jack, she produced ten adult sons and six adult daughters, losing triplets in 1701 and a stillborn son in 1704. In 1703 she had twins. Between 1706 and 1710 she was pregnant five times.

On 1 November 1714 the King deigned to have supper with the new Earl and Countess of Bristol. Such a mark of distinction served to whet Elizabeth Bristol's already considerable appetite for life at court, but with only a Princess of Wales with Household appointments to fill, a good many women of appropriate social status who might have expected to be taken into service by a queen consort were inevitably frustrated in their ambitions. Among them was Lady Bristol, who confided to Countess Cowper, wife of the Lord Chancellor, that she wanted to be a Lady of the Bedchamber to Princess Caroline. If she imagined that Lady Cowper was going to put in a good word for her, she was in for a shock. Four days after the coronation, during the course of which Lady Bristol had rashly spoken of her hopes, it was Lady Cowper who received the summons to kiss hands on her appointment as a lady-in-waiting.

Lady Bristol's behaviour was not very sagacious, and certainly not designed to make friends of the established nobility or to win the confidence of the Princess of Wales. When the Duchess of Shrewsbury, born Italian but long since naturalized, was made a Lady of the Bedchamber, Lady Bristol threatened to have the appointment challenged in the House of Commons. Perhaps not realizing that the most senior appointment in the Princess's Household, that of Mistress of the Robes, would normally go to a duchess, she then schemed, without success, to obtain the post. But the royal family do not seem to have borne her any ill will. When in March 1715 she gave birth to her fourth daughter, the King and Princess Caroline stood as god-parents. But she certainly had an odd notion of how to repay this generous gesture of royal favour, now going out of her way to cultivate the friendship of the King's German mistresses, known to Londoners as the Elephant and Castle. Both of them were up to their overmade-up eyebrows in bribery and both of whom were cordially disliked by the Prince and Princess of Wales.

Poor Elizabeth Bristol's hopes of a royal appointment might well have been finally dashed by her husband. A general elec-tion, at this time, was held every three years, and the next was due in 1718. Rather than face the expense of elections so soon, not to mention the distinct possibility of a Tory majority being brought in on the strength of the King's unpopularity, the Whigs decided to ensure they remained in office until at least 1722 by the neat expedient of proposing a Septennial Bill. Bris-tol was horrified, particularly as it was intended to introduce such an important measure in the House of Lords before the Commons. His Whig principles were affronted by the Bill itself, but he told his wife he could not 'possibly beleive that a Bill which so nearly concerns the privileges of all the people shoud be first meddled with by the Peers,' and he continued to tarry in Newmarket, whence Lady Bristol had attempted to have him return to London. Hence he missed the Bill's first reading in the Lords.

So vital to the Whig interest did the Princess of Wales believe the Bill to be that she attended the second reading, which really meant she wanted to keep an eye on supporters and opponents. By this time Lord Bristol had returned to town, and he and twenty-three other peers signed a protest, giving their reasons for opposing the Bill. Needless to say, no notice was taken of

[25]

their objections, and the Bill was passed in the Lords by 69 votes to 36, and in the Commons by 264 to 121. The Princess of Wales told Lady Bristol that since her husband had left the court to join the Tories 'he should leave them for ever'. If 'voting for the ancient laws and liberties of England' meant leaving the court, Lady Bristol retorted, 'you may depend upon it he *has* left the court for ever.' So partisan was the royal family that at the next Drawing Room the princess cut Lord Bristol dead. And yet, in 1718, by now convinced of the Bristols' loyalty to the heir to the throne and his wife rather than to the king, Caroline relented, appointing Lady Bristol a Lady of the Bedchamber at the useful salary of £500 a year, a post she held until Caroline's death in 1737.

Having left Cambridge at the end of 1715 Jack Hervey had been free to witness the controversial parliamentary events of April 1716, and could hardly have imagined in what favour with Princess Caroline he would one day find himself. In June he set out for Paris, on the first stage of the Grand Tour, sadly truncated in the event – a Tour that was to result in a meeting in Hanover with Prince Frederick. On 4 June Lord Bristol recorded in his diary: 'Munday, dear Jack sett out from London towards Paris, in order to farther his travels; wherin I beseech God Almighty to protect & perfect him ye man I wish to see him.' (Bristol's mode of speech retained, all his life, the hallmarks of a country squire; not for him the polished literary style of his sophisticated son Jack and his contemporaries.) Many young men were told to visit provincial towns rather than fall prey to the temptations, supposed or real, of Paris; the reason Jack was sent straight to the French capital was because his mother had asked him to purchase for her some expensive clothes to wear at the Prince of Wales's birthday ball, due to be held on 30 October.[2]

There was another and more important divergence from the norm in Jack's itinerary. His father really did not care very much if he failed to gaze upon the architectural ruins in Rome, for there was a political motive attached to Jack's tour. Instead of heading south for Italy he was under instructions to proceed eastwards through Flanders, for his true objective was Hanover, and the seat of the Electorate, Herrenhausen, because there resided the second heir to the throne, Prince Frederick. Left behind in the charge of a great-uncle when his grandfather became King of England, Frederick was an object of curiosity to visitors from England like Lady Mary Wortley Montagu, who had a long private conversation with the nine-year-old boy, and reported to Lady Bristol that he had 'all the accomplishments which it is possible to have at his age, with an air of sprightliness and understanding, and something so very engaging and easy in his behaviour that he needs not the advantage of his rank to appear charming.'

In point of fact, Frederick, due in adulthood to become a dutiful husband and devoted father, the first civilized Hanoverian, was at this stage in danger of becoming a spoilt little brat. He already had his own gentlemen of the bedchamber, fencing and dancing masters, doctors and fiddlers. Waited on by footmen serving meals prepared by a dozen cooks, Frederick could call at any time on the services of innumerable coachmen and postilions, and he had already discovered the pleasures of drink and cards. Without parental discipline or even the company of his sisters he had taken to dressing up and holding levees, and in July 1716 his indulgent grandfather had made sure he possessed some suitable bauble to wear by appointing him a Royal Knight of the Garter. As it happened, King George was on one of his frequent visits to Hanover when Jack arrived, and as the son of a loyal Whig earl, Jack

[27]

was received in audience. But that was a mere formality. The real purpose of his visit, on orders from his father, was for Jack to ingratiate himself with Frederick.

Indeed, Lord Bristol's commands could not have been more explicit: 'When you see and are sure ye foundation in Prince Frederick's favour is laid as indelibly as you know how I would have it, and I know you are capable of contriveing, you may think of returning homewards.' Jack, who was susceptible both to male and female charms, had no hesitation in reporting back to Lord Bristol upon the 'blooming beauties' of Frederick's 'person and character'. Bristol's plan was for Frederick to take such a shine to his attractive, well-educated twenty-year-old son that he would ask his parents to make him an entertaining addition to their household. And sure enough, by the following year, 1717, Jack had one foot firmly in the establishment door; he was appointed a Gentleman of the Bedchamber to the Prince of Wales.

Despite the success of his mission to Hanover, Jack was denied any journey further south, his mother, it seems, being fearful he might suffer some misadventure if he attempted to cross the Alps. His father wrote to say that 'Mama's tears & fears are both so very predominant whenever Italy is but mentioned, that rather than put my self into ye uneasy scituation of standing anserable for all accidents that may happen in such an expedition, I am forced not only to sacrifice my own judgement but your improvement to her foolish fondness.' It was true that axles broke, carriages overturned, village inns ran with vermin, and highway robbers lived off the rich pickings of travellers, but Lady Bristol's fussing over her oldest son seems almost pathological. It may perhaps be explained by her knowledge of his precarious health. He was in fact epileptic. Ever obedient to his mother's whims and his father's wishes, Jack duly returned home, Lord Bristol's diary entry for 19 January 1717 recording, 'Ye King arrived at London from Hannover. My son Jack came over with his Majesty from thence.'

Apart from his epilepsy, Lady Bristol would have known that in many ways Jack's health was highly dubious. In the years to come he was compelled to diet assiduously, and she may have feared that left to the mercy of ill-prepared foreign food, and doctors even more ignorant and stupid than those at home, Jack might come to serious grief if he persisted in what was usually a three-year Tour. And she had good reason to worry, for her second son, Thomas, born on 20 January 1698[3] and hence just fifteen months younger than Jack, is described by the *Dictionary of National Biography* as an 'eccentric pamphleteer' whose 'health was chronic', a verdict by no means exaggerated if it is true that for 'eleven years he was unable to lie in his bed one single night from night to morning' because he was racked by a constant fever for which, by the time he was eighteen, he had been bled more than 100 times.

Thomas is believed to have studied at Christ Church, Oxford before moving to Lincoln's Inn, but he disliked the law and was baulked in his desire to join the army. Failing, for some reason, to gain a commission 'he gave himself up to drink,' and although Lord Bristol made him an allowance of £120 a year he 'many, many times wanted a dinner'. His progress through adolescence and young manhood sounds fraught; he fought two duels, and by the time he was twenty-one it was said that his mind was unhinged. Yet we find him elected to Parliament at the age of thirty-five for one of the family's borough seats.

Even more of an astonishing achievement, if his record of woes is true, was Thomas Hervey's appointment in 1728 as an equerry to Queen Caroline (George I had died the previous year). But the *DNB*'s assertion that in 1733 he was made vice-chamberlain to the Queen is extremely hard to believe; it was Jack who was appointed vice-chamberlain in 1730, a post he held for the rest of the Queen's life. The post definitely awarded to Thomas, in 1738, was superintendent of the royal gardens, and no doubt he had minions to carry out most of the work that this sinecure entailed. He had eloped with Elizabeth, the young second wife of his great-uncle Sir Thomas Hanmer, thereby igniting a gigantic scandal and acquiring the very considerable income of £2,000 a year. The couple had an illegitimate son who, unlike his father, did get into the army, became an officer in the 1st Regiment of Foot Guards, and in 1774 was given leave to make use of the name Hervey and to bear the family's arms. Elizabeth Hanmer died in 1741, and three months later Thomas married, apparently while languishing in the Fleet Prison. This would indicate that he had gone through the whole of his mistress's fortune, for the Fleet was especially reserved for debtors.

It was said that Thomas Hervey was 'always scribbling', his semi-literate efforts consisting in the main of deeply offensive, and slightly deranged, open letters to the wronged Sir Thomas Hanmer. *Measure for Measure, or a Proper Reply to a late scurrilous Pamphlet 'A Proper Reply to a Letter'* gives some idea of the paranoid nature of the man. William Pitt came in for his share of criticism, as did a clerical baronet, Sir William Bunbury, whose name some people believe Oscar Wilde plucked from obscurity to bestow on Algernon Moncrieff's fictional friend Bunbury in *The Importance of Being Earnest*. Horace Walpole noted that Hervey 'who always obliges the town with a quarrel in the dead season, has published a letter to Bunbury full of madness and wit.' On the subject of another letter from Thomas Hervey addressed 'to the late King' (it was dated 1755 and presumably referred to George 1) and mentioning 'a civil list arrear of long standing', Walpole commented, 'It beats everything for madness, horrid indecency and folly, and yet has some charming and striking passages.' Eventually Hervey turned on two of his nephews, the 2nd Earl of Bristol and Augustus Hervey (later 3rd Earl). If Thomas Hervey was ever taken into Queen Caroline's service as an equerry it must have been as a kindness shown to Jack. Despite undoubtedly being unbalanced, and living a very rackety existence, Thomas Hervey survived to within four days of his 77th birthday, dying in Bond Street on 16 January 1775.

On Jack Hervey's return to England from Hanover his father arranged to give him an allowance of £200 a year on top of the income he already enjoyed from his grandfather's legacy, and in no time he had amassed a fifty guinea debt for gambling, a bagatelle compared with the debts rich men and women ran up in the eighteenth century but a worrying indication none the less that Jack could easily become addicted to the card table. And now that his mother was a lady-in-waiting Jack too began to enjoy what his father called the 'pompous elegant pleasures of a court,' for a room at Richmond Lodge was put at his disposal by Charles Selwyn, the Gentleman Usher to the Princess of Wales.[4] Hence whenever he wished he was free to visit his mother. The Master of the Horse, Lord Lumley, was even willing to lend him a coach from the Prince's stables. And Jack's early visits to Richmond, where later he himself would be in waiting, were to have a profound effect on his life.

Caroline boasted of her dislike of Hanover, saying she would 'as soon live in a dunghill' as return to the Electorate, and although this may have been a ploy to ingratiate herself with the British, she genuinely preferred English ladies around her to their heavyweight German counterparts. One of her innovations was to appoint a bevy of young, pretty and vivacious

[31]

maids of honour. A granddaughter (although he never married) of Prince Rupert of the Palatine, the courageous if headstrong nephew of Charles I, was one such. Her name was Sophia Howe, she was a second cousin by marriage to Caroline, and her larking about in chapel occasioned a ticking-off from the Duchess of St Albans, who told her she could not do a worse thing than giggle in church. 'I beg Your Grace's pardon,' Sophia replied, 'I can do a great many worse things!'[5]

But by common consent the prettiest and most lively of the maids of honour was Mary Lepel, always known as Molly. Born in 1700 and exceptionally well educated (she was fluent in Latin), Molly had been taken into her service by the Princess of Wales when she was only fifteen, and it was during Jack's visits to Richmond Lodge that, rather surprisingly, they fell in love. They first met at a dinner party on 28 October 1719 (dinner being served in those days in the early afternoon). It says a great deal for Molly's good nature, which endeared her to everyone, that although she had no dowry to speak of, and she and Jack got married in secret, Lord Bristol immediately welcomed her into the family. The marriage was not announced until 25 October 1720, five days after Jack's twenty-fourth birthday, but already on 20 May Lord Bristol was writing to Molly to offer his congratulations, for he had at least been let in on the secret. On 21 April he had noted the forthcoming marriage in his diary and had hastened to assure Molly that his son had 'shewn ye nicest skill in choosing you, since in you alone he could securely promise himself not only every quality essential to his own happiness, but has also made a wise provision to intaile good sense & virtue (its constant concomitant) on our (now) flourishing family.' If by these expressions Bristol meant he felt sure that Molly would pass on her own 'good sense & virtue' to her offspring, to whom indeed, according to the *DNB*, she was to prove 'an admirable mother to a large family of troublesome children,' he may have been sorely disappointed, just as he became disillusioned by Jack's choice of bride when in later years it dawned on him that she was no heiress.

There is a simple explanation for the secretiveness of the wedding. It is customary for any lady in service at court to make a formal request to marry (both Queen Elizabeth 1's and Victoria's ladies-in-waiting did so in fear and trembling), and a married maid of honour was, by definition, no longer a maid, and in the eighteenth century she was obliged to resign. As Molly Lepel was on £200 a year, by keeping quiet for six months she was able to pocket a much needed £100. Jack must have known she was not well off but, her father having been at court as a page of honour to Prince George of Denmark, the husband of Queen Anne, Lord Bristol may have surmised that she was. And having twice married rich women himself he could hardly credit that his sons would not have the sense to do the same. He was later to declare it was one of his 'greatest griefs' that Jack had not married a great heiress. In 1720 he remained in confident expectation that his eldest son and heir, Carr, would do so, although he must nearly have had a fit when in February that year Carr turned down a young lady worth £7,000 a year.

Lord Bristol should have been delighted that Henry, his fourth son by Elizabeth, managed to find an heiress for a wife, Catherine Aston, a daughter of Sir Thomas Aston. They met when Henry was stationed at Lichfield while an officer in the Dragoons. But his wealthy daughter-in-law was about all Lord Bristol did have to celebrate, once declaring that Henry was only fit to live in a jail. Lichfield's most famous son is, of course, Samuel Johnson, and although Dr Johnson thought Henry Hervey a 'vicious' man – meaning he was inclined to vice, not to cruelty – he was grateful to the young son of an earl for tak-

[33]

ing notice of him. They seemed on the face of it an unlikely couple to have got on well. Johnson's biographer Walter Jackson Bate, however, has described Hervey as hard-drinking, dissolute and self-indulgent, and presumably he was a man who could afford to disregard the great lexicographer's 'manners, appearance and dress'.[6]

Could it have been under the charitable influence of Dr Johnson, an upright and practising Christian, that Henry saw the light, reformed his ways and sought ordination, becoming Rector of Shotley in Suffolk? He petitioned the Duke of Newcastle for the see of Chester, without success, and one wonders why such an obscure clergyman who had even dropped the name Hervey and adopted his wife's maiden name was chosen in 1745 to preach at St Paul's Cathedral at the annual service for the Corporation of the Sons of the Clergy, an Anglican charity founded in 1655. He regarded himself as totally unfit for the task, and asked Dr Johnson to write the sermon for him.[7] They both seem to have felt in each other's debt, and it was to Henry Hervey, who died in 1748, that Johnson was referring when he said to James Boswell, 'If you call a dog Hervey I shall love him.'[8]

There were two reasons Lord Bristol wanted Carr to marry well: he still dreamed of replacing his modest Lodge with a grand Palladian house, and his own resources were not sufficient to enable him to make a suitable provision for his own daughters. But at twenty-nine years of age Carr remained obstinately a bachelor. And by the autumn of 1720 he was in desperate financial straits. A trading enterprise called the South Sea Company had been set up in 1711 by Queen Anne's Treasurer, the Earl of Oxford. In 1719 the South Sea Bill was passed, enabling the company to open large subscriptions, which were swiftly snapped up. There was no trade, but for some extraordinary reason almost everyone saw investment in the bogus South Sea Company as an infallible way to make a fortune. Against his father's better judgement, in the summer of 1720 Lord Hervey sold his Lincolnshire estate to invest the proceeds in the South Sea Company, and his half-brother Jack was rash enough to borrow several thousand pounds from his ever in-dulgent father. Jack sold out just before the bubble burst in October, and made a considerable profit. Carr, on the other hand, according to his stepmother, was 'utterly ruined both in reputation and fortune'.

But even without Carr getting married, by 3 August 1721 the Bristol title seemed relatively secure when Molly Hervey gave birth to a son, destined to succeed his grandfather as the 2nd Earl. The choice of Christian names for the boy, George William, was no surprise, for both the king and the Princess of Wales had graciously consented to stand as godparents. Al-though Lord Bristol did not trouble to attend the christening, he undertook to pay the child's nurses ten guineas each and to finance his grandson's education. Now without a home of his own, Carr had retreated to Ickworth Lodge, where by January 1722 he was seriously ill. Jack thought it might be amusing to cheer him up by sending ribald accounts of the recent death of the Duke of Bolton. It was not surprising, given Carr's physi-cal and mental state, that in March 1722 he lost the family's parliamentary seat.

In October that year Lord Bristol was received by the King, ostensibly to add his assurances of continued support to those of others loyal to the House of Hanover who were girding their loins for a possible Jacobite uprising. But having once attained his ambition of an earldom Lord Bristol seems to have been dilatory in his parliamentary duties, not even troubling to at-tend the House of Lords for a debate to decide the fate of

Francis Atterbury, the incorrigible bishop of Rochester whose allegiance to the exiled James III had become an episcopal embarrassment; he was deprived of his see and sent abroad. Bristol was quite content to receive reports of the bishop's trial from Jack, 'as full as clear yet succinct an account of the B[ishop]'s tryal, together with the passages in the other House relating to the Papists Bill, as, had I been present, I could not have understood them better', his proud father recorded. Jack was getting in some practice for the invaluable political memoir he was to commence writing six years later.

On 15 April Molly gave birth to a girl, rather oddly given her mother's maiden name, Lepel, as a first name. And two more children, Augustus John, born in 1724 and later 3rd Earl of Bristol, and Mary, born in 1725, appeared at annual intervals. For a man who was frequently unfaithful to his wife, both with men and other women, Jack Hervey cannot be said to have been inattentive to Molly; the boy destined to become Lord Bristol's third grandson to succeed to the earldom, Frederick, was born in 1730, William two years later, Emily in 1734 and finally Caroline in 1736. No man was ever found who was not a little in love with Molly, and while many slanderous aspersions have been cast on the character of Jack (in his biography of Queen Caroline, W H Wilkins says he possessed 'some of the worst vices of courtiers; he was double-faced, untrustworthy and ungrateful')[9] when they were young the pair of them were serenaded as an especially good-looking and happy couple. Chesterton wrote

> Bright venus yet never saw bedded
> So perfect a beau and a belle
> As when Hervey the handsome was wedded
> To the beautiful Molly Lepel.

Interestingly, the little Lepel Hervey's godfather was William Pulteney, with whom Hervey was to fight a duel. Pulteney had been a Whig member of parliament since he was twenty-one, was immensely wealthy in his own right and had married a very rich as well as beautiful heiress. But a far more illustrious godfather, Frederick, Prince of Wales, was waiting in the wings to lend his own name in 1730 to the future 4th Earl. Meanwhile Jack's youngest brother Felton, now aged twelve, was in disgrace. Having survived an attack of smallpox and been appointed a page of honour to the Princess of Wales, he proved a troublesome lad and had to resign for misconduct, and when his misconduct continued at Eton he was expelled. Yet Jack's relations with the royal family remained undisturbed, as did Molly's; in June the couple were at Richmond with the Prince and Princess. But now Jack began to be plagued with a form of ill health from which he was seldom to be free; Lord Bristol put it down to 'that detestable and poisonous plant, tea', but it may have been a duodenal ulcer. Only two remedies occurred to doctors unless they believed in the array of quack medicines on ready display; bleeding or the waters at Bath. Jack sensibly chose Bath, where as it happened his half-brother Carr lay seriously ill. On 14 November 1723 Carr died. Jack now assumed his father's courtesy title, becoming Lord Hervey of Ickworth and heir to the earldom of Bristol.

Carr Hervey has frequently been charged with the paternity of Horace Walpole, briefly 4th Earl of Orford and officially the fourth son of Sir Robert Walpole. But the story's pedigree is extremely dubious. There was no hint of it until it was first put about in the nineteenth century by Lady Louisa Stuart, who is supposed to have got it from her grandmother, Lady Mary Wortley Montagu (who died when Lady Louisa was just five). In his biography of Horace Walpole, R. W. Ketton-Cremer argues convincingly that had Horace Walpole been illegitimate both his and his father's enemies would have made malicious use of the fact at the time. 'But,' he writes, 'in no contemporary letter of a friend or enemy, in none of the pamphlets or lampoons directed against [Robert or Horace Walpole] is there any whisper of a doubt as to his paternity.'[10] Horace Walpole was decidedly effete, almost certainly homosexual, a man of fastidious habits, essentially a dilettante – admittedly as dissimilar as he could have been from the robust Sir Robert but equally as dissimilar as he could have been from Carr Hervey. It might have made more sense had the finger of rumour been pointed at Jack, although he and Lady Walpole seem an unlikely alliance. And what unquestioning commentators have failed to realize is that many of the delicate and eccentric strains in the Hervey family were transmitted not by Lord Bristol, Carr's father, or his mother but by his stepmother, Elizabeth Felton.

In 1725 some judicious manoeuvring in the appropriate establishment quarters ensured that the sitting MP for Bury St Edmunds would be made a judge and thus elevated to the House of Lords. Lord Bristol's desire to see the constituency once more in Hervey hands could be put into effect. Who more suitable to become the new member for Bury, his dubious health not withstanding, than the new Lord Hervey? On 3 April a triumphant Lord Bristol was able to inform his wife, 'My son was yesterday chosen Burgess for Bury in the most honourable manner, as his father and good grandfather had always been before him, having had the votes of every member of that substantial Corporation, to which choice the Town gave their universal approbation by lining every street and window between my house (from whence he was attended by all the gentlemen and clergy of Bury and its neighbourhood) and the Guild-hall, crying as we passd along with musick, drums and morrice dancers before us, "A Hervey, a Hervey, long live & flourish that noble and honest family".'

3

———•◦•———

A SHARP AND BLOODY DUEL

All sorts of absurd theories have been put forward to explain Lord Hervey's ability to move his family from a house in Bond Street which he had called a 'deal-box' to a far more expensive and commodious residence in Burlington Street; Molly Hervey is even supposed to have flirted with the King and been paid off by him. In fact, Hervey called in all his gambling debts, and no doubt drew on the capital he had acquired when he got out of the South Sea Company in the nick of time. And it was from Burlington Street off Piccadilly that he made his muddy way to the House of Commons. Nevertheless, in an age addicted to satire, lampoons and smut, Molly came in for her share of scurrilous attention. Lord Stanhope of Shelford, a Gentleman of the Bedchamber to the Prince of Wales since 1715 and better known as Lord Chesterfield (he inherited his father's earldom in 1726), came up with:

> Heaven keep our good King from a rising!
> But that rising who's fitter to quell

Than some lady with beauty surprising;
And who should that be but Lepel?

Molly was mature enough to prefer to be looked over rather than overlooked, and almost certainly failed to take offence. It was said that her 'good sense and good nature won for her the esteem of the ladies as well as the flatteries of the wits.' If she did flirt with the king she would have done so platonically, and in order to enhance her husband's favour at court. She was fun but virtuous and always loyal to her husband, turning a Nelsonian eye in the direction of his own sexual adventures.

Whether Hervey was 100 per cent bisexual, as very few people are, or predominantly heterosexual or predominantly homosexual, it is impossible to say. But in his own flamboyant day he was regarded as excessively effeminate, and took to rouge and camp behaviour to such an extent that Alexander Pope called him Lord Fanny. There have been numerous candidates, among them Lord Chesterfield, Lady Mary Wortley Montagu and, rather surprisingly, Voltaire, who greatly admired Hervey, for authorship of the quip that when God created the human race he made men, women and Herveys. This could be taken as a reference to the family's genetic eccentricity; it may also have been a sly dig at Lord Hervey's bisexuality, which he did very little to conceal. Pope, who could be vitriolic when he felt like it, seems to have been in no doubt about Hervey's ambiguity. He wrote:

Amphibious thing! that acting either part,
The trifling head, or the corrupted heart!
Fop at the toilet, flatterer at the board,
Now trips a lady, and now struts a lord.

[42]

But that was mild compared with Pope's allusion to Sporus in his *Epistle to Dr Arbuthnot,*where, delineating the character of Sporus (Hervey himself), he wrote:

> Let Sporus tremble – 'What, that thing of silk,
> Sporus, that mere white curd of ass's milk?
> Satire or sense, alas! can Sporus feel?
> Who breaks a butterfly upon a wheel?'

It would have been common knowledge among Hervey's classically educated contemporaries that Sporus was a boy understood to have been castrated on the orders of Nero who 'used him in every way like a wife' and eventually 'married' him. Pope's other insinuations were gleaned from an anonymous lampoon on Hervey's maiden speech in the House of Lords in 1734, describing Hervey as 'a skein of silk' and 'a perfect curd of ass's milk'.

The first man with whom we know Lord Hervey fell in love was Stephen Fox. Born in 1704, he was the elder son of Sir Stephen Fox, a Tory who had made a shady fortune as Paymaster General to Charles II; his brother Henry was the Whig politician later ennobled as Lord Holland, whose third son, Charles James Fox, was to become the boon companion of George IV. Initially it was to Henry Fox that Hervey had taken a shine, when they met in Bath in 1726. 'I have an unbounded Curiosity with regard to those I love,' Hervey wrote to Henry after they had parted company. He was well aware that Henry Fox's predilection was for the company of women, and after many genteel professions of affection, he was soon posting to him 'a dozen preservatives from Claps & impediments to procreation [in other words, some form of primitive contraceptives], which at the rate of two doses a week I have computed will be physick enough for You whilst You stay in the Country.' Early in 1727 Henry Fox was due in London, but he had to postpone the visit for some reason connected with his brother Stephen. 'I hate your Brother,' Hervey told Henry, 'without knowing him (which is perhaps the only way one can hate him) for postponing another Week a pleasure I have waited for so long.'

Fortunately there were always political distractions: the return from exile of Lord Bolingbroke had resulted in an exchange of anonymous pamphlets, Hervey joining in the fray on the side of Robert Walpole who had stood in 1725 as godfather to Hervey's fourth child, Mary. And during the parliamentary session of 1727 Hervey took part for the first time in the business of the House without, however, actually speaking. His willingness to tackle Lord Bolingbroke, the most dangerous opposition campaigner of his day, had so indebted him to Walpole and the King that he was awarded an annual pension of £1,000 from the privy purse. Another recent addition to the House of Commons was Stephen Fox, in receipt of £5,000 a year from his late father's estates, and in January 1727 he and Hervey met. The fact that Stephen sat as a Tory was neither here nor there. By the time Stephen had returned, in May, to his country house at Redlynch in Somerset, Hervey was sufficiently enamoured of him to write, 'I won't tell you how I feel every time I goe through St James's Street because I don't love writing unintelligibly.' His early letters to Stephen were a means of teasing out the younger man's feelings for him; they soon grew dangerously passionate.

John Hervey kept a number of balls in the air simultaneously, and quite successfully; he loved Stephen Fox, he loved his wife, he later took a mistress, he enjoyed a facility for writing that has placed him alongside the greatest memoirists, and he revelled in the life of a courtier, not because of the glamour or comfort it afforded (life at the court of the first three Hanoverian sovereigns was tedious in the extreme) but because it gave him access to social and political intrigue.

The year 1727 marked not only Hervey's meeting with Stephen Fox but the start of a new reign. On 14 June that year Robert Walpole heaved his considerable bulk on to his horse and rode as fast as he could from Chelsea to Richmond to fall on his fat knees before the Prince of Wales with the news that he was king. 'Dat is von big lie!' the Prince exclaimed, still clambering into his breeches, for he and Caroline had been having a siesta and the Prince suspected that Walpole's visit was a plot to see how he would react to the news that his father had died in Hanover. But George I really was dead, and those who had long taken the part in family and political squabbles of the Prince and Princess of Wales could expect rewards. Lord Hervey's came eventually by way of appointment as vice-chamberlain, a post which would give him almost inexhaustible access to the queen, and thus a splendid position from which to report back to Walpole; for George II was governed by Queen Caroline, and whoever governed Caroline (Walpole was determined it should be he) governed England.

Just as he had been in the front line of Hanoverian sympathizers to scurry to Greenwich on the arrival of George I, so Lord Bristol now hastened to Leicester House, on the north side of what is now Leicester Square, the London home of the former Prince of Wales, to intercede not on his own behalf but on that of his son Jack. He told the new King his son's establishment in His Majesty's favour 'is ye thing in this world I have most at heart, & therefore beg Your Majesty should on this happy occasion promise some way or other to provide for him. His affection and fidelity I will stand bound for. His abilities I hope will answer for themselves.' Bristol was hoping John

[45]

Hervey would be given a major appointment in Walpole's new ministry, but at this stage there was no certainty that Walpole would be called upon to form one; his first instructions from George II were to send for Sir Spencer Compton, the Speaker of the House of Commons, in the opinion of Lord Hervey 'a plodding, heavy fellow with great application but no talents'.[1] But Walpole managed to convince the King he could secure for him an enormous civil list if he was retained as first minister (which indeed he did: £900,000 for the King to include £100,000 for his heir, Prince Frederick, still resident in Hanover, and a further £100,000 for the Queen – twice as much, Lord Hervey observed, as any queen consort had ever had before), and Compton was shuffled off to the Upper House as Lord Wilmington.

Until the Hanoverian succession Walpole had been a comparatively poor man. Born into the Norfolk squirearchy, he was the third of a family of nineteen children, but on the death of his two eldest brothers he inherited his father's estate at Houghton. Initially content with the lucrative post of Paymaster, within three years of George I's accession Walpole was a rich man, and between 1722 and 1735 William Kent virtually lived at Houghton Hall, producing for Walpole what remains 'the most complete and sumptuous Palladian house in England'.[2] One of those who enjoyed Walpole's lavish hospitality was Lord Hervey, who recorded that Walpole invited friends to Houghton 'to hunt, be noisy, jolly, drunk, comical and pure merry during the [parliamentary] recess.' He remembered: 'We used to sit down to dinner a little snug party of about thirty odd, up to the chin in beef, venison, geese, turkeys etc; and generally over the chin in claret, strong beer and punch. We have Lords Spiritual and Temporal, besides commoners, parsons and freeholders innumerable.'

Hervey did not exaggerate the scene. Walpole's wine bill quite often ran to £1,500 a year. In 1733 he returned to his wine merchant 552 *dozen* empties. It was to a convivial gathering at Houghton that Hervey was summoned during the general election of 1727, when most candidates would have been canvassing, yet he had little difficulty retaining his Bury seat. His mother was quick off the mark, sending a note to the King's long-standing mistress, Henrietta Howard, who was also a Woman of the Bedchamber, to say, 'I remember the king used sometimes to like to hear how such sort of affairs went; and I flatter myself this will be pleasing to him, since their majesties may be very well assured whatever interest we gain will always be laid out in their service.' It was at this juncture that Lady Bristol procured for her second son Thomas the post of equerry to the Queen, with a salary of £220 a year. But it was still Jack who remained uppermost in his father's thoughts. When two of his daughters, Elizabeth, aged thirty, and Barbara, only eighteen, died in 1727 he told Jack, 'I can never make my self so completely wretched as to think ye chief ornament of my family gone as long as God vouchsafes to spare your more valuable life.'

Seriously bereaved by the death of Elizabeth, Hervey took himself off to Redlynch, there to be consoled by Stephen Fox. He 'loved me too well not to take a part in anything that made me uneasy and do all in his power to alleviate the weight of it' Hervey remembered afterwards, and rather than attend the coronation of 1728 he lingered with Stephen at Redlynch and in Bath until the autumn. On his own again in London in December, and far from well, he reported to Stephen that the surgeon 'hath putt a fresh Costick to my Cheek, but the pain I am most impatient under is from the Costick your absence has putt in my Heart.'

'I *must* see you soon, I can't live without You,' Hervey once had occasion to write to Stephen. Anyone who seriously doubts that Hervey and Stephen Fox were lovers will have to explain away a letter Hervey wrote five months after their first meeting, which can only relate to love bites and other evidence of a physical affair. 'You have left some such remembrancers behind you,' Hervey wrote to Stephen on 1 June 1727, 'that I assure you (if 'tis any satisfaction to you to know it) you are not in the least Danger of being forgotten. The favours I have received at Your Honour's Hands are of such a Nature that tho' the impression might wear out of my Mind, yet they are written in such lasting characters upon every Limb that 'tis impossible for me to look on a Leg or an Arm without having my Memory refresh'd. I have some thoughts of exposing the marks of your pollisonerie to move Compassion, as the Beggars that have been Slaves at Jerusalem doe the burnt Crucifix upon their Arms; they have remain'd so long that I begin to think they are equally indelible.' (The word *pollissonnerie*, mispelled by Hervey, may be translated as 'lewdness'.)

Hervey's physical and emotional powers of recovery were quick if short- lived; although he had not even made his maiden speech in the House of Commons he was selected to move an address of thanks following the opening of parliament by George II on 27 January 1728. A violent fever some five weeks later, however, confined him to bed and brought Stephen Fox racing to London, where he nursed Hervey day and night. And this illness explains why it was not until 1730 that Hervey was appointed vice-chamberlain. He actually feared for his life, and decided the only remedy for continual stomach upsets, fevers and giddiness was a warmer climate. On 12 July 1728 Lord Bristol noted in his diary: 'Friday, my invaluable son Lord Hervey went on board ye William & Mary yacht with ye Duke & Dutchess of Richmond & Mr Fox, bound for Ostend, to proceed thence to ye Spaw.'

It sounds a potentially ill-assorted foursome, for it has been alleged that one reason Henry Fox's request in 1744 to marry Lady Caroline Lennox, daughter of the Duke and Duchess, was initially spurned was because they disapproved of the relationship between Fox's brother Stephen and Lord Hervey.[3] It is an amusing idea to think of Hervey and Stephen carrying on their love affair under the noses of the semi-royal couple (the 2nd Duke of Richmond's father had been an illegitimate son of Charles II) as the four of them innocently crossed the Channel in the Duke's private yacht. In point of fact the Duke, an engaging young man of twenty-seven, was a delightful and entertaining companion of whose self-educated abilities Hervey thought very highly.

The visit to the spa at Ostend was a fiasco, Hervey's health improving to begin with and then deteriorating again the minute it came on to rain. After a visit to Paris Hervey and Stephen took the road to Lyons, crossed the Alps in one piece, and arrived at Turin on 4 November. For Hervey this was the culmination of the Grand Tour he had been told to abandon after his visit to Prince Frederick in Hanover; for Stephen it was a welcome excuse to repeat a journey he had made two years before. They travelled on to Florence, and then to Rome. Few Tours went without a hitch; on this occasion Stephen's valet died, and then Stephen caught a chill for which, needless to say, he was bled, and his arm became infected. It was now Hervey's turn to nurse Stephen, while letters from Lady Hervey continually arrived beseeching Stephen to take great care of her husband. The first person to learn of the safe – or fairly safe – arrival of the pair in Rome was King George, who gave the glad tidings himself to Lady Bristol; he knew because the British secret agent in Rome had reported to London the recent arrival of 'mylord Harvay et Mr Fack'.

[49]

Dissatisfied with the doctors in Rome – Hervey was now pleading with all and sundry to find a cure for his unspecific ailments – Stephen and Hervey ventured even further south in search of warmth, but that proved a waste of time; when they reached Naples Hervey became bedridden again. The return trip was more successful as regards the weather, so they remained in warm sunshine in Florence and were lucky not to become the victims of an earthquake. In the aftermath of the earthquake antiquities were going for a song, which was one reason to tarry; the other reason was for Hervey to undergo a minor but very painful operation on what has been described as a tumour under his chin. It was probably a wart.

It was in 1726 that Voltaire, while in England, first met Lord Hervey; on Hervey's return journey the two met again in Paris, and Voltaire expressed great admiration for some of Hervey's poetry. Another notable the travellers called upon, and indeed dined with, was Cardinal Fleury, Louis XV's first minister; and no doubt one reason they accepted such a prestigious invitation was because they knew the food and wine would be good. As for the Cardinal's religion, Hervey had no time for Christian faith of any kind, and presumably had the manners to avoid any ecclesiastical controversy. On 25 October 1729 he and Stephen arrived back in London 'in perfect health & safety according to my prayers' Lord Bristol recorded.

George II waited eighteen months after coming to the throne before sending to Hanover for his heir, Prince Frederick, whose only contact with his family since he was left behind had been through the visits paid to Hanover by his grandfather. He was now nearly twenty-two. He had not seen his parents or his two oldest sisters since he was nine; he had never met his three youngest sisters or his younger brother, later the 'Butcher' of Culloden (a second son of the King and Queen, George William, had died as a baby in 1718). In his *Memoirs*, Hervey wrote that the King's ministers told him 'that if the Prince's coming were longer delayed an address from Parliament and the voice of the whole nation would certainly oblige His Majesty to send for him and consequently that he would be necessitated to do that with an ill grace which he might now do with a good one.' After a nightmare journey the Prince landed on 7 December 1728, arrived at St James's Palace in a hackney coach, and alighting in Friary Court was escorted to meet his parents via the back stairs.

Frederick spoke indifferent English, had no establishment of his own, nor a stick of furniture, and the only courtier or politician he knew – and that acquaintance was so slight as to be almost negligible – was Hervey. But he was still on the Continent when Frederick arrived in England, so they did not renew their acquaintance until the winter of 1729. Hervey would scarcely have recognized the grown-up little boy he had met in Hanover, and Frederick may well have forgotten what Hervey looked like altogether. Nevertheless they instantly became friends. Much of the posthumous poor press the Prince was to receive was due to malicious comments made about him in Hervey's *Memoirs*, but it should be remembered that these were penned after Hervey and the Prince had fallen out, and that Hervey was largely reflecting the manic loathing both the King and Queen had for their son. Initially, however, the friendship between Frederick and Hervey was so warm that, in view of Hervey's susceptibility towards young men, it is reasonable to assume that he was a little in love with Frederick.

They exchanged exactly the same sort of flirtatious letters as had passed between Hervey and Stephen Fox. Frederick knew that Hervey had once self-depreciatingly referred to himself as a chicken because of his preference for following the hunt in a closed coach rather than an open and rain-swept chaise (a wise precaution in view of his uncertain health), and signed one letter 'Adieu, my dear Chicken'; in another he referred to 'Mylord Chicken' going into 'Sommerset Shire'. He was well aware of the homoerotic relationship between Hervey and Fox, and knew it would please Hervey if he likened their own relationship to that of Orestes and 'his Dear Pylades,' cousins whose companionship was as much a byword for intimate male friendship as was that of David and Jonathan. At a time when Hervey was staying with Fox, Prince Frederick wrote, 'I have many little droleries still to tell you but the time presses, so I end, but being a fraid that this letter should be opened if I sent it directly to you, so I make a direction to Mr Fox, as if it was written to You by a Lady, to make you be teazed a little about it. Adieu my Dear, Frederick P.'

'Every Body has some Madness in their Composition,' Hervey told Stephen Fox, '& I freely acknowledge you are mine.' So widespread was the knowledge, or at least the assumption, of Hervey's 'madness' that William Pulteney, later Earl of Bath, a brilliant and persuasive speaker who had nevertheless been overlooked by Walpole for ministerial office, had no compunction – although it was tantamount to inviting an action for libel – in publishing, during the course of a political quarrel, a pamphlet in which, by the clearest innuendo, he accused Hervey not only of being a homosexual but of committing homosexual acts – in law a capital offence. 'When that monstrous paper came out,' Lady Hervey exploded to a friend in January 1730, 'my Lord, who reads all the papers, saw it, and soon resolved & determined what to do.' What he did was to tell the Fox brothers he meant to challenge Pulteney to a duel, and three days later he asked Henry Fox to call on Pulteney to seek satisfaction. After some toing and froing between the

John Hervey (1665–1751), a Suffolk landowner who sowed the seeds of the Hervey family's fortunes. A staunch Whig, in 1703 he was rather surprisingly made a peer by Queen Anne, taking the title Baron Hervey of Ickworth. And in 1714, as part of the celebrations to welcome the Hanoverian Succession, Hervey was created Earl of Bristol.

John, Lord Hervey of Ickworth (1696–1743), the boon companion of Queen Caroline and chronicler of the reign of George II. In 1730 he was appointed by Robert Walpole vice-chamberlain of the Household and ten years later Lord Privy Seal.

The Hon. Mary Lepel, always known as Molly (1706-68), the prettiest of Queen Caroline's maids of honour, who married the bisexual Lord Hervey of Ickworth and bore him eight children.

William Hogarth's famously informative Conversation Piece depicting Lord Hervey of Ickworth in the centre, wearing on his waist his key of office as vice-chamberlain. Seated on Hervey's right is his lover Stephen Fox, while Stephen's brother Henry Fox, Surveyor of the King's Works, holds up an architectural plan.

George II (1683-1760), who in 1733 asked Walpole to reward the loyalty of John, Lord Hervey, by making him a peer in his own right while his father was still alive. When the new Lord Hervey of Ickworth moved an Address of Thanks in the House of Lords in January 1734 the king told Hervey it was the best speech of its kind he had ever heard.

Sir Robert Walpole (1676-1745), England's first prime minister and 1st Earl of Orford. Endemically corrupt, he epitomised eighteenth-century Whig politics and was a valued patron of the Hervey family.

Robert Banks Jenkinson (1770-1828), Viscount Hawkesbury, who in 1808 succeeded his father as 2nd Earl of Liverpool. In 1795 he had married Lady Louisa Hervey, youngest daughter of the 4th Earl of Bristol, and in 1826, whilst prime minister, he recommended to George IV that his brother-in-law, the 5th Earl of Bristol, be advanced to a marquessate.

respective parties, Henry Fox named the place for the duel – 'in Upper St James's Park, behind Arlington Street' – and the time: at four in the afternoon. It would by then have been dusk, with hopefully not too many people around, for duelling was strictly illegal, although the law was widely disregarded.

The last three decades of the eighteenth century were in fact to see a general revival of duelling. A duel might be embarked upon by someone anxious to be accepted as a gentleman, although such a motive would not have occurred to Hervey; he was already a gentleman, even a peer. And gentlemen considered they had a perfect right to kill one another, for to break the law with impunity established one's moral superiority over the common herd. As Fintan O'Toole has sagaciously observed in his biography of Sheridan, the son of a mere actor anxious to become a politician and to be accepted as a gentleman, who fought several duels: 'In a world where politics was still the property of gentlemen the dangerous ritual of the duel of honour was the rite of passage into the world of public affairs.'[4] Although by this time an MP, Jack Hervey still hovered on the brink of public affairs, and needed to test his manliness. Pulteney's insult must have come as a heaven-sent gift.

Having no idea what was immediately on foot, Lady Hervey noted how cheerful her husband seemed that morning when he left for the House of Commons. After dining with some fellow members he and Henry Fox went for a stroll in the park, where they chanced – by prior arrangement, of course – to meet Pulteney and his second, the somehow appropriately named Sir John Rushout. Before the antagonists crossed swords, having stripped to their shirts despite the cold, Hervey told Pulteney there was a letter in his pocket written in case Pulteney should kill him, explaining that it was he who had instigated the duel, and asking the King to intervene on Pulteney's behalf.

Hervey received a handful of superficial nicks; his opponent also suffered cuts to his hand. Then, according to Lady Hervey – who was not of course present, and did not even know the duel had taken place until the following day, but would have received a first-hand account from Henry Fox if not from her husband as well – 'they closed in, which in all probability wou'd have been fatal to one if not both of them but the seconds by consent rushed in upon them and seized their swords.' Hervey was already held in high esteem by Walpole; after a busy day in the Commons in February the previous year he had been invited to dine with the prime minister, and his courage in issuing a challenge to the leader of the opposition in the Commons did him no harm at all. On the contrary, at a Drawing Room at St James's Palace congratulations were showered upon him. Lady Irwin, later to become a lady-in-waiting to Prince Frederick's wife, told her father, the Earl of Carlisle, the duel 'made a great noise, and I fancy upon the whole will turn to Lord Hervey's service, he knowing well to make a merit of this at Court; and besides,' she added, with pointed reference to Hervey's well-known sexual nature, 'most people had the same opinion of Lord Hervey before Mr Polteney drew his character with so much wit.' And she clinched the explanation for Hervey taking such a risk when she told her father, 'nobody before this adventure thought he had the courage to send a challenge.'

Within three months of his fight, which featured in an illustrated broadsheet entitled, with perhaps some exaggeration, 'A Full and True ACCOUNT of a Sharp and Bloody DUEL,' Hervey duly received his reward, appointment as vice-chamberlain to the King's Household and membership of the Privy Council. In effect, his duties were those nominally performed by the Lord Chamberlain, at this time the Duke of Grafton, and involved almost permanent residence with the royal family, supervising their peripatetic life lived at Windsor, Richmond, Hampton Court, Kensington and St James's Palace. The arrangements for marriages and funerals, Drawing Rooms and receptions, concerts and balls all fell within his province. In many ways it was a job ideally suited to a socialite like Hervey, but the pay of £1,200 a year was very little for so much responsibility, as even the parsimonious king realized in 1734 when he increased it by £1,000.

But there were many perks like free food, obliging servants and comfortable accommodation. And in Hervey's case it resulted in a genuinely affectionate friendship with Queen Caroline and the princesses. From the point of view of posterity, we are indebted beyond measure to Walpole, for Hervey's ten years as vice-chamberlain have furnished us with a riveting account of life at the court of George II. Writing in *Horace Walpole*, and believing Walpole and Hervey to have been the greatest memoir-writers of their century, R. W. Ketton-Cremer paid a generous tribute to Hervey when he observed, 'Some comparison between Hervey and Walpole is inevitable; and Hervey has the advantage in every respect.' He thought that Hervey's writing exceeded Walpole's in force and eloquence, that his characters were more powerfully drawn, and that Hervey was savage and passionate where Walpole was peevish and ill-natured. '[Hervey's] *Memoirs*,' Walpole's biographer concluded, 'are his masterpiece.'[5]

Perhaps not quite accurately, Hervey's biographer tells us that on 10 June 1730 the court went into residence at Windsor where, on 'the Feast of St George,' Hervey was to organize his first major ceremony, the installation as a Knight of the Garter of the young Duke of Cumberland.[6] St George's Day falls on 23 April, however, but Hervey's part in rehearsals for the ritual is not in doubt; he sent an amusing account of events to Stephen

Fox. 'I was Yesterday from seven a Clock in the Morning till two this Morning constantly upon my Legs, excepting half an Hour that I was at Dinner, & about an Hour that I lay down in the afternoon, to compensate for which trouble I had the recreation of seeing one sett of performers Bowing till their Backs aked four Hours in the Morning; another sett eating till they spew'd, & drinking 'till they reel'd at Noon; & a third dancing & sweating till they were ready to drop at Night.'

But he found the routine of court life almost unbearable. 'What can I tell your Ladyship from hence?' he once enquired of his mother. 'The Circle of our employments moves in such unchangeable Revolutions that you have but to look at your watch any Hour in the four & twenty & tell your-self what we are doing as well as if you were here.' And he missed Stephen, assuring him, 'The only time I spend entirely to my Heart's Content when I am free from you is that in which I indulge my-self in writing to You.' On parting from Stephen on one occasion he told him, 'The Tears came into my Eyes a hundred times between Windsor and London.'

The solution to Hervey's infatuation with Fox and his constant distress at their partings was an audacious one. Hervey turfed his wife and children out of the house in Burlington Street, gave Lady Hervey a cheque for £4,000, told her she and the children could lodge at St James's Palace or stay with his father in St James's Square, and installed Stephen in the former matrimonial home. If rumours had spread about his sexual orientation, they had been fanned by Lord Fanny himself.

'I love you & love you more than I thought I could love any thing,' Hervey told Stephen. But he went on to say he wished he could love the Prince as well as he loved Stephen. Stephen's reaction to this uncalled for comparison caused Hervey to quickly backtrack. 'God forbid any Mortal should ever have the power over me you have,' he reassured Stephen. 'If I was to fill a thousand Reams of paper it would be only aiming in different phrases & still imperfectly to tell you the same thing, & assure you that since I first knew you I have been without repenting & still am & ever shall be undividedly & indisolubly Yours.' Stephen, Hervey told him in one of his indiscreet love letters, was *'mea vera & sola Voluptas'*. Breaking into French another day, Hervey told Stephen Fox he was his *'bien aimable, mon bien aimé,'* and again, *'Adieu, que je vous aime, que je vous adore: & si vous m'aime de même venez me le dire.'* Perhaps the oddest thing about these letters is that Hervey continued to address his lover in the formal second person plural.

On 1 August 1730 Lady Hervey gave birth to her third son, a 'thumping Boy' as Hervey described the child to his wife's friend Lady Murray. The christening, followed by a celebratory supper, took place on 3 February 1731, the boy being named Frederick, for the new Prince of Wales had gladly consented to be his godfather, and since that day innumerable members of the Hervey family have been given the name Frederick. The prince could easily have sent a proxy to the baptism but chose to appear in person. (His godson was to become 4th Earl of Bristol and a most improbable bishop.) On one occasion later in the year Frederick had Hervey at his home in Kew where they went on playing ninepins so long that dinner was delayed until 5 o'clock, only just giving Hervey time to make a reluctant ride to Hampton Court to play cards with the King. Hervey was by this time Frederick's principal political adviser.

But while Hervey's love for Stephen Fox still had a good deal of steam left in it, his affection for the Prince of Wales was suddenly to go off the boil. By mid-December 1731 Hervey was raging against Frederick in letters to Stephen. The basic cause of Hervey's simmering hatred of Prince Frederick was a prick to his vanity; the Prince, not yet married, had taken over as his mistress a former mistress of Hervey's, the Hon Anne Vane, daughter of Lord Barnard and a maid of honour to the Queen. This queering of his pitch was a double irritation, for Miss Vane was to introduce George Bubb Dodington to the Prince, and Dodington promptly supplanted Hervey as Frederick's political adviser. Hervey could be incredibly hot-headed; when Miss Vane was seven months pregnant with a son by the Prince he wrote her such an intemperate letter that when she read it she fainted. The innocent bearer of the letter – Hervey had told him it merely contained advice about hiring a midwife – was Hervey's brother-in-law Bussy Mansel, married for three years to his sister Elizabeth, by then deceased. Mansel vowed vengance on Hervey, and only the intervention of Prince Frederick prevented a second duel.

When Prince Frederick dispensed with the favours of Anne Vane she took up again with Hervey. It was, however, a liaison that nearly ended in disaster. Taking advantage of the rooms at his disposal in St James's Palace, not to mention the absence of his wife in France, Hervey slept at the palace one night with Miss Vane, when suddenly 'she fell into convulsions'. In his *Memoirs* he recorded 'Her convulsions grew stronger and at last she fell into a swoon that lasted so long [Lord Hervey] thought her absolutely dead.' Terrified he would be found with a corpse in his room, Hervey did not dare to send for assistance, 'nor even call a servant into the room, for not one was trusted with the secret.' Eventually Miss Vane recovered consciousness (she may, like Hervey, have been epileptic) and Hervey smuggled her out and found a sedan chair for her in Pall Mall.

By this time Lord Hervey held a title in his own right, for in 1733 the King and Queen both suggested to Robert Walpole that Hervey should be made a peer of the realm – although in point of fact Hervey had a massive miscalculation of Walpole's to thank for this singular honour. In 1733 Walpole had decided it was time to tackle what had become almost a national pastime, smuggling. Smugglers were regarded as heroes, like highwaymen. They were said to import at least three million pounds of tea a year, and operating in gangs 100 strong they ran ashore, in a variety of guises, wine, brandy, tobacco and lace. Walpole himself patronized smugglers, but realizing that smuggling was costing the Exchequer at least £1 million a year he decided to relieve the Customs officers of their responsibilities (which was no great deprivation, for a number had been murdered by smugglers) and hand over their duties to the more efficient Excise Department.

The Excise officers were given the right to enter and search shops and taverns. Walpole's enemies incited the public to believe this meant an infringement of every sort of liberty, even the suspension of Magna Carta. The King's beliefs where money was concerned were also often off beam, and he reckoned that if smuggling could be curtailed then surely the civil list, already enormous, could be further increased. As always, he equated opposition to his servant Walpole as outright disloyalty to the crown, and for opposing his wishes half a dozen courtiers were dismissed and two peers deprived of their regiments. He had not been best pleased by the Prince of Wales throwing in his lot with those who had assembled in the streets to yell 'No Excise! No Excise!' but he and the queen were more than gratified to find they could depend on Hervey's support; he spoke out in the Commons in defence of Walpole's ill-conceived measure. On the Bill's first reading the Government obtained a majority of sixty-one. By the third reading, however, it had fallen to seventeen, and with the country on the verge of riot Walpole admitted defeat.

But by this time Walpole, and the King, had lost the support of some of the best speakers in the House of Lords, and it was felt that no better way of shoring up the court party in the Upper House could be found than by sending Lord Hervey to sit there. The title he had borne since his brother Carr's death had of course been only a courtesy one, and as he was the heir to an earldom a method was devised of elevating him to the House of Lords by 'calling him up' in his father's barony. Hence he 'kiss'd his Majesty's Hand' on the writ being issued on 11 June 1733 creating him Lord Hervey of Ickworth. The following day he was introduced into the Lords, having 'run this kissing Gantlet throughout the whole Royal Family,' one of his sponsors being Lord Walpole, eldest son of the prime minister. While Lord Bristol disapproved of his son being 'kicked upstairs,' as he put it – for he feared he would become a mere puppet of the prime minister without any tangible rewards – he generously paid £143 for the cost of the patent.

Lord Bristol had retained his independence of mind, and had resisted attempts by the Queen to woo him over to the court. He told Hervey to say all he thought 'due to her Majesty for the great honour she does me in seeming to think me yet worthy of becoming her proselyte,' yet he refrained from mentioning that he was a regular subscriber to the opposition's newspaper the *Craftsman*, frequently under attack from Hervey. But Bristol's differences of opinion with his favourite son over politics did not cause any slackening of his affection for him.

It was in the year of his elevation to the peerage that Hervey began to write what he called 'Some Materials Towards Memoirs of the Reign of George II,' now simply known as *Lord Hervey's Memoirs*. He maintained his account only until 1737, but began it from memory with the death of George I in 1727, so that in effect he has provided us with a decade of English history enlivened by vivid description and utterly credible verbatim dialogue. Some of the Queen's diatribes against Prince Frederick are those of a mother demented by hatred, the King's comments are on occasion scatological, and the account of the death of Queen Caroline is enough to make one faint. Although not written on anything like the scale of Saint-Simon's account of life at Versailles under Louis XIV and the Regency, Hervey's *Memoirs* have the same sense of immediacy, the ability to transport the reader to the very scenes being described. What we have almost certainly lost is a major portion covering the period May 1730 to the summer of 1732, believed to have been torn out and destroyed by Hervey's grandson, the 1st Marquess of Bristol. As this was the period of Hervey's closest intimacy with the Prince of Wales, it is a reasonable assumption that it dealt not only with the friendship but the rift in relations between the two of them. If one takes into account the quality and value of what remains then the Marquess committed a monumental act of literary and historical vandalism.

One of the peculiarities of eighteenth-century politics was the way county families came virtually to own parliamentary seats. It was rare for one of the two Bury constituencies not to be occupied by a Hervey, however mad or bad he happened to be, and upon John Hervey having to vacate his seat in the Commons it was proposed that his brother Tom, as mad and bad as they come, should now represent the borough in parliament. While reportedly at death's door he had amassed gambling debts of £1,000, paid by Lord Bristol by the simple expedient of borrowing the money from Hervey. The election was held on 29 June 1733, Tom having spent the campaign lurking at Ickworth Lodge while, without much enthusiasm, his brother Hervey canvassed on his behalf 'without one penny given or promisd', Lord Bristol maintained. Tom was duly elected. 'Long live the honest Earl of Bristol,' an exultant crowd exclaimed as they repaired to the Guildhall, doubtless well aware that the honest Earl had provided ten hogshead of beer for their consumption.

It was apparently Lady Bristol who had encouraged Tom to boycott his own election; he did not even turn up at the jubilations when his almost inevitable victory was announced, and her 'meddling with Corporation affairs,' Bristol told his oldest son, had very nearly decided him to leave her. Both the Queen and Walpole had sent messages to Hervey to say they wished Tom to attend the election, and his refusal to do so was extremely embarrassing. Hervey blamed Tom's disobedience of a royal command on the 'vehemence of my Lady Bristol's Temper'.

Hervey made his maiden speech in the House of Lords on 17 January 1734, when he moved an Address of Thanks to the King. He told Hervey it was the best speech of its kind he had ever read, so we may rest assured it contained nothing but praise for Walpole's policies. Hervey was in any case in the King's good books, having undertaken complex arrangements for the marriage of the twenty-four-year-old Princess Royal to Prince William of Orange-Nassau. William, poor man, was physically deformed, prone to ill health, a symptom of which was bad breath, regarded by his future father-in-law as an inferior being, and treated accordingly; Hervey tells us the King sent 'only one miserable leading coach with only a pair of horses and a pair of footmen' to convoy him to Somerset House. The guns at the Tower of London remained silent; guards failed to turn out. All these discourtesies had to be explained away by Hervey. The marriage – 'a miserable match' in Hervey's opinion, 'both in point of man and fortune, his figure being deformed and his estate not clear £12,000 a year' – had to be postponed when the Prince fell ill, and eventually took place on 14 March 1734 with 4,000 people attending. At the ceremonial bedding of the couple, Hervey says that when the Prince 'was undressed, and came in his nightgown and nightcap into the room to go to bed, the appearance he made was as indescribable as the astonished countenances of everybody who beheld him. From the make of his brocaded gown, and the make of his back, he looked behind as if he had no head, and before as if he had no neck and no legs.'

But as far as Hervey was concerned, a prince was a prince, and when in January 1734 his wife Molly gave birth to her seventh child and third daughter, he did not hesitate to invite Prince William to stand as godfather. Just for good measure, he roped in the Prince's two prospective sisters-in-law, Princess Amelia (known in the family as Emily) and Princess Caroline. Needless to say, the baby, described by Hervey to Henry Fox as a 'nasty shabby Girl', was christened Emily Caroline Nassau. In 1814, by then Lady Emily Hervey and aged eighty, she died an old maid, as did Hervey's youngest daughter, Lady Caroline Hervey, in 1819 at the age of eighty-three. Hervey was never more cynical than on the morning after the Prince of Orange-Nassau had married the King of England's eldest daughter. The Queen had become almost hysterical on the subject of Prince William's physical shortcomings, and Hervey told her, 'Lord! Madam, in half a year all persons are alike. The figure of the body one's married to, like the prospect of the place one lives at, grows so familiar to one's eyes that one looks at it mechanically, without regarding either the beauties or deformities that strike a stranger.' It was perhaps no coincidence that at this time Hervey's passion for Stephen Fox was beginning to wane.

His happy relations with the Queen, on the other hand, were in full flood. 'I go to Richmond not to attend *his* but her Majesty' Hervey pointedly wrote to Henry Fox, and by now Hervey and Queen Caroline were genuinely devoted to one another. She gave him a horse, together with 'the finest Gold Snuff-Box I ever saw,' as he again reported to Henry Fox. In fact the Queen gave Hervey at least two gold snuffboxes, for it was reported in the *Daily Advertiser* that on 1 February 1734 a jeweller's apprentice had been sent to Newgate Prison for stealing a gold snuffbox, 'the property of Lord Hervey'; and six months later Hervey told Henry Fox the Queen had given him 'another fine snuff box'. But how could such a valuable royal gift have gone missing? The Prince of Wales had once been relieved of a pocket watch by a prostitute. Was the purloiner of Hervey's snuffbox also on the game? The *Daily Advertiser* alleged that the youth had robbed his master, which would indicate that the box had gone in for repairs or some further inscription, but it would have been a bold and rash lad who pocketed such an easily identifiable item from his employer's shop.

One of Queen Caroline's particular interests was in the appointment of bishops. She virtually ran the Church of England, and it was through his friendship with the Queen that Hervey was able to influence the composition of the bench of bishops, a body with far greater political weight than ecclesiastical. No one much cared who their bishop was, for the dioceses were largely run by archdeacons while the bishops busied themselves in London, dabbling in politics, collecting pluralities and in many cases enjoying the financial spoils of well endowed sees. Hervey was directly responsible, for example, for the translation of the dilatory Benjamin Hoadly from Salisbury to the Church's fifth most senior bishopric, Winchester (he had already held the sees of Bangor and Hereford). Hervey urged him to present himself at court to press his claims in person, to behave 'not as your laziness inclines you but as your interest directs, as common prudence dictates, as your friends advise, and as what you owe to yourself and your family requires.'

Despite his philandering, Hervey's own family continued to increase, his eighth child and fourth daughter being born in February 1736. She was named Caroline presumably in honour of the queen, and once again Hervey managed to whistle up a royal sponsor, Princess Mary, the fourth daughter of the King and Queen and still only thirteen. And his relations with his mother, never steady, were on the mend. By 1735 she had been married forty years, and to celebrate the anniversary Hervey and his eldest son George dined with her at Kensington. Hervey gave his mother a ring 'for a lucky entrance into the next forty years,' she told her husband. 'I think Lord Hervey and I live as well together as any mother & son wish to do,' Lady Bristol added, 'for he has not miss'd seeing me any one morning since I came, & twice breakfasted & twice din'd notwithstanding he has so many irons in the fire' – rather a sharp observation for Lady Bristol to have made, for she added 'some of which I wish were burnt out'. She may well have been referring to his love affairs.

During the King's absence in Hanover – prolonged because he managed to fix himself up with a new mistress, Baroness Amelia-Sophia von Walmoden, later created Countess of Yarmouth, – the Queen had asked Hervey to help her rehang some of the paintings at Kensington. In fact she wanted to chuck out a number of second-rate pictures and replace them with master works from the royal collection. If there was one thing the King could not abide it was change, and on his return he immediately ordered the restoration of his fat nudes. Hervey had the temerity to plead for the retention of a pair of Van Dycks. 'I suppose you assisted the Queen with your fine advice when she was pulling my house to pieces and spoiling all my furniture,' the philistine admonished him.

On 15 March 1736 occurred one of the strangest episodes in the life of John Hervey. In the library of Stephen Fox's London house he witnessed the secret marriage of his thirty-two-year-old lover to a child of thirteen. She was Elizabeth Horner who, despite her prospects of great wealth, had already been turned down as a bride by the Duke of Leeds and as a prospective daughter-in-law by another duke, Dorset. Shortly afterwards the new Mr and Mrs Fox were presented at court. Because of his wife's tender years Fox was condemned to three years of official celibacy, until such time as it was deemed proper for a girl of sixteen to cohabit with her husband. Despite a most unorthodox start to their married life – Elizabeth's father separated from his wife, who had organised the elopement – Fox and his child bride lived happily ever after.

Stephen Fox had never shared or cared for Hervey's cosmopolitan interests; he was only happy pottering about in the country. With so little in common, and with Hervey's perpetual attention to his family and his political career, it says much for the emotional and sexual ties that sustained their relationship for so long. Stephen may simply have been prolonging a previously unexplored or unacknowledged homosexual side to his nature; Hervey was such a busy bee that, despite his incandescent letters to Fox, he found it fairly easy to switch affections and alliances. It has to be said as well that one cannot read Hervey's character without making the subjective judgement that he was promiscuous. For him, as with many promiscuous homosexuals and bisexuals, the chase was more exciting than the kill. Two of the irons to which his mother had alluded, Anne Vane (who died in Bath on 27 March 1736) and Stephen Fox, had now burnt out. But another awaited ignition.

4

KEEPER OF THE PRIVY SEAL

In 1730 Lord Hervey had told Stephen Fox that when his heart
ceased to open for him it would be shut for ever, and it may be
presumed that it was Stephen's marriage that permitted it to
open again and admit another. The new light of Hervey's life
was a twenty-four-year-old Italian, Francesco Algarotti, who arrived in London in March 1736 bearing a letter of introduction
from Voltaire. He duly called on Hervey who, like all who met
Algarotti, was instantly smitten by his charm. He was said also
to be exceptionally good-looking. He was intelligent, he had
good taste. His father, who later settled in Venice, had been a
merchant in the Palladian city of Padua, and even Voltaire
seems to have been excited by the young man, dubbing him the
Swan of Padua because he glided so effortlessly from court to
court. By the time he arrived in London Algarotti had already
studied at Bologna and had lived in Rome and Paris. He had
stayed for some time with Voltaire and his mistress, Voltaire imagining his polished guest to be a marquis. Within weeks of his
arrival in England he had been elected to the Royal Society and

to the Society of Antiquaries. Hervey presented him to the Queen. Unfortunately for Hervey, he also introduced his new beau to Lady Mary Wortley Montagu, who at the age of forty-seven promptly fell in love with him.

Equally unfortunately for Hervey, at nine o'clock on the night of 27 April 1736 he was called upon in his official capacity as vice-chamberlain to assist in a very personal capacity at the nuptials of another former friend, now a sworn enemy, His Royal Highness the Prince of Wales. He had to conduct both the bride, Princess Augusta of Saxe-Gotha, and Prince Frederick to their places in the Chapel Royal, and then to stand next to the King. It had long been the Queen's wildly impractical wish that her younger son the Duke of Cumberland should succeed to the throne, so she consequently went out of her way to cast aspersions on Frederick's virility, even trying to wish his son by Anne Vane on to Lord Hervey. The morning after the royal wedding she and Hervey had a good old gossip, as recorded by Hervey himself: 'The Queen and Lord Hervey agreed that the bride looked extremely tired with the fatigues of the day, and so well refreshed next morning, that they concluded she had slept very sound.' In other words, the marriage had not been consummated. Whether or not the marriage was consummated on the first night – and it may well not have been, for the Princess's first child was not born until 31 July 1737 – Augusta was to bear nine children in fourteen years, all of them unquestionably fathered by her husband.

The next contentious issue dreamed up by Hervey and the Queen concerned the disinclination of Princess Augusta, a Lutheran, to attend Anglican church services, and in particular to receive Communion in the chapel at Kensington Palace. Walpole suggested the Queen speak to the Prince, who said he had already remonstrated with his wife, whose response had been to burst into tears and talk of her conscience. Whereupon Hervey suggested to the Queen that she tell the Prince to tell the Princess that the provision in the Act of Settlement of 1701 (to which the Hanoverians owed their English throne), which stipulates that the sovereign must be a communicant member of the Church of England, could be said also to apply to the wife of the sovereign. This was nonsense, and presumably Hervey was confusing the Act of Settlement with the Bill of Rights. This specifically bars the throne to a Roman Catholic, and hence automatically proscribes a Catholic male or female spouse of the sovereign, for under canon law they would be obliged to bring up their children as Catholics. At any rate, Hervey's dubious intervention did the trick, and he was able to record, 'All these arguments and conferences had their effect at last so well that the Princess dried her tears, lulled her conscience, and went no more to the Lutheran Church, but received the sacrament like the rest of the royal family.'[1]

It is possible that Hervey's infatuation with Franceso Algarotti was a case of finding love on the rebound, that Algarotti was merely a not very convincing replacement for Stephen Fox. Hervey's letters to his new inamorato, while clearly imbued with sentimental passion, cannot be construed as definite evidence of a sexual relationship, as can so many of his letters to Fox. Aware that Algarotti was planning to return to Italy before very long, Hervey wrote to him, 'If you stay or if you go, do not forget me, my dear, for I will never forget you all my life.' He went on, 'I assure you simply that at present the thing in the world that I wish most for is to be able to keep you in England for the rest of your life.' But it seems to have been rather a one-sided affair, for on Algarotti's last night in London before sailing to Italy he declined an invitation to supper with Hervey on the grounds of a previous invitation from Martin

Folkes, chairman of the Society of Antiquaries – only to sup in fact with Lady Mary, a coup about which she went round gleefully boasting.

Despite his deception, Algarotti was pursued across the Continent by post, Hervey assuring him, 'I love you with all my Heart, & I beg you never to forget the affection I have for you, nor to let the affection you have expressed for me grow weaker.' Hervey was now forty-one and the father of eight children; there was a world of difference in age, if not in wisdom and ability, between him and the youthful Italian, and it would be tempting on his behalf to see Hervey's affection for Algarotti more in terms of paternal interest, except that his language is high-flown even for an age in which men were not ashamed to express affection for one another quite openly. Not only was Hervey seventeen years older than the object of his ardour, he was by now far from physically attractive. Even if we discount the aged dowager Duchess of Marlborough's assertion that Hervey had 'a painted face and not a tooth in his head' (for good measure she thought him 'the most wretched, profligate man that ever was born'), he was no Adonis, and it is difficult to see what he had to offer the handsome young Algarotti other than platonic adoration.

Yet it was clear he was in love with Algarotti. From Kensington Palace, two weeks after Algarotti's departure, he wrote indiscreetly to Henry Fox to say, 'I write like a Fool, think like a Fool, talk like a Fool, act like a Fool,' and asked him to burn his letter 'as soon as you have read it, & pray allow it the only merit it pretends to, which is being a Piece of my silly Heart that I would trust to few Eyes & few Hands but your own.' To Algarotti himself, Hervey wrote, 'I wish you were here every day & almost every moment.' In another letter the young man was told, 'You cannot imagine how often I think of you, with how much regret I think of your Absence, & with how Steady an affection & perpetual admiration I remember every mark of Partiality you express'd towards me.'

Hervey could be mawkishly sentimental; he could also be extremely witty. Writing to his mother from Kensington, an 'almost depopulated Palace', he complained of his isolation imposed by the state of the roads in London, remarking, 'There are now two Roads through the Park, but the new one is so convex & the old one so concave that by these two different Extremes of Faults they both agree in that Common one of being impassible,' so that Londoners remarked 'that there is between them & us a great Gulph of mud fix'd,' Gulph being the family name of the House of Hanover.

Towards the end of 1736 John Hervey came within a whisker of succeeding to the earldom of Bristol. Told that his father was seriously ill, he hastened to Ickworth Lodge 'notwithstanding the Parliament was still sitting,' Lord Bristol was well enough to record in his diary, '& staid with me till Thursday ... for which I hope & pray that God will please to reward him for this fresh instance of his piety towards an aged father, as well as for his constant, dutiful behaviour towards me ever since he was born.' At seventy-one, Bristol was indeed, judged by the times in which he lived, pretty old, but he made a good recovery and eventually outlived his delicate son and heir.

It was Lady Bristol who was becoming unhinged. Early in 1737 she asked Hervey not to send his children (she referred to them as 'vermin') to Ickworth as they were not in need of country air; and when Hervey, not unnaturally, told his father of his mother's decision Lord Bristol 'fell into a violent passion'. Old Sarah Marlborough was aware of the family squabble, and Lady Bristol said she hoped the Duchess would tell Lord Bristol her opinion of 'this Treacherous villain ... the worst of men and sons.' It seems that Lady Bristol had taken a leaf out of the

Queen's book, Caroline's loathing of her elder son causing her to brand him a coward. While Hervey was visiting his father, Lady Bristol declared that he had only come in the hope that his father would die and he would inherit the estate. She then tore up her will and made a new one, almost entirely disinheriting Hervey in order 'to secure what few things I have of my own from the plunder of a vile son.'

Hervey had found himself at the centre of a stupendous row in the royal family when, on 31 July 1737 at Hampton Court, the Princess of Wales went into labour. The Prince was determined to display his independence, took it into his head that the next heir to the throne should be born at St James's Palace, bundled his wife, her two dressers and his valet, who claimed to be a surgeon and a midwife, into a coach and made a headlong dash for London. According to Hervey, within forty-five minutes of her arrival at St James's, where there was not even a bed properly made up, Princess Augusta was delivered 'of a little rat of a girl, about the bigness of a good large toothpick case.' The Queen had always feared that Frederick would try to introduce a warming-pan baby, for she remained convinced he was impotent, and when the escape from Hampton Court was discovered she rounded up the two eldest princesses still at home, the Duke of Grafton, Lord Essex (a lord of the bedchamber), a couple of ladies-in-waiting and Lord Hervey and set off in hot pursuit. Although the Queen arrived too late to witness the birth, she was relieved to discover the child was a girl rather than a boy; the 'little rat' became the mother of George IV's disastrous wife.

Hervey's infatuation for Francesco Algarotti and the marriage of Stephen Fox had done little to dim his need for Fox, who was reminded by post 'I have loved you ever since I knew you, which is now many years, so much better than most People are capable of loving any thing ... I only wish it was in my

Power to show you how well I love you, that all your Pleasures & Wishes depended on me only, & if they did you would find your-self ever deprived of the one, or disappointed of the other.' As for Algarotti, he was eventually summoned to Berlin, to yet another court – that of Frederick the Great. It was not, however, with Frederick I of Prussia, who despite his enforced marriage was indelibly homosexual, that Francesco fell into bed but with the young male secretary of the French Ambassador in Berlin. Frederick cannot have been too upset; in December 1740 he made Algarotti a count.

Towards the end of 1737 Hervey's life was to change dramatically with the loss of his patron and friend, Queen Caroline. At the birth of her last child, Princess Louisa, in 1724 the Queen had suffered a rupture. On 9 November 1737 she developed acute stomach-ache and vomiting, and having been pointlessly bled and purged she was supplied by Hervey with 'snake-root with Sir Walter Raleigh's cordial'. After enduring the agony of having her stomach opened and her intestines pushed about by seven unsterilized quacks, she not surprisingly died. The main prop and purpose of his life having been removed, Hervey now fell into a paranoid depression, for in contrast to his affairs with Stephen Fox, Anne Vane and Francisco Algarotti the Queen's affection had been disinterested, and Hervey's loyalty a part and parcel of his political ambition. The Queen had died on 20 November. On 1 December Hervey wrote to Walpole to say it was obvious he was considered fit only to carry candles and set chairs and he wanted advancement; and if none was forthcoming he was prepared to quit public life.

Robert Walpole prevaricated. He assured Hervey he thought the world of him, but offered no alternative employment and in fact persuaded him to remain vice-chamberlain so that he could report on the King. Hervey had to wait until 1 May 1740 before

[73]

Walpole got around to giving him a seat in what was called the Cabinet Council. He wrote a teasing letter from St James's Palace to Lady Mary Wortley Montagu, languishing in self-imposed exile in Venice, to inform her of the fact:

> This is the last letter, dear Madam, you will receive from me dated from this Place, for this Morning I resign'd the Gold-Key that entitles me to reside here – nor do I flatter my-self that you are in great Pain till you hear whether Disgrace or Promotion is the Occasion of this Change; & as I hope that your long distance & absence, tho they leave you in a total Ignorance of what relates to me have not reduced you to a total Indifference to what does so, I will keep you no longer in Suspense, but let you know the King has been so gracious as to reward my little Services with the great Dignity of Keeper of the Privy-Seal.

This was not in fact a Crown appointment; Hervey had been made Lord Privy Seal on the recommendation of Walpole, although in theory the King could have objected. Certainly Lord Bristol, who had always distrusted Walpole and had hoped in vain to lure his son away from the court party, could have been expected to express disapproval, but he generously noted in his diary, 'Wednesday, the king delivered the Privy-Seal to my son Lord Hervey, with many gracious expressions of past services etc.' Hervey's salary was now £3,000 a year. If he could not be happy, at least he was able to feel miserable in comfort. He became increasingly disillusioned, remaining a supporter of Walpole for another five years, but a reluctant one.

Hervey's appointment to the cabinet did not mean he was relieved of functions at court, which he greatly enjoyed. At the wedding of Princess Mary to the Landgraf of Hessen-Kassel he walked in procession in front of the non-royal dukes, and the following day, so he recounted to Lady Mary Wortley Montagu, he had to dress in great haste 'in order to pass the Day most agreeably in the Succession of a Levee, a Drawing-Room, a Feast & a Ball.' And a week later, when the King set sail for his beloved Hanover, Hervey was appointed one of sixteen Lords Justice, the King declining, as ever, to appoint the Prince of Wales Regent.

It was on 1 May 1741, a year to the day following Hervey's appointment as Lord Privy Seal, that his mother died. She had been seriously ill at Bath the previous summer, and while being carried in her sedan chair in St James's Park she had what was described as a fit. She was taken back to the Bristols' house in St James's Square, and there she died, unreconciled with the son she had for some reason come to hate. Her body was removed to Ickworth, where she was buried on 9 May 'in the same vault', her husband recorded, 'with my most valuable & ever to be lamented first wife.' A portrait of Elizabeth Felton attributed to a little-known painter called Enoch Seeman can be seen at Ickworth House, together with the sedan chair in which she may have died. Lady Bristol left most of her property to Hervey's youngest brother Felton, now thirty, and Hervey received a chest and a couple of screens. But a pleasant surprise awaited him on his arrival at Ickworth Lodge two days after his mother's funeral, which it seems he did not attend. His father told him he was planning to make him a gift of £10,000. In his turn, Hervey was able to do his former lover Stephen Fox a good turn; he persuaded Walpole to give him a peerage, although some of the credit has to go to the king's mistress, Lady Yarmouth, who almost certainly creamed off a substantial bribe.

There is endless evidence of Lord Bristol's generosity towards Jack Hervey. The £10,000 he was waving around probably came to him by way of a reversion on Lady Bristol's marriage settlement, which he could easily have kept, and now he made over to Hervey the house in St James's Square; this was so palatial that it took forty workmen to lick it into shape. Along with the house, Hervey took possession of all his father's pictures and furniture. But before he could move in he became violently unwell. He was not joking when in May 1742 he wrote to Lady Mary, 'I am still alive, & still Privy-Seal; it is all I can say for the Pleasure of one or the Honor of the other.' By January 1742 Walpole had been in such trouble in the House of Commons, pursued by enemies disgruntled by his corruption and buffeted by an unsuccessful, and hence unpopular, war with Spain, that he had offered to pay the Prince of Wales's debts, amounting to an embarrassing £200,000, if he would call off his obstreperous friends. But it was too late and he had lost the support of the House of Commons once too often; on 1 February he was received by the King and offered his resignation.

The reason why Hervey, when he wrote to Lady Mary in May, was still in government was because George II declined to have him ousted from office. It had only been with the greatest reluctance that the King parted with Walpole, conferring upon him the earldom of Orford, granting his illegitimate daughter the style and dignity of the daughter of an earl, promising him a pension of £4,000 a year – not knowing, perhaps, that his former First Lord was about to walk off with £7,000 from the Secret Service Fund – and finally falling on Sir Robert's neck, weeping and kissing him and begging to see him frequently.

But for Hervey the writing was on the wall; he had made too many enemies to be able to rely on the King's goodwill for ever. In a last desperate attempt to hold on to office Hervey very stupidly made off to Ickworth with his seals of office. He then seems to have gone as batty as his mother and his poor brother

Tom, who, when he voted against Walpole in the Commons, exclaimed 'Jesus knows my thoughts! One day I blaspheme, and pray the next!' In June the King offered Hervey a pension of £3,000 if he would resign, and still he refused. In the end Hervey told the King he would accept a political sacking, not a personal one, and that a few intimations of His Majesty's favour would not come amiss. For instance, he wrote the next day to say he would like to become a Lord of the Bedchamber. But by now the King had had enough. Hervey was summoned to appear at court and surrender his seals of office, which he only forced himself to do after making further unfulfilled demands and delivering a lecture to the King on his and everyone else's shortcomings. It was a bitter and futile conclusion to his twelve years of political influence.

After a time of seeming indifference, Hervey went over to the opposition, blithely lampooning the King and Lord Orford, to both of whom he owed everything achieved in his career, his status, influence and income. He even attempted to coerce Stephen Fox, now with him in the House of Lords as Earl of Ilchester, to desert the King. Only Lord Bristol responded to Hervey's lonely pleas, assuring him he would make an effort to attend the Lords if he could be 'of the least use to our sinking country or to your self'. But rather than speak, Hervey contented himself with writing anti-government pamphlets, his literary style being so distinctive that few people doubted who the author was. On the domestic front things were far more satisfactory; his eldest daughter Lepel, now nineteen, made an advantageous marriage to the twenty-one-year-old Constantine Phipps, later Lord Mulgrave and a grandson of the immensely wealthy Duchess of Buckingham, the illegitimate daughter of James II by his mistress Katherine Sedley, Countess of Dorchester. It was the Duchess's husband who built Buckingham House, later purchased by George III, on the site of the present Buckingham Palace. There would now be royal Stuart blood flowing in Hervey veins.

Hervey must have known the Duchess well, for she appointed him one of her executors, and as it happened, she died only a fortnight after her grandson's wedding. Hervey had called on her at Buckingham House, where she conducted herself as though she was a member of the royal family, on the anniversary of the execution of Charles I, her grandfather; the drawing room was draped in mourning, as was the grande dame. Just how well the Duchess had known Hervey may be judged by the fact that she also left him Buckingham House for his lifetime. Hervey however was well satisfied with the house his father had given him in St James's Square and handed over Buckingham House, probably the grandest private residence in London, to his daughter and her husband. The least Lepel Phipps could do was attend the Duchess of Buckingham's funeral as chief mourner, the proud and vain old lady ending up in Westminster Abbey. Lepel herself died suddenly in 1780 at the age of fifty-seven.

Hervey's health began to worsen noticeably, and on 18 June 1743 he wrote a dismal letter to Lady Mary Wortley Montagu, now languishing in Avignon. 'The last stages of an infirm life,' he told her, 'are filthy roads, & like all other roads, I find the further one goes from the capital the more tedious the miles grow, & the more rough & disagreeable the ways.' A week later he performed what on the face of it was one of the most disgraceful acts of his life; he was a rich man, and bequeathed dowries and annuities to his children, but to his loyal, long-suffering wife he left only what he was obliged to do by the terms of their marriage contract – £300 a year. His conduct was considered at the time both spiteful and inexplicable. Nothing could alter the view of his father, however, that when Hervey died on 5 August, prematurely aged at forty-six, he had lost a son with 'excelling genius and rare talents,' which in fact was true. Pope's final verdict was that Hervey was 'a Fool of Quality'.

Queen Caroline's 1904 biographer, W. H. Wilkins, came down on Hervey like a ton of bricks: 'Lord Hervey was a man of considerable wit and ability, and undoubtedly an amusing companion. But he was a contemptible personality, diseased in body and mind, incapable of taking a broad and generous view of anyone or anything; ignorant of lofty ideals and noble motives himself, he was quite unable to understand them in others, and always sought some sordid or selfish reason for every action.'[2] He was certainly a man of considerable wit; as to his ability, he was a memoirist of genius. But his alleged inability to understand lofty ideals or noble motives in others may perhaps be attributed to a general lack of such adjuncts to eighteenth-century public life, in which the acquisition of sinecures, ownership of rotten boroughs and wholesale plundering of government funds was regarded as perfectly acceptable. Hervey operated during a period of endemic corruption, and his splenetic character has to be judged against the mores of his time and his chronic ill health.

It is hard to say who suffered at his hands other than his wife, but there may be a rational explanation even for his ill-tempered will; after his death Lady Hervey built for herself a house in St James's Place, presided over a literary salon, where she received David Hume and Edward Gibbon, and travelled on the Continent. Surely the answer to the riddle of Hervey's will is that he knew his wife was already well provided for. The *DNB* says that although she suffered 'from severe attacks of the gout, she retained many of the attractions of her youth long after her husband's death'. When she died on 2 September 1768 the family did not hesitate to have her interred at Ickworth beside her wayward husband, and had she harboured any grudge against him she could easily have requested burial elsewhere.

What is certainly very strange is that Hervey had entrusted his second daughter, Mary, who later married George Fitzgerald and died horribly in a fire when she was eighty-nine, to the care of a Mrs Strangeways Horner, whom apparently Hervey knew but no one else did; but she explained to Hervey's widow that she was unable to comply with his request, which had come to both herself and Lady Hervey as a complete surprise. Their eldest son George, now twenty-two, became heir presumptive to his grandfather. Hervey was buried on 12 August, spoilt by his father to the last; the normal woollen shroud was dispensed with and a more expensive one was purchased, and for this infringement of the law Lord Bristol happily paid a fine of £5.

5

MANY MOST BEAUTIFUL NUNS

George William Hervey, Lord Fanny's eldest son, was said to be even more effeminate than his father. On 2 June 1739, three months before his eighteenth birthday, he had joined the army as an ensign (the equivalent of a second lieutenant) in the 38th Regiment of Foot, known as the Duke of Marlborough's Regiment, the Duke at the time being the 1st Duke's grandson. A year later he had transferred, again as an ensign, to the 1st Regiment of Foot Guards and on 27 January 1741 he had been promoted captain in the 48th Regiment of Foot. It was in August 1742 that his father and grandfather had persuaded him to resign his commission. Had he remained in the army he might – just might – have done as well as his brother William, Lord Hervey's fourth and youngest son, who became a general. General the Hon William Hervey died in the year of Waterloo, at the age of eighty-two.

But George's sights seem to have been set on a diplomatic career. On 1 December 1743, four months after his father's death, he took his seat in the House of Lords as the 3rd Lord

Hervey of Ickworth, and on his grandfather's death on 20 January 1751 he succeeded to the earldom of Bristol and the valuable Suffolk estates. Here he seems to have pottered around in wealthy idleness, having declined an offer on the death of Frederick Prince of Wales in 1751 to become a Lord of the Bedchamber to the twelve-year-old future George III. On 5 April 1755 he was sent on a mission to Turin as envoy extraordinary, and in June that year he found himself appointed minister to the King of Sardinia. He must have acquitted himself well, for three years later he was appointed ambassador in Madrid, and it was while the 2nd Lord Bristol was in his Spanish post that George II died, in farcical circumstances, on 25 October 1760. Having risen as usual at 6am he had a stroke while in his closet. Hearing 'a noise louder than the royal wind' and then a groan, his valet rushed in to find the King on the floor with a cut to his face. He was already dead.

George II was succeeded by his ill-educated but amiable twenty-two-year-old grandson, who does not seem to have taken umbrage when Lord Bristol quit Madrid on 17 December 1761 without even taking leave; on 26 September 1766 George III appointed him Lord Lieutenant of Ireland and a privy counsellor. The King had written to the Earl of Chatham (the newly ennobled William Pitt) to say he expected Lord Bristol to reside in Ireland for as long as he held the post of Lord Lieutenant, but Bristol had the gall to pocket £3,000 intended to defray his travel expenses and then to resign the office the following year without ever having set foot in Ireland. Which makes his appointment two years later to his father's old ministerial office of Lord Privy Seal very strange indeed. Stranger still, when Bristol relinquished his cabinet post on 29 January 1770 the King made him Groom of the Stole and a Lord of the Bedchamber. He was only fifty-five when he died at Bath in March 1775 'of a palsy from a repelled gout'. He never married – unusual for a man of his wealth and position – and if it really was true that he was more effeminate than his father, then it does not seem unreasonable to surmise that he was homosexual; if appearances are anything to go by, and judging by a pastel portrait painted in 1761 by Anton Mengs, he almost certainly was. But like his father he did not lack courage. Having been insulted by Lord Cobham, who felt free to spit into his hat, he demanded satisfaction, and only an abject apology from Cobham prevented another Hervey duel.

If the 2nd Earl of Bristol had been dilatory in his duties, leaving Spain without saying goodbye and not even turning up in Ireland, he was well outshone in eccentricity by his heir presumptive, his brother Augustus John, who now succeeded to the family titles at the age of fifty-one. Augustus inherited also the manuscript of his father's *Memoirs,* and left instructions in his will that they were not to be published during the lifetime of George III. In the event, it was not until 1848 that a censored edition first appeared, and by that time the head of the family was Frederick William, 1st Marquess of Bristol and a nephew of the 3rd Earl.

In the eighteenth century there were only five professions open to the younger sons of the nobility; the diplomatic service, politics, the law, the Church or the army or navy. Many entirely unqualified peers and their offspring were dispatched on diplomatic missions in the hope that, lacking brains or diplomacy, at least the envoy's title would carry some weight at a foreign court. A great many went into politics in the hope of securing rich sinecures. Quite a few minor scions dabbled with the law but most gave up out of sheer boredom. As for ordination, few clergy were expected to be men of God or to spend much time in their parishes, and the same went for bishops, chosen almost exclusively on the grounds of their political reliability one way or the other. The large number of younger sons who opted for ordination and were presented by aristocratic patrons to well-endowed parishes explains the existence of so many large eighteenth-century country rectories, built to house their families, entertain their friends and stable their horses.

Born on 19 May 1724, and never imagining he would one day inherit his grandfather's earldom and estates, Augustus Hervey, who was clearly born to be a sailor, joined his Uncle William's ship, the *Pembroke*, as a midshipman at the usual age of eleven. Captain William Hervey, John Hervey's second brother, was spoken of by some as a fine seaman and competent commander, but he was written off by the often unreliable naval biographer John Charnock as 'very ill-qualified for a naval command', even as 'an object both of terror and hatred to his people.' Not much is known about Augustus's formative years at sea although, thanks to a diary he kept, a disastrous marriage he made and his later creditable naval career we know a great deal about him from 1744 onwards. For in that year, aged twenty and by now holding the rank of lieutenant, Augustus attended a race meeting at Winchester where he chanced to meet a young lady described by the *DNB* as 'the notorious Miss Elizabeth Chudleigh'. The daughter of Colonel Thomas Chudleigh, at one time lieutenant governor of Chelsea Hospital, who died while she was a girl, Elizabeth had her first love affair when she was fifteen and at one time was the mistress of William Pulteney. On 4 August 1744, at dead of night and by the light of a candle balanced on an upturned hat, Augustus and Elizabeth were married in an extra-parochial chapel in the grounds of Lainston House near Salisbury.

After a brief honeymoon Augustus Hervey rejoined his vessel, the *Cornwall*, flagship of the Jamaica station. He was back in

England two years later when he and Elizabeth lived together as man and wife with Elizabeth's mother in Conduit Street in Mayfair. At the age of twenty-two Augustus had his first – and by no means unusual – experience of being snubbed by George II. 'I went to Court at Kensington,' he recalled when writing up his diary, 'and was presented to the King by Lord Waldegrave [the 1st Earl Waldegrave, a talented diplomat]. His Majesty rather rumped me and looked sour.' Augustus was an ambitious young man and anxious to further his career; his brother Lord Hervey had given him a letter of introduction to the Duke of Bedford, his mother one to George Grenville, a Lord of the Admiralty. To keep him from starving his grandfather gave him eight guineas, later supplemented by a gift of £100 to enable him to fit himself out to go back to sea, but Augustus reckoned he needed £300 so he borrowed more.

Augustus Hervey's diaries cover the years 1746–59, but were actually written between 1767 and 1800. They were bequeathed by him to an illegitimate son, born to Kitty Hunter, a daughter of one of the Lords of the Admiralty, in about 1764. Baptized Augustus, the boy was known as Little Augustus, and was killed in 1782 when he was about eighteen. The diaries lay largely unread at Ickworth House until in 1953 they were published as *Augustus Hervey's Journal* by William Kimber and edited with considerable erudition by David Erskine, a grandson of the 4th Marquess of Bristol.

It was on 16 October 1746 that Augustus met up in London with his wife, whom he refers to in his diary as Miss Chudleigh, for he was writing long after he had good cause to wish he had never married her. Their reunion passed apparently 'in mutual reproaches' but Hervey remembered that 'both being very young this little quarrel passed off, nor did we let it break in on our pleasures.' He gave Elizabeth an onyx set with diamonds, and prayed that he would soon be in receipt of some prize money. And when he was 'to my great joy sworn in Captain of the *Princessa*' it began to look as though he would be. Although Augustus believed his wife was up to no good, he continued to visit her 'till 4 or 5 in the morning,' and it was at this time that she became pregnant, their child being born in October 1747 and christened Augustus Henry at Chelsea on 2 November. But he died shortly afterwards. Had he lived he might well have become the 4th Earl of Bristol. Shortly after this tragedy the couple separated, but neither of them at this time sought a divorce.

The Hon Elizabeth Chudleigh has been described by a modern biographer as 'a rambunctious lady-in-waiting' with 'ambition and a reputation to match'.[1] She was in fact only a £400-a-year maid of honour in the household of Augusta, Princess of Wales (maids of honour with no title of their own were traditionally accorded the prefix The Honourable). Among the entertainments staged in 1749 at Ranelagh Gardens, opened in Chelsea seven years previously, was what Horace Walpole described to Horace Mann, at one time envoy in Florence, as a subscription masquerade, in which 'Miss Chudleigh was Iphigenia, but so naked that you would have taken her for Andromeda.' Walpole's description was borne out by another witness, Mrs Edward Montagu, for fifty years the reigning hostess to London's intelligentsia and the first so-called bluestocking. She wrote to her sister, 'Miss Chudleigh's dress, or rather undress, was remarkable; she was Iphigenia for the sacrifice, but so naked the high priest might easily inspect the entrails of the victim. The Maids of Honour (not of maids the strictest) were so offended they would not speak to her.'

George II was not so particular, and fancied himself in love with Elizabeth. Writing again to Horace Mann, on 22 December

1750, Horace Walpole told him that at a Drawing Room two days previously 'the gallant Orondates', as he referred to the King, had told Miss Chudleigh he had appointed her mother to the profitable post of housekeeper at Windsor 'and hoped she would not think a kiss too great a reward.' The King got his kiss, Elizabeth a watch worth thirty-five guineas, and Walpole even went so far as to hint he saw no reason why the King should not marry her, even though she was thirty and he 'near seventy years'. He was in fact sixty-seven, and, although Walpole did not know it, Miss Chudleigh was married to the Hon Augustus Hervey. But by 5 May 1753 Walpole was reporting to the Hon H. S. Conway that Elizabeth had become the King's mistress. Two years later she was taken over by the 2nd Duke of Kingston, a nephew of Lady Mary Wortley Montagu.

Horace Walpole, who had played with Elizabeth Chudleigh when they were children together in Chelsea, could write as amusingly as anyone, and to John Chute, in April 1754, he retailed an anecdote about Miss Chudleigh at the opera. 'One of the dramatic guards fell flat on his face and motionless in an apoplectic fit. The princess [Augusta] and her children were there. Miss Chudleigh who *apparemment* had never seen a man fall on his face before, went into the most theatric fit of kicking and shrieking that ever was seen. Several other women, who were preparing their fits, were so distanced that she had the whole house to herself; and indeed such a confusion for half an hour I never saw!'

The year 1748 found Augustus Hervey off Leghorn, where with great courage and skill he prevented the British ships being destroyed by fire. The *DNB* reminds us of another of Hervey's naval feats for which he was generally acclaimed, when in 1757 he distinguished himself 'by driving the *Nymph*, a French frigate of thirty-two guns, on the rocks off Majorca, and, on a refusal to surrender, sinking her.' The year 1748 also found Hervey taking a well-earned respite in Florence, where dinners given for him he found 'very agreeable and entertaining. The conversations were equally so, as the ladies are the most gallant of Italy and the husbands the least jealous in my opinion.' His intimates in Florence, he tells us, were the Marchesa de Pecori and the Marchesa Acciaioli, but he seems to have dallied with any number of other women at 'the bridge of La Trinita,' where assignations became so flagrantly conducted that Horace Mann, who happily connived, 'was obliged to suppress it a little and light up his dark walks and recesses.'

Augustus Hervey's unbuttoned diaries leave one in no doubt where *his* sexual orientation inclined him; the list of his conquests on the Continent includes princesses, duchesses, marchesas, countesses, the wife of a Doge, artists' models, publicans' daughters, actresses, singers, dancers – even nuns. Moving on from Florence to Lisbon he had a great outing one morning with the Duke de Bagnos and the Comte de Vergennes, when they 'went in cloaks to upwards of, I verily believe, thirty ladies houses – ladies of pleasure I mean.' On his immediate return to England he was now so well off that he gave his wife £500 to pay her debts. But by 25 January 1748 – he noted the date very precisely – he 'had come *eclaircissments* as to Miss Chudleigh's conduct with her ... In short, I took a resolution from this afternoon of going abroad and never having any more to do in that affair.' Things were going no better at court, where Hervey was again presented to the King 'who took no notice of me'.

Like so many men in public life who were spurned by George II, Augustus Hervey had no hesitation in paying his respects to the heir to the throne. At Carlton House, Hervey recorded, Prince Frederick 'was mighty gracious to me, talked to me a great while about this Bill,' the Bill in question being an attempt to alter conditions of service for naval officers on half pay. Apparently the Prince of Wales told Hervey it was 'shameful for Lord Anson and Lord Sandwich to make so many brave men slaves.' He promised Hervey he would 'certainly serve me when in his power'. Unfortunately the Prince was to die only two years later. Interestingly, Hervey offers historians his own version of the cause of Frederick's death, a cold caught while playing tennis – a variation on the generally accepted explanation provided by Horace Walpole. (A story that refuses to lie down, that Frederick died because he was hit on the head with a cricket ball, was manufactured by his enemies, as much as to say, how stupid could he have been, and is sheer myth.)

In the sense of immediacy that Augustus Hervey creates in his diaries, he is the equal of his father. 'As I was packing my things the 2nd June [1749],' he wrote, 'to set out next day, tho' in all this time I had never heard from Miss Chudleigh, yet she suddenly came in upon me at Mrs Aston's, which I impute to their having sent to her and told her of my design [of going abroad and having nothing more to do with his wife]. But I was deaf to all the siren's voice.'

Hervey lived a truly privileged life; by the summer of 1749 he was running round Versailles, observing that Louis XV's mistress Madame de Pompadour, at her toilette, was 'the handsomest creature I think I ever saw, and looked like a rock of diamonds'. In Paris he rode, danced, fenced and practised on the harpsichord, which still left him with the energy to pass his nights with two women, one a dancer at the Opéra. As an alternative attraction to the dancer there was always Madame Monconseil, with whom he supped. 'She shewed me the prettiest little boudoire that could be – nor did I lose my time in it.' Two weeks later he was 'at the French Comedy and Mademoiselle

Romainville, one of the principal actresses, kept by Monsieur Maison-Rouge, a *fermier-général*, had some mind for a slice of me I found, which I had no scruples about.' After another visit to the Comedy 'Mademoiselle Blotin came with her mother to me and supped with me, and whilst the mother lay on a couch in the antichamber the daughter went to bed with me, and returned home that morning.'

In November 1749 Hervey 'fell in love with the most beautiful woman in France, Madame Caze,' and in order to show his interest in her 'I did contrive it in part by pulling her gown once or twice when my mask was off and hers on'. By Madame Caze he eventually had an illegitimate son. Soon, however, he was toying with a baronne, and when his mistress was eight months pregnant decided to return to London, where he was 'presented to the King by Lord Harcourt, who took not the least notice of me.' He was nevertheless 'very well received at Leicester House by the Prince and Princess of Wales'. This was on 7 January 1751, the year that was to see the death of the Prince with a consequent collapse of the opposition, and shortly after Hervey's visit to Leicester House the death at Ickworth Lodge of his father. Lord Bristol was one of that generation of unsophisticated yeoman stock who retained many habits from the past which, by the time of his death, were much despised by the beau monde; he stuck not only to his use of the word 'ye' but on his birthday expected everyone to dance, the servants joining in with the family and guests. Augustus Hervey has left a first-hand account of the old man's burial, resting against his left cheek all his first wife's letters, 'a blue Turkeystone ring she gave him put on his finger, and his bracelet of her hair on, which he ever wore.'

In 1752 Augustus Hervey was again in Lisbon with time on his hands, so the pursuit of women recommenced. At a party given by 'the late King's favourite son' there were 'many most beautiful nuns' and everyone stayed late 'making love in the *frereatica* way (as they call it)'. He intended *freiratico*, meaning 'one who is given too much to the love of nuns,' of whom there were no shortage in Portugal at this time. The country was in the grip of religious fervour, with so many processions and feast days that the shops scarcely had time to open before they had to close again. It has been estimated that a tenth of the population of two million were in Holy Orders. Not all the 'nuns' Hervey met were necessarily under vows, however; the nunneries were packed with young girls who were wards of chancery, with women doing penance and with others genuinely wanting to be chaperoned while their husbands were abroad. Nevertheless, his partiality for the inhabitants of convents and nunneries, whether they were professed or not, surely served to provide a particular sexual frisson, a spur to what could have become a jaded palate. The story that he once raped an entire nunnery may be dismissed as fiction; Hervey's sexuality was all too readily assuaged by women who fell for his charms, and he was in any case a considerate and generous lover.

'I went often sailing up the river with Don João, and to nunneries, and that way passed my time, and making love to someone of the Portuguese ladies or other, as they are all very amorous and very intent at never losing an opportunity of amusing themselves,' he wrote. 'Here I saw and got acquainted with the Princess of Holstein [daughter of the Duke of Holstein and married to the captain of the queen's guard], and a very fine woman she was and I soon perceive she was game, which I thought would do when I returned, as I was now going soon away.' Back in Paris, having left his Princess on ice, we learn of 'two coquettish sisters' whom Hervey 'soon found which way to gain them, and fed them accordingly.'

[91]

There were certainly times when Hervey's licentiousness got the better of him, and there are entries which indicate that he was writing for his own amusement rather than for publication. It is hardly surprising that in 1953 his editor replaced with a dash a word that can have been none other than a seven-letter one that begins with 'f' and ends with 'g': 'I was now preparing to leave Naples,' Hervey wrote when recalling the year 1753, 'the carnival having almost wore me out, being one continued round of dining, supping, dancing and ...'.

Augustus Hervey's character and achievements in the sexual field have been likened, not very perceptively, to those of his contemporary Casanova; they resemble more closely those of Mozart's Don Giovanni, as related by his servant Leporello in his Catalogue Song. In 1754 he was 'very often very happy' with a 'beautiful creature about fifteen'. He eventually had his wicked way with the Princess of Holstein 'in a little closet'. There were occasions when he had to hide under the bed and he once found himself locked inside his paramour's house. One extraordinary adventure involved a mysterious, and rather alarming, abduction in order to service a lady of quality who insisted on remaining anonymous. While waiting for war to break out with France in 1755, his 'whole time passed in Love, mirth and voluptuousness'. It is sometimes difficult to remember that Hervey was a brave and resourceful officer, who ended up a Vice-Admiral of the Blue, and a close and loyal friend of the unfortunate Admiral John Byng, shot, as Voltaire sarcastically quipped, *pour encourager les autres*. The admiral had failed to relieve Fort St Philip in Minorca, and despite a plea for clemency even from those who court-martialled him, he was shot on the quarter-deck of the *Monarque* in Portsmouth Harbour on 14 March 1757. Byng left Hervey a clock, 'which clock,' he recalled, 'I have, and will keep as long as I live.' It was a French timepiece ornamented with Dresden flowers.

[92]

When in 1758 Hervey took his seat in the House of Commons, he was received at Savile House by the nineteen-year-old- Prince of Wales (the future George III), he and his brother Edward having moved there, next door to Leicester House, on the death of their father; and then Hervey went round to Leicester House to be received by Augusta, Princess of Wales, in whose household 'Miss Chudleigh' still resided. Apparently Prince George was 'very civil and spoke to me a great deal'; whether the Dowager Princess realized that Hervey was the husband of one of her maids of honour, or whether he and his wife bumped into one another, we do not know. We do know that Hervey's triumphal entry into his family constituency was a case of the bells of Horringer, Chevington and Bury ringing all the way as he passed, and three or four thousand people turning out 'with flags, morrice dancers, music and loud acclamations'. There were suppers and a ball and 'nothing but mirth and joy', and when Hervey came to tot up the bill he found 'this pretty jaunt' had set him back £358, 'besides £40 I gave to the two parishes'.

As for 'Miss Chudleigh', much of the future Elizabeth, Countess of Bristol's conduct was a foretaste of the scandalous behaviour indulged in by the wife of George IV. On a visit to Berlin in 1765 she occasioned the surprise of Frederick II, who reported to the Dowager Electress of Saxony the appearance of 'an English lady, Madame Chudleigh, who emptied two bottles of wine and staggered as she danced and nearly fell to the floor.' On her return to England 'she led a life of extreme dissipation'. But there seem to be differing versions of some of her escapades, and some glaring inaccuracies in the telling of them. According to the *DNB*, it was in 1759, hearing that the 2nd Earl of Bristol was in failing health, that Elizabeth Chudleigh, as she still called herself, so that she could retain her maidenly post at court (and she had in any case always kept her marriage to Augustus secret), made haste to the parish where she had become the wife of the man now very likely to succeed to an earldom. There finding the rector, Mr Amis, on his deathbed she 'caused him to enter her marriage in the register-book of Lainston chapel.' In 1759 George Hervey, the 2nd Earl, still had sixteen years to live, and the year in which Elizabeth dashed to Hampshire to see Mr Amis was in fact 1768. (Even then, the Earl had another seven years of life left to him.) Writing to Sir Horace Mann on 28 February 1769 Horace Walpole said that Elizabeth 'forced herself into the house' and 'by bullying, and to get rid of her, she forced the poor man to give up the certificate.' This could mean that he handed over the marriage certificate and that Elizabeth either retained it to prove, if need be, that she was Countess of Bristol or else destroyed it so that she would be free to marry her protector, the Duke of Kingston, and thus inherit his considerable wealth. At all events, Walpole went on in his usual gleeful fashion to say 'she has appeared in Doctors' Commons, and sworn by the Virgins Mary and Diana that she was never married to Mr Hervey.'

Mr Hervey now imagined himself in love with a doctor's daughter from Bath, and decided he wanted a divorce, on the grounds of his wife's adultery. But in order to get divorced he had to prove he was married. And Elizabeth appears either to have destroyed evidence of their marriage or to have quietly retained it. It was on 11 February 1769 that she decided she was not prepared to incur the scandal of a divorce, that she would much sooner commit perjury, and thus she swore an oath in a consistory court to the effect that she was a spinster. The court believed her, and 'enjoined silence on Hervey'.[2] Feeling free to go one step further by committing bigamy, on 8 March that year Elizabeth Hervey 'married' the Duke of Kingston by special li-

[94]

cence, decked out in white satin trimmed with Brussels lace and pearls.

In May 1773 Augustus returned to the attack by presenting a petition to the King in Council, asking for a new trial, and the matter was referred to the Lord Chancellor. But dramatic events were shortly to overtake everybody, not least the Duke, who in September died at Bath 'of the palsey' – this occurring on 23 September if you believe the *DNB*, on 24 September according to Horace Walpole's *Journal of the Reign of George III*. In a will dated 5 July 1770 the Duke had left his 'dear wife' his 'landed estate' for life and the whole of his personal fortune. Both in a letter to Horace Mann, dated 4 October 1773, and in his *Journal* Horace Walpole took considerable pains to prove Elizabeth's bigamy by pretending the Duke had referred to his 'dearest wife Elizabeth Duchess of Kingston, *alias* Elizabeth Chudleigh, *alias* Elizabeth Hervey.' Had he done so, it would have been tantamount to the Duke proclaiming to the whole world that his wife had been – and in the absence of a divorce still was – married to Augustus. So pleased was Walpole with this figment of his imagination that he enquired of Mann, 'Did you ever hear of a duchess described in a will as a street-walker is indicted at the Old Bailey?'

It was, however, to the King's Bench and eventually the House of Lords that Elizabeth Hervey was heading. There had been witnesses to her wedding to Hervey, but while the evidence was being gathered she sailed for Italy in the late Duke's yacht, and was received by Pope Clement XIV. This pleasant excursion was cut short by news that she was to be charged with bigamy. She decided to return to England to contest the allegation, found herself short of funds, and armed with a pistol, stormed off to the bank in Rome where her valuables had been deposited. On 24 May 1775, by which time her legal husband had become Earl of Bristol, she appeared before Lord Mansfield in the King's Bench, and was bailed in her own recognisance of £4,000 according to the *DNB*, £5,000 according to Walpole's *Journal*, and a further £1,000 each pledged by four friends. Bets were laid that she would abscond, but in fact she turned up at Westminster on 15 April 1776 looking 'well though pale and trembling'. She was dressed in black silk and, so Horace Walpole reported to the Reverend William Mason, 'she did not once squally, scream or faint ... She spoke of her innocence and of her awe of so venerable an assembly.'[3]

Well she might have done. The peers who were to try her had processed to Westminster Hall with the judges, Garter King of Arms and the Lord High Steward. The trial lasted four days, a string of hostile witnesses, including the widow of the cleric who had married her to Augustus, were produced, and the peers came to the decision she was indeed married to Augustus and only bigamously to the late Duke of Kingston; hence she was the Countess of Bristol and not a duchess. The Attorney-General could see no reason why she should not undergo the usual punishment for bigamy, by having her hand branded, but the other judges decided on mercy; she had already been branded a liar, she was fifty-six and a countess, and so she was allowed to retire overseas. She also retained the fortune she had inherited from the Duke of Kingston, but she seems to have mislaid her yacht, having to be rowed to Calais in an open boat.

On 22 January 1777 Augustus Hervey, still anxious to re-marry, and perhaps even produce a legitimate heir, applied to the consistory court for recognition of his marriage to Elizabeth so that he could then divorce her, but the court believed he had colluded in the original proceedings and told him that his mar-riage to Elizabeth was indissoluble. All he could now do was hope that Elizabeth might die, thus setting him free. Far from planning to die, the Countess busied herself fitting up a ship she had bought in Calais and then sailed to St Petersburg, sending ahead of her a couple of paintings from the Duke's collection which she thought might pave her way with the Russian imperial family, only to discover to her horror that she had parted with a Raphael and a Claude Lorrain. When she tried to retrieve them she met with a polite refusal. But she still managed to ingratiate herself with Catherine the Great, who gave her an estate; the Countess purchased a second estate near St Petersburg which she named Chudleigh, and then set about distilling brandy. But hers was a restless spirit. Soon she moved on to Montmartre and bought a house near Paris, once the home of Monsieur, younger brother of Louis XIV. Most European capitals received the honour of a visit from Elizabeth, her conduct being described as 'extremely coarse', her character 'self-indulgent and whimsical … only redeemed from utter contempt by a certain generosity of temper that extended even to her enemies'.[4] She died in Paris on 26 August 1788.

Elizabeth's mother seems to have been a lady of remarkable resource as well. Horace Walpole tells us that on her way home by coach late at night, with two old pensioners in attendance, 'she was asleep, and was awakened by three footpads, one of whom held a pistol at her breast. She coolly put her head out of the other window, and said, "Fire!" The patrol fired, and shot the robber.'[5]

We can only guess why Augustus and Elizabeth kept their marriage secret. She had no fortune, and Augustus may have supposed his father would oppose the match on that score. It is obvious too from all one reads about her that hers was a lively disposition; she was flighty and not too intelligent, although, like all the maids of honour, very attractive. According to Horace Walpole, she had 'a most beautiful face', but he thought 'her person was ill-made, clumsy and ungraceful'.[6] It certainly seems that very early on Augustus entertained serious doubts about Elizabeth's faithfulness; they had no children to survive them, and it may simply be that as they grew apart from a marriage made in haste when they were very young they decided to pretend there had never been one. A divorce would have been hard to come by, but the risks of covering up a marriage when a second union was desired were considerable.

Augustus Hervey seems to have had no difficulty combining a naval with a parliamentary career; he became a frequent speaker in the House of Commons. In 1762 he was appointed colonel of the Plymouth division of marines, and the following year Plymouth conferred on him the freedom of the borough; the same year, George III made him a Groom of the Bedchamber. By January 1771 he was a Lord of the Admiralty. He only lived to enjoy his earldom for three years, dying from 'gout of the stomach' on 23 December 1799 at St James's Square, and he was buried at Ickworth five days later. 'Active and brave, but reckless and over-confident' was the verdict arrived at by the *DNB*. He bequeathed to his ill-fated natural son, Little Augustus, £300 a year until he came of age, which he never did (and £400 a year thereafter), and had he been able to do so he would have left his son the entailed estates as well. There seems to have been some distinct falling out between the 3rd Earl and his heir presumptive, his brother Frederick, for on leaving his *Memoirs* to Little Augustus he also left instructions not to 'give, lend or leave them' to Frederick.

6

———•—•———

LE COMTE DE BRISTOL,
EVÊQUE DE DERRY

Augustus Hervey was only fifty-five when he died, and it is interesting how much longer-lived were the daughters of John Hervey and Molly Lepel than the sons. The daughters, on the death of the 1st Earl, were granted the style, dignity and precedence of the daughter of an earl which would have been theirs by right had their father succeeded their grandfather. And once again the earldom of Bristol passed to a grandson of the 1st Earl, Frederick, John Hervey's fifth child and third son. Save in wartime there can have been few instances (the Sackvilles of Knole come to mind as one, however) of a title having such trouble descending from father to son. And so stepped on to the stage the forty-nine-year-old Bishop of Derry, 4th Earl of Bristol, of whom the Earl of Charlemont, the Bishop's political rival in Ireland, observed, 'His family was indeed famous for talents, equally so for eccentricity, and the eccentricity of the whole race shone out and seemed to be concentrated on him.'[1] This remark has also been attributed to

Lord Chesterfield, who died six years before Frederick succeeded to the earldom.

Frederick Hervey had been born on 1 August 1730, and was unusual in being given only one Christian name – that of his godfather, Frederick, Prince of Wales. At Westminster School he made an important life-long friend, William Hamilton, later Minister at Naples and the husband of Emma Hamilton, Lord Nelson's mistress, a man with whom the future earl-bishop was to share a passion for antiquities. They were in fact exact contemporaries, and oddly enough both died in the same year, 1803. Frederick was still a thirteen-year-old schoolboy when his father died, from whom he received a pittance; £100 a year towards his education and £200 a year on the death of his grandfather. So that although the 4th Earl became a very wealthy man, his early years were spent in relative poverty. While at Corpus Christi, Cambridge – he arrived at the college on 10 November 1747, when he was seventeen – he toyed with the idea of a career as a lawyer, and was admitted to Lincoln's Inn in February 1748. But it was Cambridge that nurtured him for three years, even though he did not trouble to take a degree.

Just as his brother the 3rd Earl had done before him, Frederick disdained searching for a wealthy wife and married for love, hence gaining the disapproval of his grandfather. In 1752, nine days before his twenty-second birthday, Frederick was wed to Elizabeth Davers, a charming and delightful girl of nineteen. Another drawback as far as family approval was concerned was the somewhat cavalier attitude Elizabeth's parents had taken to the matter of their own lawful wedlock. Her father, Sir Jermyn Davers, had lived with Elizabeth's mother for a decade before they bothered to get married. Perhaps worse still, Sir Jermyn, like Lord Bristol a Suffolk squire, had the temerity to espouse the Tory cause in Bury. Elizabeth Davers brought with her a modest dowry of £3,000, which Frederick no doubt reckoned better than nothing. And as a dutiful wife she could not be faulted, producing three girls and four boys, by far the most notorious of whom was to turn out to be her second daughter, also named Elizabeth.

It seems that before joining the army Frederick's younger brother William had intended to seek ordination, and when he changed his mind Frederick wrote to his brother-in-law Constantine Phipps (unlike most of the family, he and his wife Lepel had accepted Frederick's marriage from the start), 'Since [William] has resolv'd not to be a clergyman I think I have determined to become one – my Inclination, my interest, and what tho' last mentioned yet first consider'd, Mrs Hervey's desire, all unite and have all been strenthen'd by my brother's approbation [he meant his elder brother, Lord Bristol], so that nothing now remains to complete my scheme but some preparation and the time to execute it.' No mention of God or a vocation; and by preparation he did not mean he was about to go into retreat and pray, merely to address the authorities at Corpus Christi on the matter of an MA being conferred without examination, a privilege accorded to the sons of peers. Just a couple of months after writing to Phipps, Frederick found a bishop – of Ely – prepared to ordain him deacon, and on 26 January 1755 he was priested. He had to wait until 1768 for an honorary doctorate of divinity, from Trinity College, Dublin; Oxford awarded him a doctorate two years later.

That Frederick Hervey had no vocation to be a parish priest goes without saying. He picked up a couple of poorly paid sinecures, and in 1761 he was appointed a chaplain to the king, which would only have entailed preaching the occasional sermon in one of the chapels royal. He seems to have performed no spiritual duties whatsoever, although not for want of trying;

[101]

even while the Dean of Bristol was 'in extreme good health on Friday last', as the Duke of Newcastle felt obliged to inform Hervey, the ambitious cleric was seeking the deanery. Attempts to dislodge the incumbent Dean of Norwich and the Master of Magdalene College, Cambridge fared no better. Rather than hang around with time on his hands, the Reverend the Hon Frederick Hervey sallied forth with his wife on the first of many Continental jaunts, the adventurous itinerary taking in Brussels, Geneva, Naples, Rome, Florence, Venice, Padua and Corsica. Once Frederick had inherited his brother's earldom, an astonishing number of Bristol Hotels sprang up on the Continent; in some flea-infested inn on the site of some of them Frederick may or may not once have stayed.

One reason Hervey was so anxious for preferment was because his family was steadily increasing and he needed a reasonable income. In 1754 his first daughter, Mary, later Countess of Erne, was born. George followed a year later, dying at the age of nine. Another son, John Augustus, had been born on New Year's Day 1757, and Elizabeth, destined to become a duchess, appeared in 1758. Another short-lived boy was born in 1761, and Louisa and Frederick William arrived respectively in 1767 and 1769. It was while visiting Naples the year before Louisa was born that Hervey nearly suffered a fatal accident. He had been climbing the crater of Mount Vesuvius, and wrote home to his twelve-year-old daughter Mary with the gruesome details. 'At last after about an hour's fatigue we reach'd the summit, where we found a great hollow of about forty feet and half a mile round: at the bottom of this were two large mouths from whence the mountain frequently threw up two or three hundred red hot stones some as big as your head, and some considerably larger. One of these struck me on the right arm, and without giving me much pain at the time made a wound about

[102]

2 inches deep, tore my coat all to shreads, and by a great effu-
sion of blood alarm'd my companions more than myself. In a
few days it became very painful, then dangerous, and so continued to confine me to my bed for near five weeks.'

You gained a bishopric in the eighteenth century in more or
less the same manner as you gained any senior position in society; through personal influence. And when his brother
George was appointed lord lieutenant of Ireland, what more
natural than the promise to Frederick of the first vacant Irish
bishopric? But that, of necessity, meant waiting for a diocesan
bishop to die, for it was almost unheard of before the twentieth century for a bishop to retire. Cloyne, which became vacant in 1767, turned out to be a poorly endowed see, and the
primary motive in being consecrated in the direct Apostolic
Succession was to gain a decent income. But Cloyne could at
least be used as a step on the episcopal ladder, and on 2 February
1767 Frederick was duly nominated. Consecration followed in
Dublin Cathedral on 31 May, the archbishop and the bishops
of Meath and Ferns laying hands on Hervey, and he had to
wait only two years before he could be translated to the see of
Derry, a very wealthy bishopric indeed.[2] It has to be said,
especially in the light of his later casual attitude towards the
duties of a diocesan bishop, that initially Hervey displayed
considerable zeal in his pastoral work, assiduously visiting
parishes, promising not to present English clergy to any Irish
living, raising clergy stipends, building roads and a new much
needed bridge over the River Foyle. Using his experience
gained at Ickworth, he helped to improve farming, and he encouraged the mining of coal. Although it is true he was to lavish vast sums of money on two Irish country mansions for
himself as well as one in England, he also supported public
building ventures, and it was said that the county and city of

Londonderry owed to him 'many of their chief architectural beauties'.

Hervey's biographer, Brian Fothergill, tells a story which shows a most unpleasant side to Frederick's nature – and he was nothing if not a man of contradictions.[3] It seems that in order to fill one particularly wealthy living, Hervey invited to dinner the fattest of his clergy (also presumably the greediest), and after dinner proposed that they should run a race, the winner to be inducted to the rich parish. But there was no winner, Hervey having sent his guests off on a course that ensured they all fell floundering into a bog. While he had little regard for the dignity of others, at least he seldom stood on his own. But so little did he care for other people's feelings that many found it difficult to discern in him a single spark of Christian charity. Emma Hamilton wrote in her *Memoirs* that 'though an ecclesiastic of such high station in the Church, the bishop was an avowed sceptic in religion, the doctrines and institutions of which he would not scruple to ridicule in the company of women, treating even the immortality of the soul as an article of doubt and indifference.' And Lady Hamilton knew Hervey well. Someone who changed their view about the Bishop of Derry as time went by was George III, who had told Hervey's elder brother in 1767, 'I am as well pleased as yourself with his being a bishop.' Later the King denounced him as 'that wicked prelate'.

By April 1770 it may be surmised that Hervey's feelings of affection for his wife had cooled, for he set off for the Continent accompanied by his thirteen-year-old son John Augustus, leaving Elizabeth in Suffolk with the other children. He remained abroad on this occasion eighteen months, no doubt content to let his archdeacons run the diocese (there were, in the Church of Ireland, no suffragan bishops, so perhaps in order for confirma-

tions to be conducted and new clergy to be ordained neighbour-
ing diocesan bishops would have been invited in to administer
the episcopal sacraments). Hervey was an intrepid traveller,
mainly on horseback, and on this journey he saw Geneva,
Rome, Trieste, Toulouse, Lyons, Rouen ... passing through
Verona 'like a flash of lightening'. He delighted in telling an
anecdote about a visit he paid to a monastery when he was mistaken for a Roman Catholic bishop, the monks all kneeling to
receive his blessing. But it is highly unlikely that Roman Catholic Religious would have mistaken an Anglican Irish bishop for
one of their own; in the eighteenth century Anglican bishops
did not even wear an episcopal ring, and the first thing the
monks would have done was genuflect in order to kiss the
missing adornment. With his English accent they would also
have assumed he was a Protestant, for although freelance
Roman Catholic bishops did roam around England in the eighteenth century (one has been reinterred in Westminster Cathedral) the Catholic hierarchy was not reinstated until 1851.

Nevertheless Hervey was a genuine ecumenist, and while in
Rome in 1771 he contrived to be received at least twice by
Clement XIV, for he was anxious to devise some way whereby
the Irish Catholic clergy could subscribe to an oath of allegiance to George III without offending their religious principles. He received a polite hearing but no action by the Vatican
was forthcoming, much to his disgust. A more creative use of
his time was spent studying the remains of Diocletian's palace
at Spalato, now Split, in Dalmatia. The effect these classical
ruins had had upon Robert Adam was to transform English
domestic architecture and interior design, and Hervey too
took back to Ireland a taste for neo-classicism; it was to per-
vade almost all the architectural creations for which he became famous.

[105]

On his death in March 1775 the Bishop's brother and 2nd Earl, George, left him a handsome legacy of £10,000, a very decent addition to his capital pending the likely inheritance of Ickworth Lodge. The Bishop was now in fact heir presumptive to Augustus, whose personal affairs were, as we have seen, in something of a muddle. Frederick had owed his bishopric to his late brother, and of all Lord Hervey's offspring they seem to have enjoyed the closest relationship. Hence the legacy. And on hearing of the 2nd Earl's death Frederick wrote to a friend, 'Within the last few days I have lost the kindest and most affectionate brother. This has blunted in me every sense of pleasure ... I cannot but regret him as long as I live.' Now that he had a considerable stipend, a decent legacy and more or less the certainty of eventually inheriting the family estates – although admittedly in 1775 the new earl was only fifty-one – Frederick felt able to begin a series of building projects that reflected his eccentricity to perfection.

For the site of his first Irish mansion, Downhill Castle, begun in 1776, he chose an exposed and windswept cliff five miles north-west of Coleraine, so exposed that it was almost impossible to grow a tree. By the summer of 1776 the agricultural reformer Arthur Young was able to inspect the outlines of the house, and reported it would be 'a large and convenient edifice when it is finished'. All Frederick's houses turned out to be large; they were seldom convenient. But he loved the bracing Atlantic gales – 'exhilarating and invigorating air' was how he described them – and he believed the atmosphere of Downhill was good for the gout. In 1779, the year of his succession to the Bristol earldom, Frederick commissioned Michael Shanahan, who had built Downhill, to design a mausoleum in memory of the 2nd Earl, based on the Roman mausoleum of the Julii at St Rémy in Provence. It was an elegant building consisting of 'a solid rectangular base in the Ionic order over which rose a lighter circular temple of eight Corinthian columns supporting a cupola topped by an urn.'[4] A statue of the 2nd Lord Bristol graced the inside of the mausoleum, a copy of Magna Carta in his hand, sculpted by a Dutchman, John van Nost the younger, who had settled in Dublin. The lord lieutenant who never set foot in Ireland was richly commemorated, until his mausoleum fell foul of a gale in 1839.

Downhill Castle became the Bishop's principal home, although he built another substantial house in Ireland, Ballyscullion, at Bellaghy, near the shore of Lough Beg. Begun in 1787, Ballyscullion was based on Belle Isle on Lake Windermere. With flanking corridors and a central Palladian porch and cupola, it was also a precursor of the monumental house he later erected at Ickworth. It contained a double corkscrew staircase inspired by the staircases at the Château de Chambord, built by François I in the early sixteenth century; a grand staircase twisting round a smaller one for the servants, so constructed that people on one could not see those on the other. Ballyscullion received few episcopal visits, as things turned out, for it was going up at a time when Frederick was almost constantly on his travels. As a domestic residence, Downhill, in no sense a castle at all, was the more compact and engaging, where 'everything is redolent of Joy and Youth, and we commonly sit down to table from 20 to 25,' the Bishop told Arthur Young. And although Downhill was soon hung with paintings purchased on the Continent – among them works by Titian, Rembrandt and Raphael – the primary purpose of both Ballyscullion and Ickworth House was to serve as repositories for the Bishop's ultimately enormous collection of art and antiques.

Frederick bequeathed both his Irish houses to a first cousin once removed, Henry Hervey Aston Bruce, who was promptly made a baronet and changed his name to Hervey-Bruce. It was he who added crenellated walls and bastions of basalt on the seaward side of Downhill Castle. Sir Henry died in 1822, and in a fire twenty-nine years later much of the interior was destroyed and many works of art lost. Rebuilding did not begin until 1870, and the house was finally demolished in 1950. It was to 'Musick and Harmony of mind' that the prelate attributed the easing of his gout while at Downhill, and he certainly proved to be a jocular and generous host, keeping open house and having many of his junior clergy to stay. But even his was not entirely a life of pleasure, at least in the early years of his episcopacy. In 1775 John Wesley, not much disposed to forgiving untoward levity, spent a Sunday with Hervey and was much impressed by the 'admirable solemnity' he displayed when celebrating Holy Communion.

It was in 1776 that Hervey's two oldest daughters married, Mary choosing a thirty-eight-year-old widower, the 2nd Baron Erne, created Viscount Erne in 1781 and Earl of Erne eight years later. He had £9,000 a year and four children by his first wife. Elizabeth chose an Irish parliamentarian by the name of John Foster, whom she married in Brussels.[5] 'I like the young man better than ever,' the Bishop told Mary, referring to Foster, 'and I think him peculiarly suited to her.' He was nothing of the sort, and the future career of Lady Elizabeth Foster was very nearly to put her aunt Elizabeth Chudleigh's in the shade.

Having settled in the builders and disposed of two daughters, the Bishop announced that ill health necessitated another journey abroad; it was to last two and a half years. At least his wife was invited to accompany him this time, along with Louisa, who was ten. Mrs Hervey was an illuminating letter-writer. From Pyrmont, famous for its healing properties, she reported to her daughter Mary that the mineral waters were beneficial and would be 'still greater if the weather were not worse than ever you saw it, even in Derry, constant rain, dirt and puddle, yet in spite of all [the Bishop] is well and cheerful and the gouty pains fly before them.' They became intimate with Princess Augusta, once the 'little rat of a girl, about the bigness of a good large toothpick case', whose controversial birth the Bishop's father had missed by some forty minutes, now married to the hereditary prince of Brunswick-Wolfenbüttel. 'We dine with her quite *en famille*,' Mrs Hervey was proud to boast. It sounds like a very jolly royal get-together. Two of Queen Charlotte's Mecklenburg-Strelitz brothers were there to dance attendance. So was the Prince of Waldeck, whom Mrs Hervey found 'vastly obliging', and Prince Augustus of Saxe-Gotha of whom she reported, 'We have taken violently to each other.' Her husband too found the place 'magical', and had some difficulty tearing himself away 'into dear Italy once more'.

If anyone doubts the inherent eccentricity of the Bishop of Derry, one need only consider that he would hold a levee – a reception at which only men were present – at six o'clock in the morning. On Maunday Thursday in the Sistine Chapel he 'most absurdly appeared in his English bishop's dress,' Sir Edward Newenham, an Irish politician, recorded in his diary. 'He was laughed at by everyone. For this piece of absurdity he was obliged to go to the lowest part of the chapel among the common people while my sons and I were in the same upper division with the Cardinals. After this behaviour the eccentric bishop was held in the greatest contempt. Scarcely a nobleman would visit him.' And one can gauge Frederick's order of priorities when in 1789 he succeeded to his brother's earldom, exchanging his episcopal signature Frederick Derry for his ennobled one, Bristol, save when he was overseas, when he ran the two together, calling himself Le Comte de Bristol, Evêque de Derry. To be fair, he was generally referred to in society as an Earl-Bishop, and as bishops only rank as barons he was strictly speaking correct in opting for 'Bristol'. There were few precedents for him to follow, the last Earl-Bishop very likely having been Odo, the half-brother of William the Conqueror, who was Earl of Kent and Bishop of Bayeux.

The year 1780 did at least find Frederick back in his neglected diocese, when he had fun hanging his newly acquired paintings at Downhill. But he was soon off again, this time to enjoy a two-year holiday in England, living at Ickworth Lodge. Here Mrs Hervey tried to effect a reconciliation, without success, between her daughter Elizabeth and her husband, John Foster, whose marriage was already adrift. 'With regard to the reconciliation,' she wrote to Mary, 'I do not think there is a ray of comfort or hope in it. It was totally against my opinion as to *happiness*, but yr Father's orders [she meant his episcopal orders] and her situation [Elizabeth was pregnant] call'd for it.' Elizabeth Foster had given birth in 1777 to Frederick; this second boy, Augustus, was born on 4 December 1780. Despite her pending separation from her husband, Augustus was not to be the last of her children. And by this time the Bishop's elder son, now Lord Hervey, was the father of a baby girl. When in April 1781 Lady Elizabeth finally parted from her husband, her father sauntered off to Norfolk, leaving his wife to cope with the mess.

According to the Bishop's niece, the daughter of Lapel Phipps, Elizabeth's 'odious husband will settle so little on her that she must be dependent on her father, which is always an unpleasant thing.' While staying at the Lodge she told her husband that her 'noble uncle' cared for nobody but himself, would not allow Lady Bristol to go to court or even to town, 'lives magnificently, has an excellent cook, is himself in high spirits, and we pretend to be so.' Lady Bristol she thought 'a charming woman', with 'great good humour and a great deal of dignity and good breeding.' Much good did this delightful character reference do her.

Like his grandfather, Frederick Bristol now began to envisage vast improvements to the estate, and in February 1782 he persuaded the influential landscape gardener Lancelot Brown to visit Ickworth. Nothing materialized at the time, and Brown may simply have been questioned about a suitable site for yet another grand mansion. The truth is that Lord Bristol was far more interested in buildings than in people – and that included his own family. After thirty years of marriage he suddenly decided to abandon his wife, leaving her behind at Ickworth Lodge in November 1782 on his delayed departure for Ireland; he rented out his London house for £700 a year, and it seems quite clear he intended a permanent breach. Lady Bristol wrote to her daughter Elizabeth, 'I leave him to Heaven, and to those thorns that in his bosom lodge to prick and sting him.'

Back in his diocese the Bishop began to flirt so outrageously with a twenty-year-old and very beautiful first cousin once removed as to cause a scandal. Her name was Frideswide Mussenden; she was married, and her father, Frederick's uncle, was a clergyman. Frederick bragged about his lady friend to Lady Erne, who was told of a land of 'eternal springs and cloudless skies' in which her father was cavorting. While the romance was almost certainly not consummated, it did result in a second architectural folly in the grounds of Downhill – the Mussenden Temple, a circular structure with a doomed roof supported by Corinthian columns. It was intended both as a homage to Mrs Mussenden and as a library, and nearly 200 years ahead of his time Frederick allowed the local Roman Catholic community to use the vault of the temple for their services. By the oddest quirk of fate, in 1785, the year that Michael Shanahan completed this pleasing building, its dedicatee died, aged twenty-two. So extravagant had the Bishop's adoration for his cousin been that in 1783 a letter, hiding behind the cowardly shield of anonymity, had appeared in the *Freeman's Journal* virtually indicting Frederick of having seduced Mrs Mussenden and become her lover. But these libels were not believed by the young lady's family; her brother, the Reverend Henry Bruce, remained so loyal to Frederick that this may well explain why he inherited Downhill and Ballyscullion. The Temple was originally built thirty feet from the cliff edge, but progressive erosion eventually left it standing just a foot away and ready to tumble into the Atlantic. In 1997 it was declared one of the most threatened monuments in the world, and it had to be saved at considerable expense by the National Trust who strengthened the cliff face.

Apparently not sufficiently occupied with building, buying pictures and conducting an indiscreet if platonic love affair, Frederick Hervey now decided to plunge head first into Irish politics, taking up the cause of the volunteer movement and causing alarm and consternation at Westminster, not least because the Bishop's clear intention was to take over the leadership of the Londonderry Volunteer Corps. He got himself appointed colonel prior to a meeting of delegates in Dublin, and his journey from Derry to Dublin took the form of a triumphal procession, he and his cavalcade of supporters being greeted en route with military honours. Coachmen, footmen and postilions were decked out in livery and Bristol himself wore episcopal purple, with a military hat and white gloves with gold fringes. He 'never ceased making dignified obeisances to the multitude' as he rode in his open landau drawn by six horses, and on arrival at the Houses of Parliament his trumpeters blew a fanfare. The fact that the members were sitting at the time does not seem to have occurred to him, and many of them ran outside to complain.

It was not an auspicious beginning to a series of meetings at which Lord Bristol was outflanked by his opponents and singularly failed to pull off his mission. Plans for reform of a lower house that contained 300 members, 200 of whom sat for pocket boroughs, and an upper house that had been, in the past twenty years, topped up with thirty-three barons, sixteen viscounts and two dozen earls as political placemen were produced of 'the wildest and most ridiculous nature'. With considerable courage, it has to be said, Bristol demanded Catholic emancipation, but it is not quite clear why, unless he was simply exercising the kind of liberal Whigism practiced by his paternal grandfather. There were two positive outcomes: the arousal of deep suspicion in the lord lieutenant's residence and at Windsor Castle, and an avalanche of fan mail from the ordinary people of Ireland, to whom the Bishop of Derry was quickly becoming a folk hero. But the secretary of state, Lord Hillsborough, thought that Lord Bristol was 'going on like a madman'. And he concluded that 'the people are as mad as the Bishop, and God knows to what length they may go. The forbearance with regard to his Lordship makes him imagine that Government is intimidated.' There was talk of impeachment, from now on the lord lieutenant had Bristol under surveillance and plans were actually drawn up to have him arrested. It was at this juncture that George III pronounced upon 'the wicked prelate'. What almost certainly saved the Government in London from the folly of arresting the Bishop of Derry was his popularity in Ireland.

William Lecky, the historian, summed up pretty fairly when he wrote:

Vain, impetuous, and delighting in display; with an insatiable appetite for popularity, and utterly reckless about the consequences of his acts, he exhibited all the characteristics of the most irresponsible adventurer. Under other circumstances he might have been capable of the policy of an Alberoni. In Ireland, for a short time, he rode upon the crest of the wave; and if he had obtained the control he had aspired to over the volunteer movement, he would probably have headed a civil war. But though a man of indisputable courage, and of considerable popular talents, he had neither the caution of a great rebel nor the settled principles of a great statesman.

7

A STUPENDOUS MONUMENT OF FOLLY

While the Bishop of Derry was amusing himself his family was falling apart. Lord Hervey had been banished from Downhill for extravagance. Mary, like Elizabeth, was now separated from her husband. And at Ickworth Lodge the sixteen-year-old Lady Louisa Hervey, whose ultimate fate was to be married to the forlorn prime minister Lord Liverpool, was reduced to a nervous breakdown, restricted as she was to the company of a French governess and a mother who had taken to extracting censored pages from the novels she read. Concerned only with his own health, the Bishop repaired to Bath, where he managed to 'crawl to the pump,' and then he was off again on his travels.

Accompanied this time by his younger son he headed first to Lyons, there to meet Lady Erne. Then they moved to Rome, whence he was pursued by Lord Hervey, who had condescended to break off an affair he was enjoying in Naples with the wife of a Neapolitan prince in the hopes of getting his father to 'quit his creditors'. But Lord Bristol gave his son the slip, only to receive, on travelling on to Florence, the shocking news

[115]

that his nephew, George Fitzgerald, the son of John Hervey's second daughter Mary, had been hanged for murder. It was George who had commanded his uncle's escort when he drove to the Irish parliament. He had by then already spent time in prison, and it seems that his was a hot-blooded temperament; while waiting to ambush someone with whom he was conducting a feud he shot another man, having already, so he boasted, taken part in twenty-six duels. Horace Mann, whose forty-year tour of duty as Minister in Florence was drawing to a close (he was now eighty), managed to keep the news of this family disgrace out of the Italian newspapers. More than somewhat subdued, in February 1787 Lord Bristol returned to Downhill.

But within a month he was writing to Mary Erne to tell her he had 'begun a *new Villa*'. The situation, he enthused, was 'beautiful and salubrious beyond all description'. This was to be Ballyscullion. The foundation stone was laid in April 1787, and in addition to its famous staircase the house was intended to be 'perfectly circular', Lord Bristol told his daughter, although it ended up oval. The picturesque was much in vogue, and in order that the 'new villa' should sit in perfect surroundings the Bishop got busy badgering the patrons of churches within sight to build spires. He was greatly encouraged in the case of one nearby church, as he announced to his daughter. 'The Worshipful Company of Drapers in the City of London have in the most obliging and flattering manner given me anonymously £100 towards building a steeple and spire at Ballynascreen, so that before the end of the year [1792] I hope to have 4 or even 5 spires in the sight of Ballyscullion built chiefly at the expense of other people to beautify the prospect.'

By the time the house was fit to live in in 1789 (he intended to allow 'young geniuses' who could not afford to travel to Italy 'to come into my house and there copy the best masters') he

Augustus John Hervey, 3rd Earl of Bristol (1724-79), an accomplished naval officer and inveterate philanderer. Like his father, Lord Hervey of Ickworth, the 3rd Earl kept a riveting journal. In 1744 he made a youthful and foolhardy marriage to the notorious Elizabeth Chudleigh, a maid of honour to Augustus, Princess of Wales, who later bigamously married the 2nd Duke of Kingston.

Frederick Hervey (1730-1803), 4th Earl of Bristol and Bishop of Derry, known as the Earl-Bishop. He was the third grandson of the 1st Earl of Bristol to succeed to the title. He travelled extensively on the continent, where he purchased priceless works of art, and built two mansions in Ireland before commencing work on Ickworth House in Suffolk. In the background of Elizabeth Vigée-Lebrun's portrait of 1790 can be seen Mount Vesuvius, on whose slopes in 1769 the bishop nearly lost his life.

Lady Elizabeth Foster (1759-1824), second daughter of the 4th Earl of Bristol and first married to John Foster, MP. She was an intimate friend of Georgiana, Duchess of Devonshire and of her husband the 5th Duke of Devonshire, by whom she had two illegitimate children.

She eventually achieved her ambition to become mistress of Chatsworth when in 1809 she became the Duke's second wife.

Left. Georgiana, Duchess of Devonshire (1757–1806) and *(below right)* her husband, William Cavendish, 5th Duke of Devonshire (1748–1811). Both were devoted to Lady Elizabeth Foster, the former Elizabeth Hervey, and at Chatsworth in Derbyshire their friendship formed a scandalous ménage à trios. Georgiana called Elizabeth her 'lovely friend', while the duke thought nothing of sleeping one night with his wife, the next with Elizabeth.

was abroad; he returned in November 1790, remained in Ireland on this occasion less than a year, and when he again departed for the Continent at the end of 1791 he had a dozen years still to live. But he never bothered to visit his diocese or his adopted country again. Ballyscullion stood empty for the rest of the Bishop's life, remained unfinished, and in 1813 it was demolished in order to avoid paying window tax. All that remains of what became known inevitably as the Bishop's Folly is the portico, at some time re-erected at St George's Church in Belfast.

Frederick Bristol liked nothing better than to champion an unpopular cause. If it was not Catholic emancipation it was an old school friend's choice of bride. For a diplomat to keep a mistress was one thing; for him to marry her meant she had the right of entrée to official receptions and dinners she would not previously have attended – indeed, to be presented to the sovereign of whatever court her husband had been accredited to. When after much nagging from Emma Hart, Sir William Hamilton eventually agreed to marry her, it was to the consternation of those who now felt uncertain whether they could receive her. But this was no problem for the Bishop, who had always greatly admired Emma's beauty, and from Blenheim Palace, where he was staying, he wrote to Hamilton on 21 December 1791 to say, 'I congratulate you, my old friend, from the bottom of my heart upon the fortitude you have shown, and the manly part you have taken in braving the world and securing your own happiness and elegant enjoyments in defiance of them.'

Why Lord Bristol left Ireland for good late in 1791 it is impossible to know for sure. His excuse every time he deserted his diocese was ill health, and on this occasion he felt so unwell (he may in fact have been a genuine hypochondriac) he made his will, signing it Bristol and Frederick Derry. The £10,000 legacy he had received from his brother had been left in trust for

[117]

Frederick's children, with the proviso that he could bequeath it to his offspring in whatever proportions he chose. This left him free to make a thoroughly diversive will, if not actually an illegal one. At the time of their marriages he had settled £2,000 each on Mary and Elizabeth; he now declared that those settlements were in fact their share of his brother's legacy, thus in effect pocketing £4,000. He then declared: 'I give to my affectionate and dutiful daughter Lady Louisa Hervey five thousand pounds and to my undutiful and ungrateful son Frederick William Hervey I give one thousand pounds.' Lord Hervey was to receive nothing from his uncle's bequest, but he was left all his father's property in England – in other words, the Suffolk estate and the London house – but these would have come to him anyway. Fate was shortly to upset Lord Bristol's spiteful intentions towards his younger son, who seems to have incurred his father's displeasure because he declined – and Lady Bristol took his side, which would not have helped – to visit the Netherlands with a tutor.

What is so extraordinary about Lord Bristol's decision to build a great new house at Ickworth is that he could cheerfully let ten years slip by without once visiting the estate, and that having paid a brief call before setting out for the Continent, first making sure his wife would be staying at Ramsgate, he conducted all the architectural arrangements from abroad. It was as though he had never planned to live in the new house, merely to have more and more pictures hung there, and that he saw himself as a great builder who was acting entirely for the benefit of posterity.

He left England in September 1792, accompanied by a chaplain with the rather exotic name of Trefusis Lovell, but as Lord Bristol was hardly likely to carry out any episcopal duties on his travels Mr Lovell was more of a companion than a chaplain.

One of the most remarkable encounters Bristol enjoyed, at Jena, was with the novelist and poet Johann von Goethe, with whom the Bishop lost no time having a stand-up row, accusing him, as a result of his book *The Sorrows of Werther*, of tempting people to commit suicide. Goethe described Lord Bristol as of 'slight frame and countenance, lively in carriage and manners, quick in his speech, blunt, sometimes even rude.' He thought, however, that the obstinate and pedantic side of his nature was balanced by 'his extensive knowledge of the world, of men and of books,' and by 'the liberality of a noble and by the ease of a rich man.' He added at a later date, 'It was sometimes his whim to be offensive, but if one treated him equally offensively he would become perfectly amenable.' After subjecting the Bishop to a catalogue of sins committed by the Church, Goethe commented, 'This outburst worked on the bishop like a charm. He turned meek as a lamb and treated me from then on, during the rest of our conversation, with the utmost courtesy and subtlest tact.'

In the autumn of 1793 Frederick's elder son John was in serious trouble. For the past six years he had been serving as British Minister at the court of the Grand Duke of Tuscany, a diplomatic post for which he appears to have had no qualifications or aptitude whatsoever. He had taken as his mistress Lady Anne Hatton, who unfortunately had also caught the eye of George III's sixth son, the twenty-year-old Prince Augustus, later created Duke of Sussex. Their rivalry is said to have caused a stir, but it cannot have been of long duration, for in 1793 the impetuous Prince was foolish enough, in Rome, to marry Lady Augusta Murray in deliberate contravention of the 1772 Royal Marriages Act. But something had excited Lord Hervey enough for him to start referring to the Grand Duke in a letter as a fool, and his chief minister as a knave. 'It will not be possible to allow him to remain after his behaviour,' Lady Webster wrote in her *Journal*. Married to Sir Godfrey Webster, she was travelling with the 3rd Lord Holland (he was only twenty, having succeeded to the barony at the age of two), whom in 1797, having given birth to Holland's son and been divorced by her husband, she married. She became, for half a century, the doughty literary and political hostess at Holland House, dying in 1845. To compound his foolishness, Lord Hervey was rude to the Grand Duke, Lord Holland himself describing Hervey's conduct as 'intemperate, indecorous and violent in the extreme'.

Discovering to her horror that her son was to be recalled, Lady Bristol begged his brother Frederick to ask for an interview with the prime minister, to seek permission to travel to Florence to break the news to Lord Hervey personally. 'Fred saw Mr Pitt this morning,' Lady Bristol wrote to the Countess of Erne (as her daughter Mary had become in 1789). 'Nothing could be more gracious, open and condescending, with very obliging professions of regard to the Family, and concern for this unlucky incident. I find they have nothing in view for him but a pension – but we must try for some distinction.' Frederick received the necessary permission to go to Florence. 'Fred's request to be messenger of *bad news* is so uncommon that I see it has struck Mr Pitt very much,' Lady Bristol reported to her daughter, 'and he has behav'd with uncommon kindness to him. It is certainly a charming thing, and I think his going to Hervey will mollify him and do a great deal of good.' She was hoping too that Frederick might effect some sort of family reconciliation at home, but her hopes were in vain. Lord Bristol did not want to know about Lord Hervey's problems, and steered well clear of Florence where, no doubt unknown to him, Lord Hervey had compounded all his previous stupid conduct by

making amorous advances to Lady Webster. 'Surprise and embarrassment have completely overset me,' she wrote in her *Journal*. 'Oh! what vile animals men are, with headstrong passions.'

Having avoided his son, Lord Bristol made a beeline in Rome
for someone he would have considered far more rewarding, a
young man of twenty-two called Charles Heathcote Tatham. He
was a friend of Sir William Hamilton who, like Vanburgh at the
start of his career, had no formal architectural training; he was
in fact intent on drawing classical ruins, which may at that time
have passed for an adequate architectural education. Tatham
wrote on 19 November 1794 to Lord Holland to say, 'The Earl of
Bristol Bishop of Derry, lately arrived in Rome, to my great surprise consulted me to make him a design for a Villa to be built
in Suffolk extending nearly 500 feet, including offices. The dis-
tribution of the plan is very singular the House being oval
according to his desire.' In the event Tatham was not entrusted
with the commission, and it seems that Bristol was merely trying out on him ideas he now carried daily in his head.

One reason Lord Bristol tarried on the Continent – if tarried
is the word to describe the abandonment of his diocese for a
disgraceful length of time – was because there was a constant
supply of beautiful women with whom, away from the prying
eyes of his clergy, he felt perfectly at liberty to flirt. One was
Emma Hamilton, who became his 'dearest Emma' and sometimes his 'dearest dear Emma'. There were royalty to be rude
to; at a music party at the Hamiltons Prince Augustus decided
to sing along, and was told by the Bishop, 'Pray cease, you have
the ears of an ass.' Another flight of his romantic folly was
aimed at a former mistress of Frederick William II of Prussia,
known as Madame Ritz and later ennobled as Countess von
Lichtenau in order that she could be presented to the Queen of Naples. They met at a concert in Munich, and Bristol immediately fell

for her combination of beauty, charm and intelligence. She soon became his *adorable amie*. He followed her to Bologna, an abortive journey as it transpired, but eventually enticed her to Naples. 'For Heaven's sake, *chère Comtesse et adorable amie*,' he had written on 29 December 1795, 'do not continue to moulder in the mire of that unhealthy town of Rome...but come and enjoy this earthly paradise.' When the Countess arrived in January Bristol paraded in public with her miniature on a chain hung round his neck, merely the finishing touch to a sartorial clutter consisting of a coat of crimson silk, purple stockings and a white hat edged with more episcopal purple.

While staying in Naples, John Morritt, a friend of Sir Walter Scott, noticed the Bishop in the company of Countess von Lichtenau, and reported home that the Bishop was 'constantly talking blasphemy, or indecently at least, and at the same time [was] very clever and with infinite wit – in short, a true Hervey.' He added that Lord Bristol courted 'every young and every old woman he knows'. But there was a brief pause in the chase when in February news arrived in Naples of the death at sea – from the prosaic cause of a common cold caught while on deck – of his elder son and heir, Lord Hervey. It was Prince Augustus who broke the news to Lord Bristol, news which, Bristol wrote to Lady Hamilton, had 'quite *bouleversée* my already shattered frame.'

Physically, Bristol really was in a bad way, and the shock of his son's unexpected death, resulting in just two possible heirs remaining, his younger son Frederick and his bachelor brother William (all his Hervey uncles were dead), seems to have exacerbated his condition. He took to his bed, his pulse, he told Lady Erne, 'scarce to be felt'. He had been 'very nearly dying' according to John Morritt, who added that he was sorry to say the Bishop was better 'and likely to recover'. The first thing

Lord Bristol did on recovering was give serious thought to Frederick's marriage, for he could see a very real possibility that the Bristol earldom might become extinct. Who should he alight upon as a potential daughter-in-law but the illegitimate daughter of his friend Countess von Lichtenau, the girl's father just happening to be the King of Prussia.

Mariana von der Mark, as she was known, was seventeen, very beautiful and very rich. Her mother thoroughly approved of the Bishop's plan for her to marry the new Lord Hervey, and set out for Berlin to try to win the King's approval. 'The good and kindly Lord Bristol is in despair without you,' Emma Hamilton wrote to the Countess, 'and awaits you with the same ardent desire as the Jews the Messiah.' The Countess, of course, had never met her prospective son-in-law, so Lord Bristol extolled his newly discovered virtues in a letter. On 26 May 1796, writing from Rome, he told her, 'The prolongation of my convalescence, dear friend, has given me time carefully to weigh our plan; the more I think, the more I dream of it, the better I augur it. [Lord Hervey] is to come to meet us at Prymont – and I have no hesitation in saying that you will be captivated and really enchanted by him. He is a perfect man of the world – versed in literature, conversant with politics; a handsome countenance, beautiful features, a striking face – natural eloquence – charming manner, English modesty and reserve.' This was the 'undutiful and ungrateful' son to whom so recently the Bishop had bequeathed a mere £1,000. There was only one unfortunate snag to be overcome: Frederick's implacable opposition to his father's matrimonial plans for him. He had already decided to marry Elizabeth Upton, daughter of the 1st Lord Templetown, better known to his intimates by his Christian name, Clotworthy; and no amount of parental bullying would budge him.

[123]

The prospect of an alliance with the Prussian royal family, with all the advantages he could envisage for himself, was not the only grandiose scheme occupying the Bishop's mind. Through his years of wandering round the Continent he had seldom ceased to think about the house he was having built by correspondence. Back in September 1795 he had been writing home about basso-rilievos – sculpture with a slightly raised design – to be painted as 'Dear Canova suggested', and by the end of that year he had met in Rome a young Irish architect he had known previously from his time in Derry. This was Francis Sandys, who returned to England with a firm commission to 'erect a Palace'. 'A stupendous monument of folly' was Lady Bristol's verdict as building operations proceeded apace, for she could see that the new Suffolk house intended to supersede Ickworth Lodge was going to be at least twice the size of Ballyscullion, with an eventual frontage of 600 feet, its central oval rotunda measuring 160 feet by 120 feet, the height of the dome from the ground rising to 104 feet. Lord Bristol was intending to live in the central rooms. The pavilions, each, as Brian Fothergill has written, 'the size of a substantial country house,' were reserved for his treasures.[1] The reason for his own rooms on the ground floor being so spacious – he wanted them thirty feet high – was because he felt claustrophobic in rooms with low ceilings. A Cambridge professor, John Symonds, was told by the Bishop in a letter written from Pyrmont on 16 July 1796 that he wished to make Ickworth House 'quite classical, to unite magnificence with convenience and simplicity with Dignity'. His chaplain, Mr Lovell, was dispatched to England with architectural instructions; a papier mâché model of the house as envisaged by Sandys, on a scale of 1 inch to 12 feet, was sent out to Italy. The designing and building of Ickworth must be a unique instance of architectural cooperation between a patron who never set foot on the site and those entrusted with putting his very exacting requirements into effect.

As the instigator of Ickworth House it is appropriate there should be likenesses of the 4th Earl on view. In the drawing room is a portrait of him by Elizabeth Vigée-Lebrun, with Mount Vesuvius, by whose crater he nearly lost his life, smoking away in the distance, painted in 1790. In the entrance hall is an almost certainly posthumous and unattributed portrait, dating from about 1805. Over the fireplace in the smoking room is a painting by William Hoare of the Bishop presenting his elder son John Augustus to William Pitt in 1771. And on his return from fighting in the American War of Independence in 1783 John Augustus had himself painted, with his dog Twitchet, by Gainsborough. This portrait hangs in the drawing room. Someone else who travelled to America and whose portrait is at Ickworth (off the east corridor) is the Bishop's brother-in-law, Sir Robert Davers, who was painted by Batoni in Rome in 1756, and had the misfortune to be murdered by American Indians near Lake Huron in 1763. The most striking portrait of the 4th Earl is to be found in the west bedroom. Painted in 1790 by Hugh Douglas Hamilton, an Irishman who specialized in depicting young gentlemen on the Grand Tour, it shows the Bishop seated in a corner of the Borghese Gardens, overlooking a detailed vista of Rome.

Impatient to welcome wealth and semi-royalty into his family, Bristol ordered a portrait of Countess von Lichtenau's daughter, sent the Countess innumerable presents, and begged in return the gift of a watch. At Civita Castellana he found himself staying in an inn previously frequented by the Countess, where he discovered her 'dear precious name' traced in her own hand on the chimney-piece in his room. He even fancied, as the wind was in the north, that each gust had come from her, having passed over her rosy lips and mingled with her zephyr breath.

On his arrival at Pyrmont Lord Bristol found the King, the Countess and their daughter all duly assembled; the only person missing was Lord Hervey. It seems that Lady Elizabeth Foster broke the news to Bristol that her brother had promised his heart to another. She was immediately roped in as an intermediary. 'Dearest Elizabeth,' Lord Bristol wrote, 'Though I would not for the world itself disappoint your poor Brother's hopes, if his noble generous heart be really engaged, nor even diminish of one obol [one-sixth of a Greek drachma] the allowance I should be able to make him, which is exactly the same I gave your poor dear eldest brother, yet I must confess it would half break my heart to see his fixed on any other than the beautiful, elegant, important and interesting object I have proposed to him. At least, dearest Eliza, if you have any interest with him, induce him, beg him, my dear, not to decide before he is able to choose'. Mariana would, he continued:

> bring him into our family £5,000 a year, *besides* a principality in Germany, an English Dukedom for Frederick or me, which the King of Prussia is determined to obtain in case the marriage take place – a perpetual relationship with both the Princess of Wales and her children, as also with the Duchess of York and her progeny – the Embassy to Berlin, with such an influence and preponderance in favor of dear England as no other could withstand. Add to all this the King is so bent upon it from his great partiality to me that doubt not his doubling the dot in case F desired it, which indeed I should not ... In short, nothing could be more brilliant, or flattering, or more cordial than his recep-

tion in case he can think with us; and indeed, Dearest Elizabeth, the example he has before his eyes in and within his own family ought fully to determine him against a love-match; 'tis so ominous a lottery, so pregnant with blanks, so improbable of success … All I desire of him is not to resolve against us, not to throw away a Pearl, richer than all his tribe; let him but see before he decides, let him weigh all we offer to his ambition, his ease, his comfort, his taste, and his pocket.

It was not, of course, Hervey's ambition, ease, comfort, taste or pocket Lord Bristol was concerned with, but his own; and as a letter from a father and a bishop this one was a disgrace. Both Elizabeth and Frederick maintained a stony silence, even though Lord Bristol continued to bombard them with talk of a dukedom and the embassy in Berlin. It was all to no avail, and in 1797 Mariana von de Mark was married to Count Frederick von Stolberg, while Frederick Hervey walked down the aisle with his chosen bride in February the following year. Frederick was advanced to the rank of a marquess in 1826 but the dukedom his father so longed for eluded him. (It is doubtful whether Lord Bristol thought it any consolation when in 1799, through his maternal grandmother, he inherited the barony of Howard de Walden. Three years after his death it devolved upon his grandson, the 2nd Lord Seaford, who became Lord Howard de Walden & Seaford.)

As the health of the King of Prussia deteriorated Lord Bristol offered a helping hand to his Countess; indeed, he offered her the protection of his 'house in England, and all my houses in Ireland. Willingly,' he told her, 'will I share my purse with the friend who monopolises my heart and all my affections.' At this time he also had a large house in Naples, which he placed at the

disposal of the king, for he had a great belief in the curative
powers of the '*atmosphère vernal de Naples*'. However, the king
appears to have recovered without leaving his own territory, for
Lord Bristol moved into one of the king's houses, Sans Souci at
Potsdam, the rococo summer palace begun by Frederick the
Great in 1745. Although Lord Bristol overstayed his welcome
and complained that the moon in Naples was warmer than the
sun in Berlin, when he left the King presented him with a fabu-
lous Dresden breakfast service. Four months later the King was
dead; accused of having taken bribes from the French, the
Countess was thrown into prison. She was also accused of being in league with the Bishop on behalf of Great Britain. Politics
in Europe were in chaos; Bristol had undoubtedly dabbled in
the mire himself and he too was to pay the price. Meanwhile, he
left his adored Countess to suffer indignity – she was later freed
and cleared of all charges – without making the slightest attempt to see her or help her in any way.

What he did instead was once again harness his entourage –
he had a cook who rode ahead in order to have a splendid
meal awaiting him at the end of the day – and pursue his almost neurotic wanderings: over the Alps, to Trieste and
Padua, back to Venice, then to Milan. The roads were bad, the
Bishop rode on horseback and progress was slow, for apart
from the dangerous terrain and 'those accumulated
Purgatories' as he described the mountain passes, his travelling carriage became increasingly laden with statues and
paintings purchased en route. The one destination he had no
intention of making for was Derry, and after he had been
absent five years, and rumours of his pending death had so
often proved premature, three of his brother bishops let it be
known that, even by the standards of absentee bishops in the
eighteenth century, his conduct had gone beyond anything

that was acceptable. The Bishop reacted in a way that makes one wonder if by now his mind was not a little unhinged. He placed three peas in a bladder and sent this peculiar package to the Archbishop of Armagh, accompanied by the following whimsical lines, which he signed Bristol & Derry:

> Three large blue-bottles sat upon three blown bladders;
> Blow, bottle-flies, blow. Burst, blown bladders, burst.

Not long afterwards his eccentricity nearly cost him his life. At Siena, during the feast of Corpus Christi, the Bishop was enjoying dinner at a hotel when the procession of the Blessed Sacrament passed by in the street below. As he disliked the tinkling of bells he picked up a tureen of pasta and hurled it out of the window. Had he not escaped on horseback he could easily have been lynched. Such an act of sacrilege would have occasioned surprise under any circumstances; an Anglican bishop normally so well disposed towards Catholics who could behave in such an outrageous manner in someone else's country can perhaps be forgiven on the grounds that he was becoming increasingly dotty.

With Napoleon Bonaparte and his family on the rampage and republics taking the place of monarchies, Lord Bristol's indiscretions in letters to Sir William Hamilton and his daughter Elizabeth (he must have known the post was frequently intercepted) became fairly breathtaking. He had come to detest the French, and he had no hesitation in saying so – while passing through their newly sequestered lands. And it became quite obvious to those in authority that the Earl-Bishop was a British spy. The fact that no one to whom he sent messages at home – Pitt, Lord Liverpool, Earl Spencer, the Devonshires – took the least heed of him failed to convince the French that he was not an official secret agent. His crackpot scheme for partitioning

France must have struck the new masters of Europe as particularly ominous.

Sensing danger too late, Lord Bristol instructed his bankers in Leghorn to ship his treasures in store there to Corsica. His bankers thought Corsica even more dangerous than the Continent and initially ignored his instructions. But when the French army suddenly appeared on the horizon they decided to act, hiring a boat for £1,800 to move valuables to the tune of £800. It would not be long before total disaster would overtake Lord Bristol's treasure trove, for works of art stored at Rome were seized by the French invaders. He thought their value between £18,000 and £20,000, but he never troubled to keep proper records of his purchases, and any one of his paintings by the great masters could be worth millions of pounds today. Sure enough, he dreamed up a madcap plan for their retrieval. He asked Elizabeth Foster to arrange with the prime minister for him to be appointed ambassador to Rome and for a Minister to be sent out from England to congratulate the Romans on their emancipation. That way he would save 'all that immense, valuable and beautiful property of large mosaick pavement, statues, busts and marbles without end, first-rate Titians and Raphaels ...'.

In April 1798, still not accredited to an embassy, and never likely to be, the Bishop set out from Venice to Rome, where he hoped he might be able to pay a ransom for his artefacts. At a village called Pedo, between Ferrara and Bologna, he fell ill, and while on his sickbed he was arrested. No specific charges were ever laid, but it was obvious the French knew he had been reporting on their activities. When he was well enough to travel he was taken to Ferrara and then to Milan, where he was imprisoned for nine months in the Castello Sforzesco. He was treated considerately, being allowed to write letters (no doubt all read by his captors before being posted), and permitted his own food and guests. His was very much the sort of genteel imprisonment suffered by medieval princes worth a ransom. The Governor of Milan was in fact paid 50,000 francs but unfortunately, while pocketing the money, he failed to release his prisoner. Nonchalantly reporting Bristol's arrest to London, Sir William Hamilton showed no surprise. 'We know little more about the Earl of Bristol's arrest and present confinement at Milan than was (as I see by the last newspaper) known in England the 29th of April, but we all know that his Lordship's freedom in conversation, particularly after dinner, is such as to make him liable to accidents of this nature.'

Bristol was released in February 1799, and the summer of 1800 found him in Florence, hobnobbing with the Countess of Albany, widow of Prince Charles, the Young Pretender; she noted that he was constantly falling off his horse. And it was in December of that year that Lady Bristol, the Bishop's much-neglected wife, died at Ickworth Lodge. Although the shades were drawing in all round, nothing could curb the Bishop's extravagance; an Irish peer, Lord Cloncurry, was in Rome in 1803, the year of the Bishop's death, and reported that he was receiving 'upwards of £5,000' every quarter which he immediately spent on works of art. Cloncurry wrote:

'In this, as in most other cases, however, the proverb became true – wilful waste made woeful want, and towards the end of the quarter the noble prelate used to find his purse absolutely empty, and his credit so low as to be insufficient to procure him a bottle of Orvieto. There followed a dispersion of his collection as rapidly as it was gathered, but, as might be expected, at a heavy discount.'

By now Lord Bristol's weird appearance on the streets of

Rome had acquired the status of legend. In April 1803 he seemed to a young Irish girl, Catherine Wilmot, as:

> one of the greatest curiosities alive, yet such is his notori-
> ous character for profane conversation, and so great a rep-
> robate is he in the unlicensed sense of the word, that the
> English do not esteem it a very creditable thing to be much
> in his society, excepting only where curiosity particularly
> prompts. I have often seen him riding and driving past our
> windows, and his appearance is so very singular that I
> must describe it to you. His figure is little, and his face
> very sharp and wicked; on his head he wore a purple vel-
> vet night cap with a tassel of gold dangling over his shoul-
> ders and a sort of mitre in the front; silk stockings and
> slippers of the same colour, and a short round petticoat,
> such as Bishops wear, fringed with gold about his knees.
> [This may have been a soutane, normally only worn in
> church or in a procession.] A loose dressing-gown of silk
> was then thrown over his shoulders. In this Merry Andrew
> trim he rode on horseback to the never-ending amusement
> of all Beholders! The last time I saw him he was sitting in
> his carriage between two Italian women, dress'd in white
> Bed-gown and Night-cap like a witch and giving himself
> the airs of an Adonis.

The Earl-Bishop only had three months to live, and the manner of his death was quite in keeping with that of his life – eccentric to the end. On the road from Albano to Rome, on 8 July
1803, he suffered an attack of what he called 'gout in the stomach' (it may have been a recurring ulcer). He was carried into a
cottage, but when it was revealed that the Italian peasant was
sheltering a Protestant bishop – a heretic in his eyes – Lord Bristol was unceremoniously dumped in an outhouse, and there he

died. His body was destined for the family vaults at Ickworth, but the crew of the *Monmouth*, a man-of-war in which the new Minister at Naples, Hugh Elliot, had planned to have his coffin transported, objected to having a corpse on board. So the enterprising Elliot had Bristol's coffin placed in a packing case and labelled as an antique statue. Could any homecoming for Frederick Hervey, 4th Earl of Bristol and Bishop of Derry, have been more appropriate?

8

———•◦•———

GEORGIANA'S LOVELY FRIEND

Anyone reading the entry in the *Dictionary of National Biography* for the 4th Earl of Bristol's second daughter, Elizabeth, could be forgiven for imagining hers was a life of demure and intellectual pursuits lived by a beautiful society hostess who fully merited marriage to a duke; that she was a woman whose sixty-five unblemished years were spent in publishing travelogues and editions of Virgil and in sitting for portraits by Reynolds, Gainsborough and Angelica Kauffmann.[1] She was certainly beautiful and she was responsible for the production of some interesting books and memorable portraits, including a rather strange, almost Pre-Raphaelite one by Lawrence, but for louche conduct the true story of her life rates alongside that of any Hervey worthy of the name.

All the *DNB* tells us is that 'in early life she married John Thomas Foster. After she had become a widow she spent some time on the Continent with Georgiana, duchess of Devonshire, and other ladies.' It will be recalled that as Miss Elizabeth Hervey, the future 4th Earl's second daughter married the Irish politician John Foster in 1776. He did not die until 1796, by which time Lady Elizabeth Foster (as she became in 1779) had been involved with Georgiana for 14 years. Again, it will be recalled that after the birth of two children her marriage ended in tears, not in widowhood, John Foster claimed guardianship of the children and Elizabeth became dependent on her curmudgeonly father for financial support.

This was the situation in which Elizabeth Foster found herself while sharing a house in Bath with her equally unfortunate elder sister Mary Erne at the time of her first meeting with the Devonshires in 1782. Georgiana had been born at Althorp in Northamptonhire on 7 June 1757, the eldest child of John Spencer, created Earl Spencer in 1765. She was therefore twenty-five when she met Elizabeth Foster, who was two years younger.[2] In 1774, on her seventeenth birthday, Georgiana was married virtually in secret, to William Cavendish, the wealthy, taciturn 5th Duke of Devonshire, who was twenty-five. Many friends predicted a bumpy marriage; Georgiana's straight-laced mother, Countess Spencer, thought her daughter 'aimable, innocent and benevolent, but ... giddy, idle and fond of dissipation'. Idle, never; her life became a whirlwind of political and romantic intrigue. But her chronic addiction to gambling very nearly brought about her husband's ruin.

Devonshire already had an illegitimate baby daughter, Charlotte, by his mistress, a former milliner called Charlotte Spencer (she was no relation to the Spencers of Althorp). After five and a half years of a childless marriage the Duke asked Georgiana to accept his bastard daughter, for his mistress was now dead. The child had, after all, been conceived before the Duke married Georgiana, and the young Duchess was only too delighted to have a 'healthy good humour'd looking child', as she described Charlotte to Lady Spencer, to look after. After adding one letter to the Duke's Christian name they decided to call the child Charlotte Williams and to pass her off as an orphaned Spencer relative.

In 1781 Georgiana suffered two miscarriages, and at the time she met Elizabeth Foster in Bath the following year she was seeking a cure for her infertility. On the return of the ducal pair to London in the autumn they were accompanied by Elizabeth, described by the press, who followed Georgiana's every movement like hawks, as the 'Duchess of Devonshire's intimate friend'. Although the newspapers' use of the word intimate was not intended to convey any sexual connotation, there has to be a strong assumption of at least a platonic lesbian bond between Lady Elizabeth Foster and the Duchess of Devonshire. 'My Dearest Dearest Love' was an expression of endearment on Georgiana's side that went well beyond the normally accepted limits of friendship, even given Georgiana's innate loneliness and the ease with which Elizabeth had managed to ingratiate herself into the Devonshire household. In a letter written in the early days of their relationship, Georgiana told Bess (as Elizabeth Foster came to be known) she must never leave her, and when plans were afoot for the Duke to be appointed lord lieutenant of Ireland Georgiana told Lady Elizabeth she was 'half mad' with the thought of being parted. Even as the prime minister, the Duke of Portland, was discussing the Irish question with the Duke of Devonshire, the Duchess sat down to write to Elizabeth to say, 'Oh Bess, every sensation I feel but heightens my adoration for you.'

Elizabeth was quite outstandingly attractive to men, and in his own quiet, less effusive way the Duke was as taken with her as was his wife. What in effect developed at Chatsworth, the Devonshires' palatial seventeenth-century home in Derbyshire, was a *ménage à trois*, and Georgiana was so well aware of the

[137]

gossip that was likely to ensue that when she and the Duke were in residence at Devonshire House in London she made sure there was alternative accommodation for Elizabeth nearby. The situation might in fact have been dreamed up by a writer of fiction, for Elizabeth Foster, the daughter of an earl, had no hesitation in accepting £300 a year to act as governess to little Charlotte Williams, a post most women of her social standing, however hard up, would have regarded as too demeaning to be contemplated. Bess had developed an alarming cough, and it was on a journey to the south of France ostensibly in search of warmth that Bess and Charlotte were seen off on Christmas Day 1782. There may, however, have been an additional reason for Elizabeth's departure. She asked the Duke and Duchess to keep her informed of 'the stories you hear of me', and one rumour circulating was that Bess was having, or had indulged in before separating from her husband, an affair with a notorious rake, the 3rd Duke of Dorset. Whatever the truth of the matter, Bess was speedily followed to France by a letter from Georgiana addressed to 'My dearest, dearest, dearest Bess, my lovely friend.'

In July 1783 Georgiana at last gave birth, unfortunately to a girl, the Duke being desperate for an heir. Christened Georgiana after her mother, the child was known as Little G. From the Continent Elizabeth Foster wrote to Georgiana begging to be allowed to come home to look after mother and child (and it should be remembered that Elizabeth's maternal outlets had been cruelly thwarted by her husband's refusal to allow her access to her own two boys). 'I shall await your directions, my angel,' she told Georgiana, and asked her to 'kiss our child for me'. As the summons failed to arrive, Elizabeth sent urgent pleas for funds, and elicited a ready response. 'I am in an agony of despair, my angelic heavenly love ... I find you are kept in

Turin for want of money,' a distracted Georgiana wrote. 'I send £50 tonight ... Canis [her nickname for the Duke] will give me the day after tomorrow 200 which I shall send, and then I will send 200 or 300 more in three weeks where you will direct me.' Elizabeth had learnt how easily she could twist Georgiana round her little finger. 'God bless you my angel love,' the Duchess concluded. 'I adore and love you beyond description.'

The money came in handy, for ignoring her mother's advice to 'have a person of character' to chaperone her, and not to 'play the coquette', Elizabeth now moved on to Naples, still with Charlotte Williams in tow. There, according to disturbing news relayed to the Devonshires, she was sharing a house with not one but two lovers. Georgiana merely cautioned prudence, but Elizabeth was not a Hervey for nothing; she had the bit between her teeth and was now in the process of throwing herself into the arms of a *chevalier* back in Turin. 'Live with women as much as you can', Georgiana implored her, 'let them be ever so disagreeable ... My angel love, the world is so alive [with stories] about you.'

By way of mitigation, Elizabeth wrote to Georgiana to say she had been presented by Sir William Hamilton to the King and Queen of Naples, and that no one in that kingdom had raised any objection to her domestic arrangements. Nevertheless she did leave Naples, and her indiscretions were never again referred to by the Devonshires. When towards the end of 1783 Lord Spencer died, Elizabeth, by now in Rome, caused surprise among the English community by ostentatiously going into mourning. It was the death of her father that prompted Georgiana to suggest the time was ripe for Elizabeth to return to Chatsworth, for 'I really feel more capable of talking to you about my sorrow,' she wrote on 3 January 1784, 'and receiving consolation from such discourse than from anything else.' The

Duke, too, was missing Elizabeth. 'There are many places in Bath that put me so much in mind of you,' he told her, 'that when I walk about the town I cannot help expecting upon turning the corner of a street to see you walking along it, holding your cane at each end, and bending it over your knee.'

But by February Elizabeth had decided she was in no hurry to return to England after all; her latest Roman conquest was none other than a Prince of the Church. So conspicuous did her constant appearances with Cardinal Bernis become that she went back to Naples, in something of a flurry, only to fall madly in love with a ladykiller by the name of Count von Fersen; he was a handsome Swedish diplomat whose departure from Versailles had only recently left Marie Antoinette in tears. By now only too aware that her romantic antics furnished correspondence between England and Italy, Elizabeth snatched up her pen to own up to her latest adventure to Georgiana before the Duchess should hear of it from someone else. 'I think better of [Ferson] than anybody I have seen,' she wrote, 'but your claims and Canis's on me can never lessen ... I do not pretend that I shall not regret him, he is in every respect amiable and estimable, but you live in my heart and to it I confess my weakness ... Oh G., are you angry with me?'

Elizabeth had good reason to fear that her promiscuous conduct might 'renew all remarks and observations and conjectures' about her. On 26 February 1783 the Countess of Clermont had written to Georgiana's mother to say, 'I hope you have talked to Lady Duncannon [Georgiana' s younger sister] about the lady in Italy. I hear there never was anything so much admired, and that she sees a great deal of company. I wish to God she would run off with somebody. I am afraid it is a wicked wish; but it is to prevent worse.' Elizabeth had suggested that Charlotte Williams might benefit from another year on the Continent – this was her excuse for trying to evade gossip in London – while Georgiana, pregnant again (and for a second time with a girl) and heavily in debt, was desperate for her lovely friend to return. Having admitted 'a very, very large debt' to her husband, Georgiana wrote to Elizabeth to say, 'You must promise, my dearest dearest, dearest angelic love, never to let Canis know I have told this secret to you.'

An election fought in Westminster in the spring of 1784 cost the Devonshires, according to the *Morning Post*, £30,000. Georgiana remained buried beneath a pile of unpaid bills, and relations with her husband had descended into stony silence. 'As much as I long to see you it is not for me to write,' Georgiana told Elizabeth. 'I am certain poor Canis's health and spirits depend upon your soothing friendship.' By now Elizabeth had tired of her self-imposed exile, and announced that she would return to England in August. In fact, she was back on 22 July. 'I saw Lady E in London,' someone informed Lady Clermont. 'She is come from Italy to pay a visit to the Duchess,' to which the Duchess of Rutland responded, 'The Duke, you mean, he is very much in love with her.' In reporting this drawing-room conversation to Lady Spencer, Lady Clermont added, 'Many other disagreeable things [were] said which I try'd to laugh off.'

The disagreeable things being said would almost certainly have referred to rumours circulating in Paris that Elizabeth and Georgiana had become lovers. 'Who has any right to know how long or how tenderly we love one another!' Elizabeth demanded to know in an indignant letter to the Duchess dated 14 January 1784.

> 'Why are excuses to be made for its sharpness and its fervency? ... Why is our union to be profaned by having a lie told about it? ... Does the warm impulse of two hearts want an excuse to be accounted for, and must your partiality to me be ushered in by another connection?'

By the time Elizabeth was living at Chatsworth during the summer of 1784, Georgiana was telling her mother Elizabeth had succeeded in making 'all the men of the house party fall in love with her'. No doubt now on the lookout for both a lesbian and a heterosexual scandal, the Dowager Lady Spencer had her spies installed. Her son George, the 2nd Earl Spencer, was there in September with his wife, the former Lady Lavinia Bingham. 'The circumstances that you wished me to take notice of when I was here,' he reported to his mother, 'I have not yet had an opportunity of observing. I do not think it is so much to be observed as is thought in general ... I never saw Lady E before ... She is certainly very pretty and sometimes very engaging in her manners.' But in case Lady Spencer thought he had not done his homework he added that Lady E's ludicrous affectations were quite sufficient for anyone not already in love with her to be disgusted. One of Lady Spencer's spinster friends, also at Chatsworth that summer, hedged her bets. 'I hope you are quite at ease about the fondness of the Husband and wife for her,' she wrote. 'You certainly may, for though to be sure nothing can be greater than it is, on all sides, yet I will pawn my life on it, it is perfectly innocent.'

It was nothing of the kind. At this stage, however, Elizabeth was genuinely unwell, and was advised by the Devonshires' doctor to go abroad again in search of the sun. Somewhat reluctantly she sailed for France, leaving behind a distraught Georgiana. 'The Duchess left town the same instant that Lady Eliz did,' Georgiana's sister-in-law, Lavinia Spencer, wrote to her husband. 'I did not see her for she was too much overcome with the separation to see anyone.'

Armed with letters of introduction from the Devonshires to friends in Paris, and supplied with plenty of Cavendish cash, Elizabeth now found all doors open to her, and she could not resist bragging to a jealous Georgiana of her reception at Versailles and the British embassy, and, most tactlessly of all, of splendid evenings spent with the Duchess de Polignac, one of Georgiana's most intimate women friends. In February 1785 she was taken aback to receive a sarcastic letter from Georgiana, congratulating her on her 'new acquaintances' in Paris. Fearing she had overstepped the mark, Elizabeth asked Georgiana if she could do both of them 'the injustice to doubt that knowing you and loving you as I have done my heart can ever alter towards you! no, never, never, never.'

This was pretty rich coming from someone who had slept with her host under the same roof as her hostess, for Lady Elizabeth Foster was at this time three months pregnant with the Duke of Devonshire's child. But then, so was the Duchess. Within days, possibly even hours, the Duke had cuckolded both his wife and his mistress. As luck would have it, Elizabeth's old flame the Duke of Dorset, happily spending £11,000 a year in the course of his duties, was ambassador in Paris. Elizabeth became his mistress again, remaining with the owner of Knole until her condition became so obvious that she decided to join her brother, Lord Hervey, in Italy. Oddly enough, from Italy she wrote to Georgiana confessing her affair with the Duke of Dorset, assuring the Duchess there was no alteration in the love she felt for her. But why should there have been, if theirs was not a physical relationship? Perhaps it had occurred to Elizabeth to pass off her child as Dorset's rather than Devonshire's, which really would have given Georgiana cause for grief, although by now Georgiana was herself beginning to look around for a possible male protector, and did eventually herself have a brief affair with Dorset.

It was on the island of Ischia, near Naples, that Hervey discovered his sister was pregnant, whereupon he insisted she should make herself scarce, by moving on incognito a little way further south to an obscure town called Vietri on the Gulf of Salerno. Here, on 16 August, in an inn that served also as a brothel, Lady Elizabeth Foster, daughter of an earl and a bishop, gave birth to the Duke of Devonshire's illegitimate daughter, Caroline Rosalie. In a diary Elizabeth kept, and doctored in middle age, she recalled 'a little staircase, dark and dirty,' a servant who was 'coarse, ugly and filthy,' and a doctor and his wife, 'the wife ... vulgar and horrible'. She says her own faithful servant wept for her. The child was found a foster home and Elizabeth rejoined her brother in Naples, where it seemed quite obvious he had not divulged her secret to his wife, the former Elizabeth Drummond, whom he had married in 1779. Lord and Lady Bristol likewise appear to have remained in ignorance about the existence of their granddaughter. The first thing Elizabeth did was begin a flirtation with the Russian ambassador. In her diary she noted: 'Misfortune cannot cure me of my vanity.' But few women, however vain, begin an affair almost immediately after giving birth and while in very considerable discomfort from the retention of milk with which Elizabeth should have been feeding her baby. One can only conclude from Elizabeth Foster's chequered career that even for a Hervey she had a very strong sex drive.

At Christmas 1785 Georgiana's brother George and his wife, who profoundly disliked Elizabeth, arrived in Naples on holiday. It was not a happy reunion. In fact, Lavinia Spencer told her husband she thought Elizabeth Foster a 'most dangerous devil'. George reported to his mother, 'She is not very well liked by the Italians on account of her want of facility in speaking their language, and her wearing perfume which is here an unpardonable offence.' He noted that Elizabeth seemed to be living with the French ambassadress, and did not seem 'to be much attached' to

Lady Hervey, her sister-in-law. 'A great many things I have heard,' George Spencer went on, 'many of which are certainly not true but some must be, I don't know what to make of her.'

Perhaps that is hardly surprising. For all her glaring faults, and like many of her clan, Elizabeth Foster had courage, and she now set about ensuring a secure future for her child. How she had come to know an elderly French aristocrat who lived in the south of France, Comte St Jules, no one has discovered, but she rescued her little daughter, travelled to Aix-en-Provence and persuaded the Comte to accept paternity of Caroline and to give her his name. Again, how she managed to pull off this coup remains a mystery. From Aix she travelled the length of France to Calais, writing to Georgiana, before she sailed, to assure her that 'without you the World is nothing to me. If you could forsake me I would not bear to live.'

Bess landed at Southampton where, when she wrote up her diary, she pretended the Duke had come alone to greet her. He was in fact on crutches with gout and on holiday with half of fashionable London, not to mention his own extended family. Bess travelled to Ickworth to see her mother and then went north to Chatsworth, where on 14 September 1786 the Duke of Dorset rolled up. Unfortunately the Dowager Lady Spencer was there too, and immediately realized that her daughter and the Duke of Dorset were having a fling. 'I am far from happy here,' she told her son – yet, like so many interfering mothers, it never occurred to her to go home. (Since the death of her husband, Lady Spencer had been living in St Albans.) Once Dorset had left, Georgiana went into a series of most peculiar muscular spasms, almost certainly brought on psychosomatically, and Elizabeth lost no time in taking charge of the household. This was too much for Lady Spencer, who ordered her own dinner to be served in Georgiana's room.

[145]

Life in the great house was becoming more fraught by the minute. As soon as Lady Spencer had departed, Georgiana owned up to her latest gambling debts to the Duke, who immediately demanded a separation. He may, of course, himself have gambled on Georgiana leaving Chatsworth and Elizabeth remaining. George Spencer was so incensed at the idea of his sister being shunted off on her own to one of the Duke's numerous hunting lodges that he offered her sanctuary at her childhood home, Althorp. But the Duke was not in a strong position to separate from his wife (a divorce would have been impossible to obtain merely on account of gambling debts). What he wanted even more than solvency was a legitimate son, and only Georgiana could provide him with one. Sending her into exile could hardly be expected to increase the chances.

The truth is that the Duke was fond of both Georgiana and Bess, but not in love with either. He was also basically an indolent man, who declined to put himself about unless he had to (he had refused to accept political office), and he rather liked having two women around him. He was in the strongest position of all three members of the *ménage à trois*, Elizabeth in the weakest. She could in all probability have persuaded the Duke to dispense with Georgiana, but unless she was married to him she could not hope to live at Chatsworth or in London as other than his mistress, and that would have meant being ostracized by many family and friends who tolerated the situation as it was. All talk of a separation eventually fizzled out when Georgiana, unexpectedly, apologised to Bess for lying about her debts; she hoped that her squandering of so much of the Duke's fortune would not make Elizabeth despise her. Elizabeth's promiscuity can in part be attributed to her low self-esteem. It was love rather than sex she had always craved, and with this turn of events she realized that Georgiana's love for her, and her need of her, were totally genuine. She now felt confident enough of her position in the complex relationship to have no further urge to usurp the role of chatelaine.

Elizabeth Foster was to become Georgiana's confidante – which placed Elizabeth in a potentially powerful and dangerous position. Today the Duchess would have been a prime candidate for admittance to Gamblers' Anonymous. She believed implicitly that however much money she lost she could recoup it by risking more. Inevitably her debts mounted; she borrowed in order to repay, and became more debt-ridden than ever. In 1787 she was writing, 'Oh God Bess, I have gone on and lost an immense sum – I dare not tell you that it is 6,000 – It is madness and I ought not to live on with Canis – but what am I to do? I must not tell him this – and you shall advise me when I return what I am to do – whether to tell him or not – it could be settled without and so that it should never come to him – you know he *could* not forgive me. My Bess I am desperate.'

Now Bess was top dog, so to speak, and the wretched Georgiana felt desperately in need of her support and protection. One of the Duchess's biographers believes it is probable that at this point Bess disclosed the existence of Caroline St Jules to Georgiana.[3] There seems, however, to be no record as to how the news was received; with little surprise, in all probability, and almost certainly no jealousy. Georgiana had long ago lost sight of a romantic marriage; her wealth, comfort, political prestige, social standing and friendship with the Prince of Wales were far more important to her, as was her emotional dependence on the mother of her husband's bastard daughter. Yet Elizabeth's position was not to be envied. Her husband still refused to give her permission to see their boys, Augustus and Frederick, both living with their father in Ireland; her daughter, albeit illegitimate, was in France; she longed to become Duchess

[147]

of Devonshire but was denied any possibility of that fulfilment while Georgiana was alive.

During the London season of 1787 Bess and her Duchess were inseparable; they went to the opera, were received at Carlton House by the Prince of Wales whom Georgiana knew so well she addressed him in letters as her dearest brother, were invited to suppers and balls, traipsed round the pleasure gardens at Ranelagh. But when the Devonshires returned to Chatsworth, Bess opted to stay on in London for the summer. This was not, the Dowager Lady Spencer imagined, because she was waiting until she had departed from Chatsworth before going north but because Bess had managed to capture the heart of the Duke of Richmond – the 3rd Duke of Richmond as it happened and the third duke to fall for her. By the time Bess had moved on to Chatsworth at the end of October she realized she was again pregnant. But whose baby was it – Devonshire's or Richmond's? Bess said Devonshire was the father, and although it seems that the Duke had his doubts, he and Bess told Georgiana immediately. Once again it would be necessary for Lady Elizabeth Foster to withdraw to France to give birth; there was always the excuse of a need for warm weather, and no woman in society could hide herself away in England for perhaps five months without causing automatic suspicion.

Georgiana even offered to accompany Elizabeth to France, but she may have had an ulterior motive; it would have made a reunion in Paris with the Duke of Dorset so easy. But in the end Georgiana remained in England, both she and the Duke travelling to Dover to wave Elizabeth off. On 10 February 1788 Georgiana wrote, 'I don't know how I shall be able to bear my parting with Bess.' The parting on Bess's side was equally traumatic. 'Oh it was bitterness to lose her,' Elizabeth wailed in her diary, 'but him – his last embrace – his last look drew my soul after him ... Oh, why could I not love him without crime? Why cannot I be his without sin?'

Elizabeth made for Rouen in Normandy where she lodged in a 'tolerable, but in a close confined street on one part and a stinking court at the other'. On 26 May she gave birth to a boy, his paternity still in very considerable doubt. Was he a Lennox or a Cavendish? Although her first son by her husband had been named Augustus, she called this boy Augustus too, and gave him the additional names William James Clifford, so we can safely assume either that Elizabeth was confident that Canis was the father or that she wanted him to believe he was; (William was the Duke of Devonshire's Christian name and Clifford was a barony created in 1628, remainder through the female line, and inherited by the Duke from his mother). The boy was always known as William Clifford. During Elizabeth's stay in France Georgiana broke off relations with the Duke of Dorset, for she had fallen seriously in love with an up-and-coming twenty-three-year-old politician, Charles Grey. There was also at this period a by-election in Westminster in which Georgiana took part, and it was shortly after the election that Bess returned, once again taking up her role as mistress to the Duke of Devonshire, if not yet mistress of Chatsworth.

In the early summer of 1789 the Duke decided to take both his wife and Elizabeth to Spa, in what is now Belgium; for Georgiana it meant that perhaps the healing properties of the water would enable her to conceive a son, and for Elizabeth it was an opportunity to be reunited with her irregular offspring, Caroline and Clifford. The three of them sailed for Calais on 20 June, Georgiana with a loan of £500 from her brother secured in her luggage. With gay abandon the party were sailing straight into the eye of the French Revolution. On 22 June the Devonshires and Elizabeth arrived in Paris. The fact that a crowd of 10,000 people had assembled in the Palais-Royal did nothing to dampen their spirits; in fact, it brought out that air of nonchalance so peculiar to the English, and to the English aristocracy in particular. Faced with a rampaging mob, Georgiana's first instinct was to mount a soap box and harangue it.

As so often happens on the verge of momentous events, life went on much as before, and Georgiana and Bess received visitors and tradesmen. Once the rioting had subsided sufficiently to make a visit to Versailles possible they were received by Louis XVI and his queen, and invited to dine. The Duchess and Bess said what would turn out to be their last goodbyes on 8 July, by which time things looked so black that both women drove to Versailles in mourning. It was Georgiana's great friend Madame de Polignac who had engineered the transfer of Caroline St Jules to Paris, and to the French Duchess as well as the Queen the English visitors expressed their thanks as well as their farewells. The Duke of Devonshire was now determined to put some miles between his party and the seat of rebellion. En route to Spa they stopped off at Brussels, and it was here that they heard of the storming of the Bastille. They heard also, to their great relief, that several of their friends, including the Polignacs, had managed to flee by night.

Having escaped the blood bath in Paris Georgiana now found herself pursued even to Spa by debts. Her banker, Thomas Coutts, discovered she had been lying to him, and declined to make her yet another loan. James Hare, the son of an apothecary and himself impoverished by gambling, implored Georgiana to let Elizabeth or himself break the news of Georgiana's latest financial embarrassments to the Duke. But a great weight of anxiety was lifted when Georgiana discovered she was indeed pregnant, and for some reason it seems to have been assumed by everyone – correctly, as it transpired – that this time she was going to give birth to a boy. The Duke cancelled plans to return to England, for he was not prepared to risk the hazards of a Channel crossing before the child had been born. The sea might in fact have been safer than dry land; rioting had spread to Brussels, and the Cavendish party were forced to retreat temporarily into France, to Lille. The oddest turn of events was when in December the Duke decided to return to England alone, leaving his wife and mistress to the mercy of mercenaries.

9

A DUCHESS AT LAST

The Duchess of Devonshire was by this time so distracted by her debts that she was contemplating retiring from London society. This prompted Elizabeth Foster to try to alert the Duke to the true state of affairs; Georgiana had even persuaded her husband's banker to make her a secret advance of £5,000. All that these advances ever did was pay off the interest on existing debts; the debts themselves were never cleared, and part of this £5,000 loan was squandered on horse races 'as the risk is so little and the gain might be so much.' There spoke the truly addicted gambler. Hints were dropped in the Duke's ear but still he refused to believe the extent of Georgiana's reckless behaviour. Bess, of course, was terrified that when he found out he would disown his wife without divorcing her, and that she, Bess, would be left high and dry with no status, official or otherwise. Everybody, Bess told Lady Melbourne, was praying for a son – Georgiana's one hope of salvation.

As anxious as anyone to keep Georgiana from miscarrying, in order to cheer her up the Duke sent her daughters over from

England, which was no simple enterprise; an army of retainers, including grooms and footmen, were posted to France to keep the two little girls in the state to which they were accustomed to live at Chatsworth. There was, in consequence, a first meeting of half-sisters, for Caroline St Jules was at Spa as well. 'She is a poor little thing', was how Bess passed off her own daughter to Lady Melbourne, who in all probability was not deceived; aristocratic indiscretions were no great novelty. Even the ever watchful Dowager Lady Spencer turned up, determined to make sure no rumours spread to the effect that a foundling baby boy had been smuggled into Georgiana's bed. Some of Georgiana's letters having been intercepted – for she could never resist meddling in politics – the house at Brussels was searched, and the Duchess and her family ordered to leave. The Marquis de Lafayette assured Georgiana she would be safe if she returned to France, and on the road her entourage ran into an obliging French duke, d'Ahrenberg, hastening in the opposite direction. He said Georgiana could use his house at Passy, close to Paris (now part of the Bois de Boulogne), which they reached on 19 May, only just in time. Within hours of arriving, Georgiana went into labour. Then the most extraordinary scene took place. Determined that her daughter, and she alone, be assigned mother of the future Duke of Devonshire, Lady Spencer ordered Bess to go into Paris and appear at the Opéra, to prove that she was not pregnant. Bess returned to the Duc d'Ahrenberg's mansion just in time for the birth, which took place in the early hours of 21 May. When they saw that the child was a boy, both Georgiana and Elizabeth knew they were saved.

There had never been any love lost between Elizabeth and Georgiana's mother, and Elizabeth had the supreme satisfaction, when Lady Spencer left with her granddaughters ahead of the other adults, of knowing that it was she who would be the first to escort her daughter Caroline up the sweep of stairs which at that time led to the entrance to Devonshire House. (They were removed by the 6th Duke.) When, in August, Georgiana and Elizabeth set off for home, the Countess of Sutherland (a peeress in her own right), ensconced in the British embassy, wrote to her friend the Marchioness of Stafford, 'I regret the Duchess's departure very much. As for Lady Elizabeth, she is nice enough but one can do without her.' It was, in its way, one of the most cutting remarks a lady of quality could have made of another. Georgiana and Elizabeth sailed in a convoy of four boats, three of them packed with luggage and servants. Elizabeth must have had her heart torn in two directions; her daughter would be waiting to greet her, safe in England, but poor little Clifford remained trapped in the turmoil of Paris.

Fresh ructions lay ahead. Lady Spencer had recruited an ally in her running battle to have Bess ousted from the Devonshire household, a stern and morally upright governess by the name of Selina Trimmer. She had been planted partly to protect the Countess's grandchildren from what she believed to be the feckless conduct of their parents, partly to spy on Bess. No doubt reminded by the spiteful Lady Spencer that initially Bess had been designated governess to the Duke's daughter Charlotte, Selina Trimmer and the nurserymaids began to adopt an insolent attitude, even declining to stand up when Lady Elizabeth entered the room. Georgiana was so outraged that for once in her life, she ticked off her mother, reminding her that Elizabeth lived with the Duke and herself because that was what they wished, and she even attributed to Elizabeth the fact that her marriage had not broken down. Recalling past services rendered by Elizabeth, Georgiana told her mother, 'Her society was delightful to us, and her gentleness and affection sooth'd the bitterness that [my] misfortunes had brought on us.'

In August 1791 the Devonshires, with Bess and the children, were staying in Bath. Fortunately for us, so was the novelist Fanny Burney, recently released after five years from the tedium of attendance upon Queen Charlotte as Assistant Keeper of the Wardrobe. She already knew the Dowager Lady Spencer, and had every occasion to call on Lady Spencer's daughter. Stories she had heard about that daughter's particular friend, Lady Elizabeth Foster, would have impelled her to the front door of their rented Bath house in any case, if only to have an opportunity of recording her disapproval. She did not care in the least for the 'little French lady', as she called Elizabeth's daughter, Caroline; she found her 'fat and full of mincing little affectations and airs'.

Fanny had already been primed by Lady Spencer to dislike and distrust Caroline's mother, of whom she later thundered, 'To the tales told about *her*, *scandal* is nothing – INFAMY enwraps them.' It was some time before the Duchess and Elizabeth appeared, and when they did Lady Spencer introduced her daughter and then 'slightly, as if unavoidably, said "Lady Elizabeth Foster".' Fanny knew perfectly well whose illegitimate child Caroline was, and her puritanical instincts made it difficult for her to stomach conversation with Bess. When she got home she wrote in her diary, 'Lady Elizabeth has the general character of inheriting all the wit, all the subtlety, all the charm and all the wickedness of the Herveys.'[1]

To say that Fanny Burney disliked Elizabeth Foster would be a considerable understatement, but to what extent her considered views were entirely her own, or to what extent they had been prejudiced by Lady Spencer, it is hard to say. But Fanny Burney's observations, although often partial, are also so often sharp that her record of her meeting with such a startling representative of the Hervey family as Elizabeth Foster are worth recalling in greater detail.

I fancied all sort of things about lady Eliz Foster- I fancied that while – from some inevitable compact with the Duke – she [Georgiana] consented to countenance her, and receive her as her own guest, she was secretly hurt, offended and unhappy ... She submitted with the best grace in her power to save her own character by affecting to have no doubt of Lady Elizabeth's, but that, in her inmost mind, she detested such a Companion, and felt a hopeless and helpless resentment of her own situation ... It is generally believed her own terrible extravagancies have extorted from her a consent to this unnatural inmating of her House, from the threats of the Duke that they should be separated! What a payment for her indiscretion ... All this I thought, I imagined I read it from time to time in her own countenance – and I found myself strongly concerned for her in the situation.

A few days after making her call, Fanny Burney came across Lady Spencer and her daughter in the town, unaccompanied by Bess, and wrote that Georgiana seemed 'more easy and lively in her spirits, and consequently more lovely in her person.' She added the devastating observation, 'It struck me also, in her favour, that her spirits had before been depressed by the presence of the odious Lady Elizabeth and were now revived by being absent from her.' There is no question that many women, for whatever reason, disliked Elizabeth, but on this occasion it has to be said that Fanny Burney could have had no inkling of the reasons for Georgiana's apparent mood swings. One half of her may well have been in cheerful mood, the other half overshadowed by foreboding. She had again managed to conceive, but the child she was carrying was not the Duke's; the father was Georgiana's lover, Charles Grey.

[157]

Elizabeth already knew of Georgiana's plight; so did Georgiana's sister, Harriet Duncannon. 'There has never existed a stricter confidence and friendship than there has [been] for many years between my sister, Lady Elizabeth and myself,' Lady Duncannon once said. During the Duke's absence from Bath, Grey had behaved with disgraceful disregard for Georgiana's reputation, calling at the house whenever he felt like it. The newspapers were no less averse to scandal and gossip in the eighteenth century than they are today, and Bess was terrified that Grey's behaviour would be reported.

Someone tipped off the Dowager Lady Spencer, by means of an anonymous letter, and she flew into action. 'Her commands are you know absolute,' Bess told Lady Melbourne, 'and her vigilance extreme.' Lady Spencer needed a scapegoat and she turned on Bess, who in fact had entreated Georgiana to take care; then Lady Spencer castigated Georgiana so severely that she capitulated and agreed to send Grey back to London. There was no question of Georgiana fleeing to France for the birth of her illegitimate child; Cornwall was the warmest spot she could retreat to without alerting the Duke's suspicions. But before Georgiana, Bess and Lady Duncannon could take to the road, someone let the cat out of the bag – it may have been Lady Spencer – and the Duke promptly arrived on the doorstep.

Angry shouts from the Duke and sounds of a weeping Duchess echoed through the house. Then the door opened and Bess was summoned, to be given a scolding for being in on the secret and not reporting it. The Duke demanded that his wife go abroad or face a separation; Lady Duncannon's health, which was truly in a bad way, could provide the cover story. 'Bess has very generously promised to go with us,' Lady Duncannon wrote to Lady Melbourne. 'I urg'd her to it almost as much on her own account as my sister's, it must have been ruin to her to stay behind.' She added, 'Lord D [her husband] and my mother still both believe we are going to Penzance, and how they will ever be brought to consent I know not.' Lady Spencer returned to Bath on the rampage, and continued to blame Bess for her daughter's interesting if distressing condition. Lady Melbourne told her to ignore Lady Spencer's insults. Bess replied, 'I shall observe all you say, but Lady S has begun as bad as possible about me – even to say I should not travel with them – but on your life say not a word of it to anybody – if the Dss goes I will.'

There was one event to bring comfort to Elizabeth, at any rate; her son had now come over from Paris but was lodged for some reason with a family miles away, in Clewer in Somerset. After endless indecision on the part of the Duke, who changed his mind hourly, he eventually blurted out to Lady Duncannon, 'If you wish to save your sister and me from the most unpleasant disclosure break off your going to Penzance and go abroad directly.' Those who were to sail to France from Southampton included the Duncannons, Georgiana, Bess and her daughter Caroline St Jules, and the Dowager Lady Spencer. When Bess heard that her arch-enemy Lady Spencer was to accompany them, she tried to back off, but had she remained in England the Duke might never have sent for Georgiana again. In his anger, the Duke sent the party off practically destitute and – more in hope than expectation one imagines – he forbad the Duchess to borrow any money. He then resorted to blackmail. Grey's child, he ordered, was to be adopted as soon as it was born, or else he would divorce Georgiana for adultery and she would never see her legitimate children again. Such was the emotional and financial power that men of his time were able to wield over women.

While Georgiana lay in bed in a house near Montpellier in the southern provence of Languedoc, expecting her baby and also quite confidently expecting to die, she made a new will and wrote farewell letters to her children in England, begging them always to be 'affectionate to my Dear friend Bess.' They were also to 'love and befriend' their half-sister, Caroline St Jules. On 20 February 1792 Georgiana gave birth to a girl. She called her Eliza. As soon as Eliza was old enough to travel she was shipped home to live in Northumberland with her paternal grandparents, Sir Charles and Lady Grey. Although Georgiana's other children knew about the illicit birth in the south of France, Georgiana was only permitted to write to and occasionally see her new daughter on the strict understanding that she never revealed to Eliza who she really was. She had to pretend to be a godmother.

Convinced that she had lost the goodwill of the Duke of Devonshire (and with good reason; he had stopped her allowance) and fearful about their daughter's future, Bess moved on with Georgiana to Aix-en-Provence for another mysterious encounter with the Comte St Jules, who was dying. With his last gasp the old man promised to adopt Caroline officially and to provide for her. What Elizabeth Foster's hold over him was nobody has found out. From Aix they travelled eastwards to Nice, where they arrived on 9 March, having braved appalling roads and the danger of daylight robbery. 'I was very happy to hear of the Dss of Devonshire getting away from the Toulon Banditti,' Lady Sutherland wrote to Lady Stafford, 'as the idea of the horrors that might have happened to her had she fallen into their hands gave me the nightmare. As for Ly Eliz, I did not care so much about it; that sort of thing for once in a way not signifying to a Hervey so much as to any other class in the animal world.'

In April they heard from the Duke. Georgiana was to stay put until he came to fetch her himself; Bess could do as she pleased. Even given the circumstances, and making due allowance for his hurt pride, he was not a very nice man. It was while they were kicking their heels that Georgiana and Elizabeth spent the summer of 1792 on Lake Geneva, as the guests at Lausanne of an old family friend of the Herveys, the great historian Edward Gibbon. The first volume of *The History of the Decline and Fall of the Roman Empire* had been published in 1776 (the entire work was completed by 1788),[2] and when in 1782 Gibbon lost his seat in parliament on the fall of Lord North's government (Gibbon was a Whig and a liberal but without any desire for democracy) he joined a fellow bachelor, George Deyverdun, in Lausanne, sharing his house on the edge of the lake. When Deyverdun died in 1789 Gibbon stayed on. He was 52 but had only two more years to live. He is said to have read some portions of his *History* to Elizabeth during her stay, and that when she expressed her admiration he invited her to become his wife. Unfortunately Elizabeth was already married, so unless she intended adding bigamy to her list of indiscretions it was a proposal that never stood much chance of being accepted. Gibbon continued to pay her lavish compliments, however, saying on one occasion that if she 'chose to beckon the Lord Chancellor from his woolsack in full sight of the world he could not resist obedience.' Gibbon may simply have been playing the gallant flatterer, but it does seem that Elizabeth was far more attractive to men than to her fellow females.

Having given up all hope of the Duke travelling to Lausanne (he was reluctant to travel anywhere if he could help it), Georgiana and Elizabeth made for Pisa, to join Lady Spencer and the Duncannons. They had a terrible journey, faced with snow and ice and only one pass, the St Bernard, open. By now the King and Queen of France had been beheaded, the French ambassador in London had been sent packing, and France had declared war on England. It was not a good time for English

[161]

aristocrats to be wandering around on the Continent. Despite their own relative privations, Elizabeth and the Duchess helped to raise money for some of the French refugees now seeking safety in Italy, many of whom were starving. Once safely across the Alps they headed south for Naples, where the court made them welcome, even though by this time Georgiana had no jewellery left to display and precious little money.

Just as she imagined herself and Bess abandoned for ever, on 18 May 1793 a letter arrived from the Duke. He wanted them home again, so Bess and the Duchess (her sister was too ill to make the journey) set out on a hike to Ostend. They found Maastricht on the Dutch border under siege, and were advised to turn back. This they declined to do, and struggled on across Flanders, only to find at Ostend not a single space on any of the boats clamouring to leave. Their extraordinary luck held, however. A friend of Georgiana's, Lord Wicklow, emerged from the mêlée on the quay. He was just about to get away in his private boat, and agreed, somewhat dubiously, to squeeze Elizabeth and the Duchess, who had still managed to retain a formidable quantity of luggage and servants, on board. With less fortunate refugees unsuccessfully imploring a place too, the English contingent headed out to sea.

They returned to a Duke angry with Bess for having left him alone so long, and they resumed their affair, the *ménage à trois* as vital as ever; Georgiana would not countenance anyone but herself nursing Bess when she fell ill. But Bess still had dreams of marrying the Duke of Richmond. In January 1796 it was Elizabeth Foster's turn to nurse Georgiana, who had developed a devastating inflammation of the eye that caused her excruciating pain. Her reward for her dutiful care came in November with the news that her husband John Foster was dead; now she could have her sons Augustus and Frederick over from Ireland.

She was of course free to marry again, and who should have become free to marry as well but the Duke of Richmond. 'The Dss of Richmond has at last slipt off merely out of attention to Ly E.F.,' Lady Sutherland wrote to Lady Stafford. 'It is odd that Mr Foster and she should have calculated so nearly.'

One reason Georgiana was anxious to invite Elizabeth's two Foster boys to join the ménage was because she was terrified Elizabeth might quit the Chatsworth domain for that of Goodwood, and there was no reason to believe the Duke of Richmond would welcome stepsons. 'Bess is ill with happiness,' Lady Spencer was informed by Georgiana when the boys turned up. 'I never saw a more touching sight. They clung to poor Bess, who cried terribly.' Mr Foster, as Georgiana referred to Frederick, she thought 'plain but a very interesting and sensible young man'. Augustus, who was sixteen, she considered 'a very fine boy'. Thinking it prudent to pretend to mourn her husband for twelve months, Bess went on holiday in April 1797 to Bath, to stay with her sister Lady Erne, where she was observed to be in very coquettish mood. While Bess was there Georgiana suffered a miscarriage, for she and her husband were again reconciled, so rather than go north with the Duke and Duchess in December, Elizabeth preferred to stay on in London at Devonshire House, holding soirées in preparation for what she confidently predicted would be her future role as Duchess of Richmond.

But Richmond's proposal of marriage failed to materialize. 'His conduct by Ly E Foster is very unaccountable,' Lady Holland (the former Lady Webster) wrote in her diary on 26 March 1799. 'He is always talking and writing as if he intended to marry her, and yet the marriage is not more advanced than it was two years ago.' She added, presumably with inside knowledge, 'Lady E is very hopeful for it.' Georgiana told her daughter,

[163]

Lady Georgiana Cavendish, it was 'an embarrassing situation,' one made no happier by the engagement of Lady Georgiana to Lord Morpeth, heir to the Earl of Carlisle and one of the great Yorkshire houses, Castle Howard. An opportunity for Bess to attract some attention herself, by an outlandish expression of grief, now presented itself, for hearing the news that her mother, whom she did not much care for, had died, Elizabeth took to her bed. Within a fortnight she had told the Duke of Richmond that she intended going abroad to cope with her grief; she was hoping that would force his hand. She did not go, and he did not propose.

The future course of Elizabeth's life – continual habitation under the wings of the Duke and Duchess of Devonshire – was settled in October 1801, when Richmond finally put her out of her misery. He admitted he had no intention of marrying her. She was understandably bitter, and told Lady Melbourne that Richmond had exposed her to 'much censure'. She needed a whipping boy and blamed the Duke of Richmond's niece, Lady Charlotte Lennox, for poisoning his mind against her. 'Lady C L is an odious being and I should like to be certain of never seeing her again', she wrote to Lady Melbourne on 20 February 1802. Sensing how much Elizabeth needed cheering up, when the Devonshires were invited to stay at Castle Howard the Duchess asked Lord Carlisle to invite her too. But Bess was tired of her dependence on Georgiana for what almost amounted to charity. So with peace declared between Britain and France, in October 1802 she left for Paris, accompanied by her daughter Caroline St Jules and her son Frederick Foster. Georgiana pursued her with a letter. 'Write me all the gossip dearest, and all the news', she instructed her.

As a result of the Revolution, Bess was disgusted to find an atmosphere of egalitarianism; everyone expected to be addressed as madame or monsieur, and the working classes now showed scant respect to the daughter of an earl. But nothing could dampen Georgiana's ardour for her absent friend. 'My dear Bess,' the Duchess wrote in December, 'Do you hear the voice of my heart crying to you? Do you feel what it is for me to be separated from you?' She must have been reassured to be told from Paris, 'Don't accustom yourself to do without poor little me.'

War was soon to break out again, and Bess arrived back in England in the spring of 1803 just in time to avoid hostilities and the likelihood of being taken prisoner. She found a war of a different kind in full spate at Devonshire House; to her scarcely concealed delight the Duke and Duchess were again at each other's throats, so from one to the other she flew in her apparently infinite capacity for providing soothing comfort. The Duke's dependence on Bess for companionship and nursing infuriated his children. His second daughter, Harriet, reported to her elder sister from Bath, 'Our mode of life is not diversified. We are still in this Hotel, Papa thinking it, I believe, Paradise regained. Lady Eliz and Sidney [the Devonshire's pet dog] both unwell, both whining and both finally as agreeable as you know I always think them. Mama, in an hotel, as everywhere else, kinder more indulgent and more unlike the Lady or the Dog than I can express.'

Kind and indulgent the Duchess of Devonshire may have been, but she was now heavily addicted to laudanum and was steadily amassing unpaid bills and gambling debts which, by the end of 1804, amounted to a staggering £50,000. The Duke was so shocked he remained entirely mute. 'There never was anything so angelic as the Duke of Devonshire's conduct,' Elizabeth wrote to her son Augustus. 'The many conversations I had with him on the subject, though it made me nervous at the time, have made me happier now, and if possible increased my admiration and attachment to him.' But the Duke kept Georgiana in suspense so long that she was obliged to borrow a further £800 – from the Prince of Wales, himself a spendthrift on a magnificent scale.

Early in 1806 Georgiana became unwell, believing she had jaundice, which she told her mother, writing from Devonshire House, was 'going off'. By 22 March it was evident however that she was extremely ill. On 25 March Bess recorded in her diary 'a better day – the attack of fever was slighter this morning though the interval was dreadful to see, but the rest of the day the Dss has been more collected.' But within forty-eight hours it became obvious that Georgiana was dying. The doctors, as they commonly did in those days, proceeded to torture her, and she died in the early hours of 30 March, with her husband and Lady Elizabeth Foster with her 'until nearly the end'.

Six weeks later, Elizabeth wrote to her son Augustus, 'The recollection alone remains, and regrets, never ceasing regrets. Regrets only to be equalled by the angelic, the unequalled qualities of the friend of my heart, my dear, my loved, my adored friend.' She told him Georgiana had been 'the only female friend' she ever had, which was probably true. Now without Georgiana's protection, Bess and her two illegitimate children were in a most uncertain position, except that Georgiana had effectively appointed Elizabeth her literary executor. This meant that while Elizabeth undertook the task of sorting through thousands of letters, she remained under the Devonshire roof with a definite task to perform; it also meant she was free to censor anything detrimental to her own reputation.

When both the Duke and his son the Marquess of Hartington fell ill, Bess began to organize the servants and make herself totally indispensable. 'She is a disgusting beast' was all the thanks she got from Lavinia Spencer. By November one sister was telling another that Bess was shameless in 'laying down the law when Lord M [Morpeth] and you are away'. Her conduct in usurping the duties of hostess were particularly commented on. 'Lady E F is very disagreeable in doing the honours instead of me,' Lady Morpeth was told. Within two years of Georgiana's death, Lady Morpeth broke the news to Hartington of 'the most painful event'; their father was to marry Bess. The engagement was announced in the autumn of 1809. When the Duke informed his former mother-in-law on 17 October, he wrote, 'I wish you, my Dear Lady Spencer, not to answer this letter, as it must be disagreeable to you to do it.'

Within the immediate family cold hostility turned to outright hatred. To his cousin Lady Caroline Lamb Lord Hartington wrote, 'Hardly til I see it can I believe that the woman could have the assurance to take that name always so sacred to us, and hence forward to be so polluted.' Matters were hardly improved when the Duke settled £30,000 on Caroline St Jules when she married, but only £10,000 on his second, legitimate, daughter.

The Duke's second marriage did not last long. He died on 29 July 1811. Any lingering doubts those who knew her may have had regarding the character and dubious judgement of Elizabeth Cavendish, Duchess of Devonshire, would have been dispersed when she began to demand family jewels from Lord Hartington (now the 6th Duke) and possession for life of Chiswick House. Her worst crime in contemporary eyes was to disclose that the 5th Duke had been the father of Caroline and Clifford. She even claimed that Clifford, although illegitimate, had a right to use the Cavendish arms. Despite his reservations, the new Duke behaved well, settling money on his stepmother and his half-brother and half-sister. Bess duly moved out of

Chiswick and for five years she divided her time between a new house in Richmond and the West End. Then she decamped to Rome, where an old friend of Georgiana's, Sir William Gell, reported that her room was filled with books, for literature was 'now the pursuit in which she takes, or pretends to take, an interest'. There was however a rival interest; yet another Prince of the Church, Cardinal Consalvi. Her ancient antagonist the Dowager Countess Spencer needed no further excuse to refer to Bess as 'That Witch of Endor the Duchess of Devon.'

Elizabeth survived Georgiana by eighteen years, and by a most peculiar chance she died, in Rome in 1824, on exactly the same day as Georgiana – 30 March. With her was her stepson the 6th Duke of Devonshire, who very decently had her buried with his mother and father. The former Lord Hartington was equally magnanimous to Clifford, ensuring he was appointed Gentleman Usher of the Black Rod, and again using his influence to have him created a baronet. Augustus Foster became a diplomat and was knighted by William IV in 1835.

Ironically, in view of the struggles undergone by the 5th Duke and Georgiana to provide an heir to the Cavendish titles and estates, the 6th Duke never married, for he was homosexual, platonically if not physically in love with the great beautifier of Chatsworth, Joseph Paxton. His father might have been a little disappointed; neither Georgiana nor Elizabeth would have been in the least perturbed. In 1828 he purchased 14 Chichester Terrace, Brighton, adding on to it a year later its nextdoor neighbour, No. 1 Lewes Crescent. Across the road was a vantage point from which 'he liked to watch boys bathing.'[3] In his honour it was called Duke's Mound, and it remains to this day a popular resort for gentlemen of a similar persuasion.

[168]

10

———••◦••———

MAYFAIR PLAYBOY NO. 1

The 4th Earl of Bristol's elder son, John Augustus, who had pre-deceased his father, had one daughter, Elizabeth Catherine Caroline, by his wife Elizabeth Drummond. She later became Lady Seaford. And it was because there had been no son that on the Earl-Bishop's death in 1803 he was succeeded as 5th Earl by his younger son, Frederick William.

He was thirty-four, an attractive and intelligent-looking man as depicted in a portrait by John Hoppner now in the dining room at Ickworth House. He bore no resemblance physically or in character to his father. According to his mother, Frederick passed his examinations at St John's College, Cambridge 'with such wonderful credit and éclat that he was declared first of his year in every subject.' In 1796 he was returned to parliament for the family seat at Bury, which he retained until he entered the House of Lords in 1803. Under Henry Addington, prime minister from 1801 to 1804, Frederick served as under-secretary of state at the Foreign Office. The foreign secretary was his brother-in-law, Viscount Hawkesbury, who succeeded as the 2nd Earl of Liverpool in 1808; Hawkesbury was married to his sister Louisa, which may well have accounted for his swift appointment.

The marriage of Louisa to Lord Liverpool was to prove beneficial again, for in 1812 Liverpool became prime minister. He remained in office nearly fifteen years (he was the longest-serving prime minister of the nineteenth century), and what more natural than for Liverpool to do a little something for his wife's family by advising George III to advance his brother-in-law to a marquessate? Hence in 1826 the 5th Earl of Bristol became Marquess of Bristol.[1] Having decided to retain the Bristol title, he needed a new earldom for use as a senior courtesy title. The 4th Earl's father-in-law had been Sir Jermyn Davers. In 1612 Sir Robert Jermyn of Rushbrook Hall had provided a wife for Sir William Hervey. The 1st Earl had lived in Jermyn Street, which runs parallel with Piccadilly. So Earl Jermyn it was.

Meanwhile, the 5th Earl had domestic and financial problems to solve which were inextricably linked. His unreliable father had done the unforgivable thing, leaving most of his money to his cousin Henry Hervey-Bruce and practically nothing to his son and heir except an entailed estate to run and a house half built. Frederick had to accumulate rents before he even felt able to recommence work on the great Rotunda in 1821, which for two decades had served as nothing more than a tourist attraction. Matters were not much helped by the fact that the house in St James's Square required extensive modernization. As for the intended flanking corridors and the east and west wings of Ickworth, in 1813 it was recorded in *The Beauties of England* that 'the interior of this neglected edifice exhibits a mere shell, with a kind of open staircase to ascend the roof and take a view of the adjacent country,' while 'the wings, and the galleries connecting them with the edifice in the centre, have been run up to the height of only three or four feet.'

There seems to have been a certain lack of initiative in the choice of names for Hervey boys. The 5th Earl was Frederick William. He called his eldest son, born in 1800, Frederick William. To this eventual 2nd Marquess the cash-strapped 5th Earl wrote in 1819, 'What you say of the new house at Ickworth makes me regret that I had not money enough to complete the body next year ... If I could have mustered five or six thousand pounds I would have begun it directly, but I must have patience.' It had been assumed by many who paid a visit to the site that the Earl was planning to demolish his father's folly and sell the building materials for scrap. But driven on partly by innate perseverance, partly by a reluctance to endure the cramped conditions of Ickworth Lodge any longer than necessary, the Earl eventually called in a London builder, John Field, to revise his father's plans, aimed as they had been at creating an art gallery rather than a home. What the 5th Earl required was a house in which his family of nine children could live. He decided that the east wing would be provided with family accommodation divided into reasonably sized rooms while the Rotunda would accommodate three principal requirements on a grander scale – a drawing room on the east side, a dining room on the west, and, facing south, the largest room of all, the library. Halfway along the corridor between the Rotunda and the east wing there would one day be a smoking room. The house would have looked most peculiar and unbalanced had not at least the exterior of a west wing been completed; and on the south front of this wing was constructed an orangery.

Drawing a deep breath, Lord Bristol began his own major building project in 1821, having previously taken the precaution of purchasing a collection of pictures and furniture to replace the treasures lost by his father. To do this he took his wife and children to the Continent in July 1817. They spent the whole of

1820 in Paris, and did not return to Ickworth until May 1821. Perhaps one should regard the 5th Earl of Bristol's poverty in relative terms. They travelled through Belgium, Germany, Switzerland and Italy; in Florence Lord Bristol commissioned busts from Bertolini, in Rome drawings from the German painter and engraver Friedrich Rehberg. Paris supplied furniture, clocks and porcelain. He acquired a charming portrait of the six-year-old Spanish Prince Baltasar Carlos by Velázquez, now in the library. And he managed to rescue an enormous marble group by Flaxman called *The Fury of Athamas*, which can be seen today as the centrepiece of John Field's classical entrance hall. It had actually been commissioned by the Earl-Bishop in Rome in 1790 for £600. The story it depicts is not a very nice one and may justly be thought to illustrate the bishop's fascination with the macabre. It represents the scene in Ovid's *Metamorphoses* in which Athamas, driven mad by the Gods, snatches his infant son from the arms of his mother and dashes his head against a rock.

In the dining room at Ickworth is a late-eighteenth century marble chimneypiece which, like the chimneypiece in the library, was almost certainly purchased on the Continent by the Earl-Bishop and somehow found its way to England. Until 1812 it was stored in a warehouse in London, listed as 'certain chimney pieces marbles etc late belonging to the late Frederick, Earl of Bristol.'

John Field was not merely a builder; he was hired as an architect and proved to be an interior decorator of genius, carrying out designs for the doors and window-surrounds in the dining room, which the 5th Earl got round to decorating and furnishing between 1824 and 1829. It was not Field's fault that construction work took so long; delays occurred for the simple reason that Bristol kept running out of money, even on occasions selling land in order to finance the house. One cannot help feeling that he became as passionate about building as his father had been, and certainly he deserves the credit for Ickworth ever being finished and made habitable. Shortly before he became a marquess he wrote to his eldest son, 'God help you my dearest Hervey – your mother is much better – so am I, but I shall be better when these sales are over and the essential part of the new house up and paid for – I have lived so long upon this stretch that I feel sometimes as if I should fail suddenly.'

It was 1829 when the 1st Marquess and his brood took up residence in the family quarters in the east wing, but for another fourteen years they had to pick their way through builders' rubble; the Rotunda was not completed until 1832 and the west wing, which was always intended to remain unoccupied, not until 1841. To celebrate his advance in the peerage Bristol sat in about 1827 for Sir Thomas Lawrence, probably the most fashionable portrait painter of his day.

Determined as he had been to defy his father's wishes and wed for love, the 1st Marquess provided ample evidence of a happy and fruitful marriage. Augusta was born in 1798, the year of Bristol's marriage to Elizabeth Upton. Their first son, the 2nd Marquess, arrived two years later; when he was thirty he married Lady Katherine Manners, daughter of the 5th Duke of Rutland. Another boy, George, followed in 1803 but he died at the age of thirty-five. William, who fathered two boys and two girls, followed two years later, and then came Arthur, born in 1808; in 1869 he was consecrated Bishop of Bath and Wells, and became rather more assiduous in his episcopal duties than his grandfather ever was. There were yet two more boys and two more girls.

Not content with the items he had purchased in Paris, Lord Bristol commissioned furniture from a firm called Banting,

France & Co. While not strictly Regency – the Regency period ended in 1820 – Banting, France's products were in the height of fashion; George IV himself would have been delighted to have seen them in the Royal Pavilion at Brighton. Busts of Hercules and the Roman Emperor Lucius Verus repose in the entrance hall at Ickworth on scagliola pedestals supplied by Banting, France in 1829. The same firm was responsible for the hall chairs, decorated with the Bristol coat of arms; also, in the entrance hall, stands an enormous oak table with a white marble top from their workshop. It is thought the dining-room table and chairs came from St James's Square, having been supplied by Banting, France to the 1st Marquess's specifications in 1821. Likewise the gilt side table. Only in an English mansion could a pair of candelabra be found, as they can in the dining room at Ickworth, presented to the 1st Marquess by his tenants, in gratitude for not putting up rents during periods of agricultural depression.

More work by this important firm Banting, France, including four rosewood bookcases, can be seen in the library. This room also contains a bust by Bertolini of Lord Bristol's oldest daughter, Lady Augusta Seymour. As for the books in the library, many volumes were added by the 1st Marquess, but the oldest belonged to Sir William Hervey who lived from 1585 to 1660. There are some rare eighteenth-century publications, and some of the most valuable belonged to the 1st Earl and his daughter-in-law Molly Lepel.

The library also contains an interesting link with Molly's daughter, Lady Mulgrave. She was a close friend of James Wolfe, the less than brilliant general who in 1759 lost his life in a final, and ultimately successful, assault on Quebec. To such an extent did Wolfe become a national hero that forty years after his death Benjamin West was busy painting four idealized versions of the imagined scene, the fourth having been commissioned by the Earl-Bishop, who regarded Wolfe – although not many of the men and officers who fought under him would have agreed – as a 'military saint'. But the Bishop had a special interest in the whole affair. Not only was Wolfe a friend of the family; his ADC in Canada, Captain Hervey Smith, was a grandson of the 1st Earl, and can be seen in West's painting in the library at Ickworth standing to the left of the dying general.

In this beautiful sunlit library is a rosewood piano made by Clementi about 1820, presumably purchased by the 1st Marquess. But one of Lord Bristol's grandest acquisitions was a pair of Sèvres vases with portraits of Louis Philippe and Queen Amélie of France, now in the drawing room. The royal couple had sought refuge in Bury St Edmunds following the revolution of 1848, and in 1850 they made Lord Bristol a present of them. Two years later the exiled French royal family arrived incognito on the south coast for a two-week visit.

For not content with the east wing of Ickworth in which to live as well as a town house, the supposedly impoverished 1st Marquess had in 1831 taken possession of 19–20 Sussex Square in Brighton, part of the glorious domestic development undertaken by Thomas Kemp, MP for Lewes, in the wake of the Prince Regent's patronage of the original fishing village of Brighthelmstone. The house, built by Henry Kendall junior for £16,000, is situated in the north-west corner of the square, with superb views out to sea from the upper windows; it is now called Bristol Mansions. And just as the 4th Earl had given birth to so many Continental Bristol hotels, so his son lent his name to streets in the Kemp Town area of Brighton, and even to a public house – for he purchased fifty acres of land to the north and west of Sussex Square and then gave a good many plots away.

For instance, in 1836 Lord Bristol made a gift of nine acres to help establish St Mary's Hall, a boarding school in Eastern Road for daughters of the clergy. What was called an extra-mural cemetery in the Lewes Road received a parcel of six acres. By 1853 it was decreed that no more burials were to take place in the original parish church of Brighthelmstone, St Nicholas, so in April 1856 the Marquess offered twenty acres of land east of the Lewes Road. At about the same time he paid for a Renaissance-style chapel to be added by William Hallett to the Royal Sussex County Hospital, opened in 1826. He paid for St Mark's Church, and twenty-nine years after his death some of his land was even incorporated into Brighton racecouse. In numerous ways the memory of the 1st Marquess's largesse in Brighton lives on. In the year of his death the Reverend Henry Wagner and his sister added on to the Percy and Wagner Almshouses in Elm Grove in his honour; they were destined to become listed buildings in 1971 and were restored five years later.

Sussex Square became quite a family habitat. The 1st Marquess's wife died at No 19–20 in 1844. Their daughter Augusta lived at No 34 from 1832 to 1847 and a younger son of the 2nd Marquess, Lord Francis Hervey, died at No. 42 in 1931. The 4th Marquess parted with 19–20 Sussex Square at the beginning of the Second World War.

Neither the 1st Marquess nor his son the 2nd Marquess lived long enough to know that their fourth son and third brother respectively, Lord Arthur Hervey, was to follow in his grandfather's footsteps by becoming a bishop. Born on 20 August 1808, at 6 St James's Square, Arthur spent the years between his ninth birthday and his thirteenth with his parents on the Continent, where he was taught by a private tutor. In 1822, when he was fourteen, he was sent to Eton, and from there, in 1827, when he was nineteen, he progressed to Trinity College, Cambridge, taking a first-class degree in the classical tripos. Not only was he a champion tennis player – he was that rare creature, a Hervey with real brains, and the *Dictionary of National Biography*'s verdict that he was 'not intellectually brilliant' though 'accurate and painstaking' seems rather grudging. As well as being a classical scholar Lord Arthur studied Hebrew, Arabic and Sanskrit, and spoke French fluently. Between 1870 and 1884 he helped revise the Authorised Version of the Old Testament, and in 1885 he received an honorary doctorate of divinity from Oxford.

It is also quite obvious that Lord Arthur had a genuine vocation, for at the earliest opportunity, when he was twenty-four, he was ordained deacon and immediately afterwards priested. (Today he would have had to wait a year before being ordained to the priesthood.) There was no problem finding him a living; his father was patron of thirty of them, and he became in effect parish priest to the family, for in November 1832 he was instituted to the parish of Ickworth-cum-Chedburgh, and eventually became rector of Horringer and Ickworth.

Preferment came in 1862 when Lord Arthur was appointed archdeacon of Sudbury, at that time in the diocese of Ely.[2] In 1839, when he was thirty-one, he had married Patience Singleton. As Lady Arthur Hervey she lived until 1904, having provided her husband, described by the *DNB* as 'a handsome and well-made man,' with six sons and six daughters. After serving seven years as archdeacon, at the somewhat advanced age of sixty-one Lord Arthur was offered the bishopric of Bath and Wells. Gladstone had been anxious to increase Liberal representation in the House of Lords, and he asked a friend of the archdeacon to tell him in confidence what he thought of Lord Arthur's political leanings, 'a subject which,' Gladstone explained, 'though I could never consent to make it paramount,

I cannot in the office I now hold leave wholly out of view.' The archbishop of Canterbury, Archibald Tait, was of course consulted, and he assured the prime minister 'If not what is called in party language a Liberal, [Hervey] is most truly liberal and enlightened in his views.'

As far as churchmanship was concerned, Lord Arthur veered towards the evangelical wing of the Church of England (Gladstone was vaguely High Church), but it was said that he was trusted by all his clergy, ruled his diocese with tact and fairness, and was 'universally popular in it'. In later years Lord Arthur told Gladstone he had always been 'most generous in not claiming from me any political *obedience*'. Lord Arthur was consecrated on 21 December 1869, and took his seat in the House of Lords on 8 February the following year. As Bishop of Bath and Wells, he was succeeding another peer, the 3rd Lord Auckland. Both noblemen would have felt thoroughly at home in the palace at Wells, and it was in that cathedral city that in 1894 Lord Arthur was buried, having died in office, crippled by gout, at the age of eighty-five.

Arthur Hervey had not escaped liturgical squabbles in his diocese. From 1877 to 1879 he became involved in a lawsuit over a cleric he had declined to institute. The case ended up before the Privy Council; judgment with costs was given in Hervey's favour, but as he was unable to recover the costs he found himself landed with a bill for £1,558. A whip-round in the diocese produced a contribution of £978. But his biggest bugbear was George Denison, the archdeacon of Taunton, a bigot who was determined to carry battles on behalf of the Oxford Movement into areas where any moderate diocesan at the time was virtually compelled to take action. In the words of Denison's biographer, he was 'incapable of compromise: he could not ever be liberal or tolerant'.[3] Apart from the stipend and gracious living quarters there was little incentive to take on a diocese in Hervey's day, for he was not the only bishop faced with liturgical experiments that according to canon law were strictly illegal. But at least the quarrels in Bath and Wells were conducted by Christian gentlemen. Archdeacon Denison always acknowledged the Bishop's 'uniform kindness' and when Lord Arthur died Denison is said to have 'suffered pangs of genuine grief'.

Frederick William, 1st Marquess of Bristol, died in 1859, at the age of ninety, and was buried in the Lewes Road Parochial Cemetery in Brighton, now called Woodvale. His son Frederick William, Earl Jermyn, succeeded him – but only for five years. From 1841 to 1846 he served as Treasurer to Queen Victoria, but he spent most of his adult life – he died at the age of sixty-four – assisting his father with building and embellishing Ickworth House. He and his wife had four sons and three daughters, the eldest son having been born in 1834. He at least had John tagged on to his first two Christian names – Frederick William – and was only thirty when he inherited the 30,000-acre estate and the marquessate of Bristol. In 1862 he had married Geraldine Anson, who became an avid collector of fans, now on display on the Museum Landing at Ickworth.

The 3rd Marquess, before going to the House of Lords, broke with family tradition by sitting in parliament for West Suffolk as a Conservative. From 1886 until his death in 1907 he served as lord lieutenant of Suffolk, and thought nothing of driving from his Brighton house in Sussex Square to the races at Goodwood in a coach and six. His most important contribution to Ickworth – a truly stunning one – was the creation in 1879, halfway along the west corridor, of what is known as the Pompeian Room. The designs are based on Roman wall-paintings uncovered in 1777 at the Villa Negroni on the Esquiline Hill in Rome. It is a magnificent addition to the house.

Two daughters were born to the 3rd Marquess and his wife, but no son, and his brother Lord Augustus Hervey never succeeded, for he died at the age of thirty-eight. He and his wife Mariana Hodnett became great friends of the Prince and Princess of Wales. Lord Augustus was appointed a Lord of the Bedchamber, and both he and Lady Augustus were frequent guests at Marlborough House. There Queen Alexandra in order to demonstrate that, despite her slight build and a very stiff knee which caused her to walk with a limp, she could pick up Lady Augustus, would 'carry her round the room on outstretched arms, and laughing, fling her on the sofa.'[4] (Other members of the Hervey family were in the service of Edward VII and George V, as lords of the bedchamber or chaplains.)

Lord Augustus died in 1875 and his oldest son, Charles Henry Augustus Hervey, in 1893, at the age of thirty-one, so that when the 3rd Marquess died in 1907 it was his nephew and Lord Augustus's second son, another Frederick William, who succeeded. In 1896 he had married Theodora Wythes, a marriage which again produced only two daughters. So in 1907 Herbert Hervey, aged thirty-seven, became heir presumptive to his brother. Theodora Wythes was the granddaughter of the Victorian railway contractor George Wythes, and although she never produced an heir she did provide an enormous personal fortune, a great deal of which she spent on maintaining and improving Ickworth. As her husband was colour-blind she had a free run when it came to decorating, replacing some of the Regency decor with modern Edwardian colours and designs. More importantly, she expressed her horror at the inadequate living quarters allocated to the servants in the east wing, introduced more bathrooms and electric light, engaged a leading architect of the day, A. C. Blomfield, to make radical alterations

A family breakfast in the library at Ickworth House in the mid-nineteenth century, at a time when Frederick William Hervey (1800–64), married to the former Lady Katherine Manners, was 2nd Marquess of Bristol.

Top. The Duke and Duchess of Anjou and Cadez were among many distinguished guests entertained at grand dinners given by the Monarchist League when Victor, 6th Marquess of Bristol (1915–85), was Chancellor.

Bottom. For the Roman Catholic christening in 1976 of his elder daughter Victoria by his third wife, the former Yvonne Sutton, the 6th Marquess of Bristol designed for himself a pale grey morning dress to which he attached a sword and a galaxy of orders and decorations bestowed on him by sometimes rather dubious foreign potentates.

In 1988 Frederick William John Augustus Hervey, 7th Marquess of Bristol (1954-99), was sent to prison in Jersey for a year on a charge of smuggling cocaine, the first of two prison sentences he was to serve. He became a hopeless drug addict and died at the age of 44.

A view from the south front terraced walk of the great central rotunda of Ickworth House in Suffolk. The eighteenth-century mansion was begun by the 4th Earl of Bristol and completed, only through the sale of land, by his younger son, Frederick William Hervey (1769-1859), who in 1803 succeeded as the 5th Earl and in 1826 was created Marquess of Bristol. The house is now the property of the National Trust.

to the Entrance Hall, and had the pictures catalogued and cleaned and many of the books rebound.

The 4th Marquess had been born in Dresden, on 8 November 1863, where his father was an attaché. At the age of nine he entered Tonbridge School, leaving when he was twelve to join HMS *Britannia*, for he had set his heart on a career at sea, becoming a midshipman when he was fifteen. In 1883, at the Royal Naval College in Greenwich, he obtained the Beaufort Testimonial, and because he did so well in the examinations, taking firsts in all subjects, he was promoted lieutenant after only six months as a sub-lieutenant. Three years later he won the £80 gun prize. By the age of thirty-three he had attained the rank of commander, and six years later he was promoted captain.

For a time he relinquished active service in order to stand as Conservative MP for Bury St Edmunds but his parliamentary career was cut short after only eighteen months by the death of his uncle, the 3rd Marquess, which coincided with a state visit from the King and Queen of Spain. Lord Esher, the First Sea Lord, selected the new Marquess of Bristol to command the battleship *Renown* in which the royal guests sailed to England and home again, and presumably it was in recognition of this minor service to Edward VII that he was made a member of the Royal Victorian Order. In 1911 he retired from the Navy with the rank of rear-admiral, and at the age of forty-eight he decided to devote the rest of his life to Ickworth and county affairs; from 1915–34 he was chairman of the West Suffolk County Council.

There is a splendid portrait of the 4th Marquess in the dining room at Ickworth, resplendent in his captain's uniform before becoming an admiral. Also in the dining room are two portraits of his wife, whose personal fortune was to provide an endowment for the house when in 1956 the estate was transferred to the National Trust. An instructive glimpse can be gained into

[181]

the perhaps rather laconic frame of mind of the 4th Marquess from his entry in *Who's Who*; 'Owns 32,000 acres, possesses a few good pictures of the Italian, Spanish and English schools.' It was, word for word, a replica of the 3rd Marquess's entry.

Schools chosen for the education of Hervey boys were nothing if not varied. Lord and Lady Augustus Hervey sent their third son, Herbert Arthur Robert, who eventually became the 5th Marquess, to Clifton College, founded only in 1862 but already immensely successful under its Rugby-trained first headmaster, John Percival. Lord Herbert, as he became in 1907 when the children of Lord Augustus were granted the titles and precedence that would have been theirs had their father succeeded as marquess, arrived at Clifton in 1886, when he was already sixteen. His older brother having been born at Dresden would indicate that the boys were taught by a tutor before being sent to public schools, and Clifton may have been chosen for Herbert rather than Tonbridge because at the time Clifton had a strong emphasis on European languages, and Herbert was heading for the Consular Service.

He seems to have left little impression on the school. There is no mention of him in the school magazine, the *Cliftonian*, for the two years he was there, but he did move from the top fourth form to the sixth. One of the oddest things about his less than distinguished school career is the frequency with which he swapped boarding houses. He started off in what was called a waiting house, entering Brown's in 1887. By April that year he was to be found in Watson's for a term; by September 1887 he was back in Brown's, the housemaster, T. E. Brown, being a Manx poet of some renown. Even odder, Herbert was singing in the school choir as a treble at the age of sixteen.

In 1892, when he was twenty-two, Herbert Hervey joined the Consular Service, becoming a commercial attaché in 1913; this may explain why at Clifton, given the chance of three divisions, Classical, Military and Modern, he chose the Modern as it was tailored for boys going into business or commerce. In 1914 he married Lady Jean Cochrane, daughter of the 12th Earl of Dundonald, and on 6 October the following year their only son Victor was born. The marriage lasted nineteen years, ending in divorce in 1933. He became 5th Marquess of Bristol in 1951 on the death of his eighty-seven-year-old brother the rear-admiral, and then only because the third son of Lord Augustus Hervey, Lord Walter Hervey, had died in 1948, (he had married the Hon Hilda Calthorpe but they were childless).

In 1952, nineteen years after his divorce, the new Marquess married again. It cannot have been by chance that his second bride was Señora Dora Frances Enblim, the widow of Don Pedro de Zulueta, for it seems fairly obvious she had some connection with Herbert Hervey's diplomatic wanderings. They had taken him, in 1892, to Iquique in Chile as consul. For a year he served as chargé d'affaires at Montevideo and Guatemala. He was consul in Abyssinia from 1907–9, and for the next three years in Bilbao. The year 1919 saw his appointment as Minister to Colombia, and from 1923–8 he was Minister to Peru and Ecuador. He retired in 1929, at the age of fifty-nine, clearly by this time unlikely ever to be offered an embassy.

When the 4th Marquess died in 1951, leaving £$1^1/_4$ million, 15,000 acres of land had to be sold to pay death duties of £750,000. The 5th Marquess was already eighty-one when he succeeded to the title. Within a year of his second marriage, the exotic marchioness was dead. He had a town flat in Basil Street, and he can have entertained no ambitions now to spend much time at Ickworth. As there was a real danger of death duties falling on the family twice in rapid succession, he decided in 1956 to make arrangements for the National Trust, in consideration of an endowment fund of £185,000, to take over the ownership of Ickworth House, at the same time granting a ninety-nine-year lease enabling the family to retain occupation of the east wing. The end came for the 5th Marquess when in March 1960 he fell in the bedroom of his London home. He underwent an operation, and on 9 March was reported to be progressing. A week later a spokesman for University Hospital said he was 'not so well'. He died in hospital on 5 April.

His only son Victor Frederick Cochrane Hervey, since 1951 Earl Jermyn, was now, at the age of forty-five, 6th Marquess of Bristol. Long before inheriting even the courtesy title he had shown that his reign as head of the family was to reflect many of its seemingly hereditary tainted traits. Some stories about Victor Hervey are well attested; but his antics were such as to attract other tales, the truth of which is most unlikely. As a little boy he had a governess for a year; he then attended Heatherdown, a preparatory school at Ascot. And at some stage during his not very distinguished time at Eton (he entered the College in the summer of 1929, when he was thirteen, was absent for the first half of 1931, and left at Christmas that year, only just sixteen, not seventeen, as he claimed) he is reputed to have knocked a boy out with a knuckleduster. If he did resort to fisticuffs as a boy he would not have been the first to do so, and certainly not at Eton, where the chapel register records Edward Cockburn, in 1730 'murdered by Thomas Dalton, his Schoolfellow'. It is true that when he played for his house in the Lower Boy Field Game ties in 1929, Victor earned the comment 'Not a skilled player but he goes hard. He goes into his man well and is a dangerous player to play against.' It is also a fact that when grown up, Victor was generally regarded by his friends as a very gentle person, with 'soft hands and a very light handshake'. It seems more than probable that if he did knock a boy out, the

[184]

knuckleduster was appended to the story in the light of a latter and rather better authenticated event – his part in a couple of robberies in 1939.

Again, in later life Victor has been spoken of by one friend as a 'serious and intelligent man,' but there was scant evidence of intellectual ability at Eton.[5] He joined the College in III Form, 'very low down,' and according to the College archivist 'does not seem to have risen very high. Several boys who arrived after him overtook him in the school order.'[6] Leaving school so early, with no discernible attainments, may well have ranked as the first of many disappointments that were to dog his life, and for which he was to seek compensation in the fantasy world of the Monarchist League.

Victor's poor performance at school and some of his early delinquent behaviour may have been attributable both to physical ill-health and emotional deprivation. His mother was not a maternal woman; until Victor was fourteen his father was more frequently overseas on diplomatic missions than at home; and Victor sought some sort of substitute family life at Ickworth with his uncle, the 4th Marquess, and his wife. On days at Eton when parents may be expected to turn up he seldom received visits from relatives, and his absence from school in 1931 is almost certainly accounted for by an attack of osteomyelitis, an infectious inflammatory disease of the bone, which necessitated some time in bed and left him with intermittent back pain and a slight limp.

With no serious prospects of inheriting family money or the Ickworth estate for a good many years – if at all, for in 1931 his uncles, the 4th Marquess and Lord Walter Hervey, were only sixty-eight and sixty-six respectively, and his father, heir presumptive after Lord Walter, was only sixty-one – Victor considered a career in the army, if only in a half-hearted sort of way,

[185]

for he candidly admitted, 'I knew perfectly well that I was never cut out for the life of an officer.'[7] Nevertheless he entered the Royal Military College Sandhurst (it is now the Royal Military Academy) on 2 February 1934 at the age of eighteen, where he displayed early signs of entrepreneurial flare, at the same time establishing his initial rapport with the West End. It seems the College ran a bus service into London from Camberley for cadets who wished to have a night out. Victor claimed that he chartered two buses of his own in order to transport cadets at cut-price fares, saving them, on a return journey, the equivalent of about 12p. His buses held thirty 'in comfort' but 'the cadets were so keen on taking advantage of the cheaper tickets that they were willing to ride the whole way on somebody's lap.' A stop was put to this fairly harmless racket after three weeks, and it has been alleged that Victor was 'thrown out of Sandhurst after the commandant called him "temperamentally unsuited to be an officer"'.[8] Victor's version of events was that 'having thought it over very seriously, I left without taking my commission.' The truth is that in July 1934 he failed the junior examination, and on 27 November that year he was 'permitted to be withdrawn from the Royal Military College'.[9] His ignominious army career had lasted just ten months, and obituary notices in 1985 alleging he was educated at Eton and Sandhurst were somewhat off the mark.

At Eton Victor had received an allowance of £1,000 a year, a grotesque sum for a boy to be given; the average industrial wage was probably not more than £300 a year, and a middle-class family man would have jogged along quite comfortably on £800. It was small wonder he acquired a taste for money so early in life. Having in effect been expelled from Sandhurst he went into the City, joining a firm of stockbrokers 'on a half-commission basis'. He recollected in 1939 that for the first time in his life (he was still only 19) he saw 'the easy money starting to roll in', and during his eighteen months on the Stock Exchange he made '£2,000, roughly,' worth today perhaps £100,000. He recalled his early life in a series of articles supposedly written by himself in 1939 for the *Sunday Dispatch*, under the headline 'The Astounding Truth About Victor Hervey, Mayfair Playboy No 1', and published immediately after he had been sent to prison for three years for theft. It is quite possible, despite his rather tenuous links with the higher reaches of the aristocracy (he was still only fourth in line to the Bristol titles), that at the committal stage at Marlborough Street magistrates' court on 6 June 1939 an enterprising journalist realized that this Mayfair toff had a story to sell. The articles were couched in classic journalese, and either Victor suddenly developed outstanding writing skills or he dictated his adventures, real or imagined, and they were jazzed up in the newspaper's offices, ready for instant publication if Victor was found guilty at his Old Bailey trial. This seems by far the more likely explanation, and it is even possible that Victor first approached the *Sunday Dispatch* himself, for he was ever on the lookout for ready cash.

'I wanted to get into the real money,' Victor wrote, and that came 'when I crashed into the armaments business,' a reference to his supposed gun-running and double-dealing during the Spanish Civil War. 'But before I did this I dabbled in film production and floated three companies.' In order to celebrate launching a film company he gave a party that lasted thirty hours, 700 guests turning up, of whom about 400 were gate-crashers. Victor says they drank their way through more than 1,000 bottles of champagne, ate caviar by the bucketful and ran up a bill for £3,000.

This period was the tail end of Evelyn Waugh's Mayfair, inhabited by gay young things intent on endless inebriated self-indulgence. The articles sowed the seeds of Victor's future reputation, even if various facts and figures have become distorted with time, or were scarcely believable from the start. By the age of twenty-one, Victor told his readers, he had been made bankrupt for £5,690, shortly after he had given a party, while living in South Audley Street, that continued for three days. 'On this jamboree,' he boasted, 'we did an awful lot of damage.' Such conduct seems to have come quite naturally to him. 'The most exuberant joke I perpetrated in my calf days completely escaped punishment. That was when I drove a car into a row of taxis, just to see whether or not they would buckle up like a concertina. They did, in a mild sort of way. I backed out quickly before I could be stopped, and got away with it.' It is no wonder, even if he 'got away with it' on that occasion, that he admitted, 'There isn't much sense in pretending that my arrest a few weeks ago was the first time I was ever in the hands of the police; it wasn't.'

His bankruptcy in 1937, aged twenty-one, to the eventual tune of £123,955, was a result of his bungled gun-running operations. It came, he recalled, 'as a complete surprise to me'. And he wrote that during the Spanish Civil War 'while I was dealing in armaments I found more excitement than most people would find in the whole of their lives.' He was, according to an article in *The Times Magazine* for 19 February 1994, 'incompetently corrupt, attempting a double-crossing arms deal ... which was to have netted him £30,000, a bribe from the Francoists for betraying a shipment already paid for by the Republicans, but which went wrong.'

Victor was to become, if he was not at the time, a passionate monarchist – and that is putting it mildly. His own godmother had been Queen Victoria Eugenie of Spain (she has been transmogrified from time to time into his grandmother, or even more improbably his great-grandmother; his grandmothers were

Lady Augustus Hervey and the Countess of Dundonald). However inept his dealings may have been on behalf of the monarchist forces under Franco, the Spanish royal family seem to have forgiven him; he was later to be on intimate terms with the Duke of Anjou and Cadiz and the Count of Barcelona, father of King Juan Carlos. He said himself, 'I took it as a compliment that both sides in the Spanish [Civil] War remained willing to know and do business with me.'

It will never now be possible to disentangle all the facts from Victor Hervey's fantasies. His articles were ghosted in such a way as to portray him in the light of a dashing adventurer. His claims to have sold planes and submarines as well as Bren guns, and to have survived three murder attempts (his would-be assassins must have been very poor marksmen indeed), may all be taken with a large pinch of salt. As he had a rather poorly developed sense of moral responsibility, his claim to have traded with both sides in the Civil War is just about the only fact of which, at this distance in time, we can be sure.

There is a long tradition, from Dick Turpin to the Great Train Robbers, of coating the conduct of criminals with glamour, and with his highly romantic nature Victor, as Oscar Wilde put it in a slightly different context, enjoyed the thrill of feasting with panthers. 'I suppose I have always had the knack of collecting odd characters,' he wrote in the *Sunday Dispatch*. 'In consequence I got to know any number of the "boys", and became *persona grata* with the racing "spivs" and the "con" men, the small timers and the big timers in the twilight world of Soho ... Always in my meanderings around the town I found as much amusement in knowing what you might call the low life as I did in knowing the fashionable set.'

This explains how he landed up in the dock with three characters very nearly as disreputable as he. Or this at least was the conclusion of the judge at the Old Bailey, Sir Gerald Dodson, for Victor, who gave his address as Upper Berkeley Street, received the longest sentence of all four. He had after all been involved in not one but two robberies: Victor Hervey, a twenty-three-year-old called Arthur Hering of Great Cumberland Place, and William Goodwin, aged thirty, a silversmith from West Kensington, had stolen £2,860 worth of jewellery from a woman called Mrs Gabrielle Burley, who was reported as living in Seamore Place, Park Lane.[10] And along with Hering and Geoffrey Coop, also twenty-three, and also from a smart address – Conduit Mews, Paddington – Victor was found guilty of breaking into a flat in Queen Street, Mayfair and stealing jewellery valued at £2,500 from a woman called Mrs Pauline Daubny.

Victor's father valiantly turned up to the committal proceedings and was asked, 'When all your just debts are paid, are you worth £2,500?' He said he was and his wayward son was released on bail, having managed to find a second surety of £2,500, the condition of his bail being that he report to the police 'as and when' required. As is so often the way when journalists are confronted with the complexities of the honours system, errors became two a penny. The *Daily Mail* referred to Lord Herbert Hervey, Victor's father, as 'Lord Hervey'. *The Times* had Lord Herbert's age wrong by eleven years. And when, in 1994, that newspaper was researching a resumé of the Hervey family's misdemeanours, they tagged on to Victor the prefix 'The Hon', imagining his father to have been a peer of the realm.

On 7 July 1939 the *Daily Sketch* reported: 'Society women and film stars were among those who packed the Old Bailey yesterday when sentences on the four Mayfair men guilty of robbing two women of jewellery worth more than £5,000 were passed.' Victor got three years' penal servitude; his chum William Goodwin, although he had amassed four previous convictions and had been to prison before, got only two years. Hering went down for eighteen months and Coop for a lenient nine months. None of them had come from what used to be called the criminal classes. Coop, it was said, had 'lived in the West End writing poems and lyrics' to try to pay off debts. Hering, a freelance journalist, had been 'living by his wits'. Victor's excuse was the best of all. The court was told he had been 'awaiting an £83,000 fortune – his share in commission due on a sale of arms to China.' A 'close friend' told the *Daily Sketch* that Victor had not been able to draw this money because delivery of the arms had not been made.

Victor obviously behaved himself at Camp Hill Prison on the Isle of Wight, for he received a full twelve months' remission. A story believed by some, that Victor had the distinction of being the last man to be flogged in a British prison, is nonsense. So too is the loyal contention held by friends of Victor still alive, who knew him as an older and possibly wiser man, that the theft of the jewellery was really just a silly prank that somehow went wrong. A prank may go wrong once, but it stretches credulity too far to imagine that two separate thefts, one involving a break-in, were some kind of freak accident. Victor Hervey was a burglar, pure and simple.

Prison for someone educated at Eton and in line for a peerage would have been degrading and uncomfortable, the daily grind accompanied by appalling food, but the outstanding consequence of Victor's crass behaviour and its aftermath was a lifelong fear of social ostracism, and against this possibility he now set about creating an edifice of homespun grandeur.

11

IN A LEAGUE OF HIS OWN

Victor Hervey was quick to realize that not only do the English love a lord, they are extremely tolerant, even fond, of eccentrics, and along with the aura of grandeur he believed necessary to carry off his future titles he would be well advised to create an effect of eccentric behaviour. 'There goes that jolly old card Victor Hervey' was what he hoped people would say rather than 'There goes that aristocratic jailbird.' He even joined something called the Eccentrics Club. Perfectly capable as he was of amassing a considerable amount of money by legitimate means (apart from his business interests he was adept at buying and selling shares), money much needed with which to finance a lavish lifestyle, one does wonder if the story that he once embezzled the entire gold reserves of Costa Rica was not invented by himself. For a man who could not manage to make off with £5,000 without getting caught, that would have been quite a feat.

He claimed – and there is no reason not to believe him, for many would have been offshore operations – to have been a director of twenty companies. Someone who knew him well for the last twelve years of his life does not rate him as an astute businessman. 'He was too emotional, and too kind-hearted. He could easily be taken in. He was once conned by a bogus vicar. He was what I would call entrepreneurial rather than a hard-headed business man.'[1] Anyone can easily be conned, for conmen are often so plausible. Victor's second wife, Lady Juliet Tadgell, believes, on the other hand, that he had 'a very good head for business.'[2] But it was certainly with a fine entrepreneurial flourish that he advertised himself in *Who's Who* as 'an expert on Central American affairs and adviser to Governments'. His estates extended from 'west, north and east Suffok' to Dominica. The most important business of which he was chairman was de Jersey & Co (Finland) Ltd, and apparently he was military adviser to the Finnish government, although whence he obtained his military expertise it is hard to say.

For a man who listed his recreations as power yachting, shooting, antiques and beautiful women he delayed marriage for some considerable time, until he was thirty-four, when he married Pauline Bolton. That was in 1949. Towards the end of 1953 Earl and Countess Jermyn, as Victor and Pauline had by now become, moved into 15 Chapel Street off Belgrave Square, a house that has remained in the family to this day and is now inhabited by Victor's third wife and widow. After five years of marriage Pauline gave birth to a son, on 16 September 1954. Baptized at St Peter's, Eaton Square, the boy was given a low-key start in life in contrast with Victor's later children; he had just two godfathers and two godmothers, without a title between them. Given the names Frederick William John Augustus he chose to be known as John. He was destined for a pretty horrible life.

The Earl and Countess's marriage had just another four bumpy years to run. Citing his wife's adultery with a Newmarket racehorse trainer, Edward Lambton, Victor was granted his *decree nisi* in June 1959. The suit was undefended, custody of little Lord Hervey was given to his father, and Mr Lambton was ordered to pay Lord Jermyn's costs.

Victor's manners towards both men and women were said to have been those of extreme courtesy. Lady Juliet Tadgell has recalled that the first ten years of her marriage to Victor were extremely happy, and she has paid him a sincere and generous tribute. 'He was very attractive to women,' she has said, 'but got on well with men as well. He had great charm and was very intelligent, an extremely good host and raconteur. To his friends he was a very kind and considerate person.'[3]

Lady Juliet concedes that his interest in women did sometimes tip over into sexual affairs, but these were not the cause of his second divorce. Matters were more complicated than that. Lady Juliet had the misfortune to suffer miscarriages; she lost a little girl, and after the birth of her son Nicholas she was anxious to have more children. It seems that for all his attentiveness to women, Victor Bristol lacked empathy with the problems faced by women in relation to childbirth, and once it became apparent that he had lost interest in Lady Juliet's maternal ambitions, 'Things,' she says, 'did rather begin to fray at the edges.' It was small wonder that she fell in love with someone else. Victor having denied his second wife more children, it may strike some readers as odd that he went on to father three more children by his third wife, a turn of events that has prompted Lady Juliet Tadgell to exclaim, 'I am also puzzled!'

The least judgemental of people, Lady Juliet must have been upset when she read her stepson's comments about Victor quoted in *The Times* in 1994, alluding to his second divorce: 'It was for a good reason. If you want to screw hookers when you are married, you make damn sure you are not caught.' Swallow-

ing this filial bile hook, line and sinker *The Times* did not hesitate to weigh in with its own moral bias, stating that Victor had
been divorced twice 'when his wives could no longer stomach
his infidelities.' For a congenital philanderer to have got away
with one wife failing to defend a divorce petition brought on account of her own admitted adultery might be regarded as good
luck; for such a thing to happen twice is surely cause for the
husband to be given some credit for discretion. For when Victor's second marriage, in 1960 to Lady Juliet, failed, as it did in
1972, the case was again undefended. Aged 37, Lady Juliet (as
the daughter of an earl she naturally reverted to her courtesy
title on divorce) admitted adultery with sixty-year-old Somerset
de Chair, a former Conservative MP for South Paddington
whom she married in 1974. Pauline was said by gossips to have
left Victor because she could not stand his habit of keeping the
radiators on all night. This sounds like a rather weak excuse to
leave any man, and it must have been a rare occurrence, as it is
today, for the judge to award custody of the child of the marriage to the father. Whatever the precise cause of the breakdown
of two marriages, and despite being declared legally the innocent
party, these events would have been notched up by Victor as further failures, desertions even, and when the chance came to start
all over again, as it did in 1974, he seized it with both hands.

Notwithstanding the circumstances of Victor's divorce from
Pauline, no Anglican priest would have agreed to his remar-
riage in church. But as luck would have it his mother was
Church of Scotland, and it was at Crown Court Church of Scotland
in Covent Garden that on 24 April 1960, the year he succeeded as
Marquess of Bristol, Victor married Lady Juliet Fitzwilliam, whose
father had been the 8th Earl Fitzwilliam. In view of Victor's somewhat colourful background, certain members of the wealthy and
well-connected Fitzwilliam clan were 'rather startled', no doubt

[196]

because Victor had been bankrupt once and Lady Juliet was a wealthy woman. But it was fortuitous that Juliet and Pauline knew one another well, and in future never hesitated to liaise equally over Juliet's stepson John, who, as the six-year-old Earl Jermyn, dressed in a dark blue velvet court dress, had been a page at his father's second wedding. The reception was held at the Institute of Directors in Belgrave Square, a favourite haunt of the bridegroom.

On their return from a Continental honeymoon Victor and his new wife were soon caught up in a busy social life, some of it disguised as business. In September they hosted a dinner at the Savoy for a Finnish government mission. In January the following year they gave a dinner at Chapel Street for the Finnish ambassador. The Finns were certainly well fêted; in February the Bristols gave a reception at Ickworth for the Finnish minister of defence and his wife, who were staying in the house. In March it was announced that the Marquess of Bristol had given a private luncheon at 15 Chapel Street to welcome the Finnish minister of communications.

On 14 July 1961 Victor took time off from entertaining to wade into a controversy being waged in the letters column of *The Times* about arrangements at London Airport:

> Sir, May I suggest that the basic point here is not the lack or otherwise of porters upstairs. It is simply the ridiculous layout of this part of the building, where the luggage comes up on a moving band directly opposite the customs benches, behind which there is the moving band going down.
>
> All that is required is a rearrangement of the customs hall so that passengers' luggage is dumped right by the customs officers by the moving band. But such simple so-

[197]

lutions do not appear to have occurred to the great brains running London Airport.

Having got the taste for expressing blimpish sentiments, Victor fired off another letter to *The Times* on 1 August, comparing a then current supply of 'about £180 million per annum as a subsidy to various countries' to a recent cut in teachers' salaries.

> The teachers are the salt of the earth. They are dedicated people ... I hope your readers feel ashamed at the shabby treatment meted out to them recently ... teachers have for too long been grossly underpaid and undervalued, and the chief sufferers from this gross injustice will be the children ... The sins of the fathers, &c ... To conclude. The present argument is over a sum of just less than £5m., which is a fraction of the amount we have pumped out gratuitously to certain territories, many of which will assuredly give us a good resounding kick in the pants directly they know that they can get no more cash from us.

On 26 November 1961 Juliet Bristol gave birth to a son. On 8 April the following year he was christened at Ickworth, and given the names Frederick William Charles Nicholas Wentworth. It was as Lord Nicholas Hervey that he was known, and Victor had managed to round up a rather more impressive list of godparents than he had for his first son and heir; they included – what a surprise! – the Finnish ambassador, Lady Grizel Hamilton, and Princess Iris Galitzine, a member of a widespread Russian aristocratic family, many of whom had made their home in London following the revolution.

In February 1963, no sooner had the Bristols turned their backs on Ickworth to enjoy a holiday in Spain and Morocco than thieves broke into the house and made off with a quantity of silver – apparently silverwear being the only object of their interest. They were 'believed to have carried the stolen property on bicycles to a car waiting on the main road more than a mile away.' Most of the items stolen had been collected by the Bristols themselves, not by ancestors, and the insurance money was spent replacing them.

After a decent interval of six months following his father's death, Victor had taken his seat in the House of Lords on 26 October 1960. On 8 October 1963 he held a reception at the Lords, not only for fellow Members of Parliament but for 'heads of missions accredited to the Court of St James's'. He had no automatic entrée to the diplomatic corps, but there was no reason for him not to offer them hospitality, and this was his way of asserting his social status. By now he knew there was no chance of his being received by the British royal family, so he would invite the Queen's courtiers to the court of Lord Bristol. There was also of course an element of what is now rather vulgarly known as networking. Every setback spurred him on to regain what he saw as lost ground. In February 1964 the planning committee of East Suffolk County Council rejected his application to establish a yacht and power boat marina at Shotley, near Ipswich, so he got his own back for this slap in the face by establishing an annual reception at the House of Lords. And on the evening of 7 October 1964 it must have been a case of standing room only. The huge guest list included, in addition to ten ambassadors, three duchesses, representatives of three Continental royal houses, the head of the diplomatic corps, Bridget D'Oyly Carte, a distant relative of the Queen Mother's and the fabulously wealthy Nubar Gulbenkian.

Victor could be as concerned about other people's honours as his own, and Lady Juliet Tadgell's testimony has been born out

[199]

by one friend, Brian Cronan, who has described him as 'an extremely warm man, a humorous man full of anecdotes, who was very sympathetic and in return greatly appreciated small kindnesses.'[4] On 11 January 1967 Victor fired off a letter to *The Times* remonstrating with 'those in charge of the honours list' for never putting forward Donald Campbell's name for a knighthood. As by this time Campbell was dead, Lord Bristol suggested 'the proper gesture would be to award a posthumous George Cross to this man.' His advice was ignored. In 1968 he had the dubious distinction of having a spurious public house named after him; it was listed in the Cambridge telephone directory, but Victor was none too pleased about its position. 'It is rather amusing,' was his comment, 'but to appear in the tradesmen's section is something of a let-down.'

An even bigger let-down, indeed, an event designed to undermine much of the work he had so assiduously undertaken in order to rehabilitate himself, occurred on 17 April 1970 when Victor pleaded guilty at Marlborough Street magistrates' court (the very court where he had been granted bail in 1939) to driving his Rolls-Royce 'after having consumed more than the permitted level of alcohol'. Described as 'independent, of Chapel Street, Westminster' Victor was banned from driving for twelve months and fined £75 with £8 costs. As he could well afford a chauffeur the penalty would only have affected his pride. Oddly, a charge of driving while unfit through drink was dropped.

So far as Victor's general drinking habits are concerned, reports conflict. Lady Juliet Tadgell would say, quite reasonably, that 'Victor enjoyed a drink', and had a good head, only drinking perhaps rather too heavily when upset – as on one occasion when a close friend was killed in a car accident. His third wife is said to have found it necessary to ration his alcohol intake. At all events, news of the disgrace at the magistrates' court may not have circulated as far as Cyprus, for on 14 July Victor was 'received in gracious audience' by the president, Archbishop Makarios. Victor congratulated the Archbishop on 'his recent miraculous escape – no doubt through divine intervention – from the dastardly and criminal attempt on his life,' and then presented him with a facsimile of Titian's portrait of Caterina Cornaro, the last queen of Cyprus, obviously thinking it prudent to leave the original on the wall at Ickworth.[5]

Signing himself 'Hereditary High Steward of the Liberty of St Edmund', on 5 October 1972 Victor was again expressing, in a letter to *The Times*, his displeasure over local planning applications:

> Sir, I have long been astonished at local development attitudes as at last publicly revealed in your correspondence columns.
>
> Being a major landowner in the area and a lover of the aesthetic, it has pained me to view the marching desecration and suicide of this beautiful town [Bury St Edmunds] of national importance.
>
> There is land available marching with what Sir John Betjeman ... describes as industrial estates, on the western side of the town where new building could cause no traumas as it could not be worse than the existing. However, the planners for subtle reasons of their own do not wish to utilize the areas already submerged with such estates (let's face it, people have to live somewhere) but wish to gobble up the only unspoilt areas on the eastern side, for quaint reasons of their own.
>
> I happen to know that the interests on the western side are ready and willing to make land available for development and, in fact, a planning application was turned down

a few weeks ago for a small area of 30 acres or thereabouts for excuses in the usual planning jargonese (sic). One wonders what is going on?

Victor's letters to the press were typed by a secretary, but those personal letters he wrote by hand were invariably written in purple ink. Another of his quirks was to insist, whenever he could control the matter, on his title being spelt 'Marquis', in the French manner. And woe betide anyone who failed to address an envelope to 'The Most Hon' the Marquess of Bristol. He was a stickler for etiquette, and could spot a phoney order or one incorrectly worn a mile away. The arena in which he was able to give full rein to his foibles was the Monarchist League.

The League had been founded in 1943 by one of the Church of England's more notable eccentrics, the Reverend John Bazille-Corbin. He was a barrister of Lincoln's Inn and Rector of Runwell St Mary, near Wickford in Essex, a living he had experienced no difficulty in obtaining in 1923 as he happened to be the patron. One of his earliest adherents was Hugh William Peel, better known as the humorist Gillie Potter. The objective of the League was 'to uphold the principle of monarchy against the disintegrating forces of Bolshevism and socialism,' all its founder members being 'believers in the divine origin of the monarchical institution'.[6] Father Bazille-Corbin described himself as a Legitimist, celebrated the Sarum Rite in his parish church, and in 1948 applied for *sub conditione* validation of his Anglican orders to something known as the Catholicate of the West. Having duly received conditional baptism, confirmation and ordination at the hands of someone calling himself the Universal Patriarch of the Old Catholic Orthodox Church, Bazille-Corbin was promptly consecrated to the episcopacy, and henceforward styled himself Mar Marcus Valerius, titular

Bishop of Selsey. He also became Chancellor of the Glastonbury Patriarchate of Western Catholicate.

But his career was to become even more fantastical. He was made Rector-Provincial for Canterbury in the Order of Corporate Reunion, and in 1958 he became Archbishop *ad personam*. He was already Chancellor of the Order of the Crown of Stuart, and in 1957 he received a highly dubious doctorate from Prince Theodore Lescaris Commenus, whose father was a claimant to the throne of the Byzantine empire. Decorations and titles were now showered upon him: he became a Knight Commander of the Order of St Eugene of Trebizond and was awarded the Grand Collar of the Order of Santa Agata di Peterno, together with the dukedom of San Giacomo; from the would-be *de jure* King of the Two Sicilies, Bazille-Corbin was admitted to the Order of St Michel, and His Majesty was good enough to make him Marquis de Beuvel as well.

For some years the Monarchist League itself lay dormant, but in the mid-1950s it came to life again, and in 1963 what has been described as a takeover occurred. Bazille-Corbin was ousted from his position as Warden-Founder and Major Julian du Parc Braham was installed in his stead as Chancellor. The death of Father Bazille-Corbin a year later has been attributed to the shock of losing office. What he never lost was his Church of England living, for in his day a parish priest, however oddly he might behave, enjoyed his freehold for life, and was virtually unsackable.

It has not been possible to pin down the precise year that Victor Bristol joined the Monarchist League, for records were kept haphazardly, if at all. But by 1973 he had risen to the exalted rank of Deputy Chancellor, having previously served as a member of the Grand Council. In his day one might fairly describe the League's *raison d'être* as a means of encouraging the concept

[203]

of monarchy world-wide while providing good dinners for its supporters and for members of exiled royal families. Even while Victor was Deputy Chancellor, the 'Temporary Chancery – No Callers' was listed as 'Bristol House', 15 Chapel Street, and the Council of Honour included such notables as Don Carlo Colonna dei Principi di Stigliano, Duke of Marsi, and Don Beltrán Alfonso Osorio y Diez de Ribiera, Duke of Alburquerque. The Grand Council contained a brigadier general who styled himself Lord of the Honor of Assington, while Victor gloried in the titles 'The Most Hon the Marquis of Bristol, Hereditary High Steward of the Liberty of St Edmund, Grand Officer of the Order of St Alexander, Grand Master of the High Steward Association, The Lord High Interrogator, etc, etc.'

Some of the etceteras no doubt related to the array of foreign orders and decorations with which he festooned himself on the occasions of Monarchist League dinners. Whereas, for example, King Simeon of the Bulgarians (whose wife was Spanish, another clear indication that whatever Victor had got up to during the Civil War, the Spanish royal family had forgiven him) would arrive in tails and wearing just one discrete collar badge, his host (and it was widely understood that Victor underwrote these grand occasions, sometimes held at the Savoy Hotel) had himself decked out in his own version of court dress, complete with lace ruffs and buckled shoes, with a vast crimson sash over his right shoulder and the star of an order that looked remarkably similar to the Garter, a sword hanging at his side, a collar badge and an assortment of medals. Lady Juliet Tadgell says 'It amused him to dress up' and it would be nice to think there was some element of self-mockery in Victor's excessive devotion to his finery.[7] He was not the only member of the League to receive royal favours. In 1975 it was announced that the Chancellor, at that time Julian du Parc Braham, now a lieutenant colonel and already apparently an officer of the Order of the Cross of Boyaca, had been granted permission by the Queen to accept from the President of Colombia the Grand Cross of the Order of San Carlos.

The League had branches at home and overseas. When the chaplain of the League in Australia died (he was also the branch representative of the League in the Queensland and Papua New Guinea Region) the journal of the Monarchist League surprisingly allowed a solecism to slip through, referring to him as 'The Rev. Freshwater'. There was an Imperial Monarchist League to be found in Aberystwyth, under the patronage of His Imperial Highness Grand Duke Wladimir. Many of those who attended dinners in London in Victor's day were bank clerks from dreary places like Slough, who would save £10 from their meagre wages just to rub shoulders with foreign queens and princes. Many bestowed upon themselves outsize cardboard stars and badges. But the League itself was not above inventing spurious titles; at the annual banquet in 1975 held at the Apothecaries' Hall in London, someone calling himself the Much Hon Lumsden of Cushnie put in an appearance.

By 1976 Victor had succeeded Colonel Barham as Chancellor, and the chancery was shifted to 3 Belgrave Place – but still no callers were permitted. At this time an angelic photograph of HRH the Prince of Spain was reproduced in the League's journal, together with two pages of detailed information about 'The Law of Succession and the Spanish Royal Prerogatives'. One would need to be besotted (as many members of the League were) with the complex byways of foreign royalty to wade through the turgid articles that regularly appeared in The *Monarchist*. But how else would one ever discover there was a Princess Royal of the Two Sicilies, or a Bavarian prince called His Royal Highness Infante D. Luis-Alfonso de Baviera y de Borbon? How

[205]

else could one ever hope to learn of the existence of the Illustrious and Noble Brotherhood of St John the Evangelist of La Laguna, founded in the Canary Islands in 1649? A story was told of a member of the League turning up to a dinner looking remarkably unprosperous but wearing the (perfectly genuine) order of the Golden Fleece; when Victor's beady eye spotted the impostor, he admitted he had picked it up in the Portobello Road. Thanks to the Monarchist League, little was allowed to slip by unnoticed. One year no fewer than 300 members turned up at the Chapelle Expiatoire de Paris to attend a Requiem Mass for the repose of the souls of 'Their Very Christian Majesties King Louis XVI and Queen Marie-Antoinette.'

Life members of the Monarchist League can even be found in California, whence one of them wrote to point out that an article 'Orders of Chivalry The Royal Order of St Maurice and St Lazarus of Italy' was 'wrong on two counts'. Someone else flew to his desk to explain that in a previous letter he had inadvertently referred to 'the Imperial Russian Family' when what he should have written was 'the Russian Imperial Family'. A careful watch was kept on important royal events. When a telegram was sent to 'HRH The Princess Margrethe of Denmark upon her 21st birthday' readers were breathlessly reminded 'HRH may one day be Her Majesty The Queen.' When the Shah of Iran was deposed, the League suggested to the prime minister, Margaret Thatcher, that he should be offered asylum in England. Scarcely a royal birthday went unremarked: on 9 May 1979 Her Imperial Majesty Empress Zita of Austria celebrated her 87th birthday; the birth of the 37th grandchild of Their Royal Highnesses the Count and Countess of Paris was duly noted. So was the death of His Majesty Yang di-Pertuan Agong Yahya Petra of Malaysia. Tags were kept on the Imperial House of Turkey. By the age of eighteen Lord Nicholas Hervey, Victor's second son, had been roped in as president of the International Youth Association of the League, and he too was soon contributing articles.

By October 1971 Juliet had already separated from Victor, William Hickey in the *Daily Express* announcing that 'undaunted by the prolonged absence of his wife, the Marquess of Bristol has bravely decided to go ahead with the reception he holds every year in the House of Lords for Government ministers and diplomats.' It transpired that Somerset de Chair, with whom Juliet now intended to live, and Victor had previously been close friends, but Victor told the gossip columnist, 'Mr de Chair certainly won't be at either of my parties this year [at the Lords or at Ickworth at Christmas], unless as a gatecrasher.'

By the time of Victor's third marriage, to Yvonne Sutton in 1974, he decided it was necessary to become a tax exile, and he acquired a home in the Place Beaumarchais, Monte Carlo. He also acquired a new lease of life; for a man approaching sixty, whose hobby was 'beautiful women', he could not have chosen a more attractive wife of twenty-nine. Nor could that marriage have been better blessed than with the birth of two beautiful daughters, although unfortunately Victor did not live to see them grow up. (Victor had little rapport with children, and his death when his third family was very young may have been a greater deprivation for them than for him.) When his first daughter, Victoria Frederica Isabella, was born in 1976, he had no trouble rounding up a galaxy of eight godparents, including the King and Queen of the Bulgarians, Queen Susan of the Albanians and the Princess of Luxembourg. While the christening took place at Ickworth Church, a Jesuit, Father Alfonso de Zulueta, who gloried also in the title Count of Torre Diaz, administered baptism, in deference to the new Lady Bristol's religious persuasion; according to an elaborate Roman Catholic order of service, decorated with a pink tassel, he did so by kind

[207]

permission of the Reverend H. Price Jones, the Anglican incumbent.

'Lord Bristol was always very supportive to me in having all three of our children baptized as Roman Catholics' Yvonne, Marchioness of Bristol has told the author. And there was probably no doubt that Victor was thrilled to have a daughter (he had found John tiresome only when he left the nursery and, had he lived long enough, he might have been a very good father to both daughters). For the christening, and the lunch party afterwards, he designed for himself an amazing pale grey morning dress, complete with lace ruffs and a cummerbund, to which he attached his sword; he also wore a collar badge. Several medallions dangled from his right breast; on the left breast of his suit were pinned no fewer than four stars pertaining to various foreign orders. In this frankly ludicrous get-up he posed for a photograph with his hand resting on Lady Bristol's shoulder, while the infant Victoria Hervey lay comfortably snuggled in lace. It was most unfair of a *Daily Express* photographer to snap Lord and Lady Bristol before they had taken up their positions for the official photographs – a picture showing a nurse holding the baby some distance from the parents. 'A yawning gap between master and servant as the Bristols pose for a christening day photograph' was the snide and grossly misleading caption. Lady Victoria later went to Benenden, grew up as beautiful as her father could possibly have wished, and became hot copy for gossip columnists. Described by one reporter as 'magnificently, stupendously inarticulate', she took to posing scantily dressed in hotel rooms and never developed any inhibitions about asking for payment for interviews.

Victor took up permanent residence in Monte Carlo at the end of March 1979, explaining to the press, 'During the past 15 to 20 years I have given the tax man £15 million which I earned through my own endeavours. The tax system in this country is penal to people like myself, and I decided that enough was enough.' His new tax arrangements meant he was unable to leave his safe haven in Monte Carlo until the following summer, and for the birth of her son, Frederick William Augustus, Yvonne was obliged to fly to London on her own, having decided to place herself in the hands of an obstetrician she knew 'rather than an obstetrician we did not know in Monte Carlo. Lord Bristol's concern was purely for my health and that of our baby.'[8]

High rates of taxation were not, it seems, Victor's only source of complaint. 'It is no longer safe to walk the streets with one's girl friend or wife any more,' he declared. 'Not that I am at all unnerved to go out alone, because I have a black belt in karate. But I wouldn't dream of taking my wife for a stroll – even in Belgravia. There is no crime rate in Monte Carlo, or it is negligible, and one has much more security and peace of mind there.' He said his London home was now up for sale, but evidently plans to part with 15 Chapel Street were abandoned.[9] Warming to the theme of Britain having gone to the dogs, the Marquess added, 'People will really have to get down to work and earn a living. Take the Civil Service and all those pen-pushing parasites at Whitehall. We could do with 80 per cent less of them because they are all no-goods who got the job because they couldn't get a job anywhere else.'

Victor was allowed back in the UK for ninety days a year, and by 4 June 1980 the coast seems to have been clear, for Lord Frederick's Roman Catholic christening took place that day at St James's, Spanish Place, the Count of Torre Diaz again officiating. Unlike either of his half-brothers, Frederick rated two crowned heads (although one of them, King Rached al-Mandi, an honorary godparent on account of being a Muslim, is believed by some to have had scant legal claim to call himself King of the Tunisians). The other sovereign, also of course a Muslim, was genuine enough even if he no longer had a throne; he was King Ahmed Fouad of Egypt. Prince Tomislav of Yugoslavia and Prince Nikita Romanoff of Russia brought with them a whiff of the Orthodox Church; the Princess of Luxembourg again obliged. Lord Nicholas Hervey stood as a godfather to his half-brother – but not Lord Jermyn, who by now was in disgrace. In 1976, aged twenty-one, he had been on a drink–drive charge, the start of a life of criminality, degradation and ultimately self-inflicted death.

Victor choreographed the christening as if it was a state occasion, and when he came to record the proceedings for The *Monarchist* his children's titles were all firmly spelt out, in the manner of a parvenu. 'Your Chancellor is happy to tell you that Grand Council Members and Officers of the Monarchist League played a significant part in the Christening Ceremonies of our infant son The Lord Frederick William Augustus Hervey,' he wrote. 'Herald Trumpeters announced the movement of the procession to the appropriate seats facing the High Altar. This was headed by Mr Jeffrey Finestone, Editor of The *Monarchist*, walking four paces in front of your Chancellor with The Marchioness of Bristol, who held the infant child. Next were the two nurses, between them our pretty little daughter The Lady Victoria Frederica Isabella Hervey, aged nearly four, then the Godparents, in sequence ... then The Lord Nicholas Hervey, son of your Chancellor, and the famous hostesses, Mrs Peter Black and Mrs B Rosenfeld.' He completed the Alice-in-Wonderland scene with the picturesque observation, 'The procession was tailed by Captain Francis Skilleter.'

It is easy enough to write off Victor Bristol's obsession with royalty and his exaggerated mode of dress as the conduct of a

self-professed eccentric, but an article he contributed to The
Monarchist in 1979 with its air of bombast, its indiscriminate use
of capital letters and exclamation marks, and its unmistakable
hint of paranoia, does incline one to wonder if he had not become mentally unbalanced. The dividing line between the reac-
tionary aristocrat playing the buffoon and the untitled
inhabitant of a madhouse is often a very thin one. He claimed to
be a 'happy Tax Exile,' who nevertheless had 'been chased out
of the UK by Mr BLOODSUCKER and his team, those people set up
in office by the Social Government [he must have meant Social-
ist] and for vote-catching reasons not yet having been abolished
by the Conservatives – or likely to be exterminated for the same
ridiculous political reasons.' Clearly there had been no time in
which to tidy up his syntax, so inflamed was he by the thought
of paying tax, and he was now in full flight.

'The BLOODSUCKER Department,' by which he meant Her Majesty's Inspectors of Taxes, he described as 'throwouts [whatever a
throwout is], dropouts, drugouts, long-haired morons, idiots'.
Overlooking the fact that a republic cannot also be a monarchy,
he ranted on; 'This great Monarchy of ours has been debased in
Government to a fifth-rate third-world Republic.' The charge of
drug addiction levelled at civil servants was an unfortunate one;
within four years his eldest son was narrowly to escape being
charged in New York with conspiracy to distribute heroin and cocaine. (When the charge was heard in June 1983 it was dropped
for 'lack of sufficient evidence to proceed'.)

'As I write these notes' Victor explained, 'I am sitting on a
beautiful balcony at the Chancery where I have a good sight of
the Yacht Harbour, part of the Casino Gardens and the top of
the famous Casino itself also the upper midriff (sic) of the Hotel
de Paris. I should add that your Chancellor enjoys the Casino,
the throng, the tenseness, the beautiful rooms, the food and the

gorgeous women, but does not gamble himself unless it is on a good lunch or dinner in the Principality, which in this haven of all havens bears no risk whatsoever of not providing full value and satisfaction.

'Perhaps as a MONARCHIST I am prejudiced in favour of the benevolent Administration afforded by His Serene Highness Prince Rainier III assisted by Her Serene Highness, the Charming Princess Grace.'

He concluded with a panegyric on the low level of crime in Monte Carlo, attributable to the 'courteous Police,' who were, in fact, 'the first, finest and most tactful in Europe, in every respect'. Of course, the occasional bad egg did fall through the net, but as the observant Marquess pointed out, 'anyone with any psychology can detect that a squat fellow with a flat bulgy nose, little beady eyes and a pig-like expression is someone to avoid, as in all levels of life!!'

This tirade was severely frowned upon by the Grand Council, notwithstanding one of its members was Lord Nicholas Hervey, by this time also one of two Vice-Chancellors. At their meeting on 28 August 1980 it was noted that 'Great concern was expressed about the tone of the Chancellor's Notes in *The Monarchist*. It was felt that references to Tax Exile should not be published in The *Monarchist*.' Miles Jackson-Lipkin, a judge of the high court in Hong Kong, said he would speak to the Chancellor and report back to the next meeting. 'Meanwhile,' this minute continued, 'it was unanimously agreed that all articles should be carefully edited including the Chancellor's Notes.' Victor's status as a tax exile was well and truly underlined by the sum of money he was to leave in England: £7,507. No doubt he had been in the habit of retaining a small reserve of pocket money in the United Kingdom to pay for visits to his favourite London hotel, Claridge's, where in fact he lunched just eight weeks before he died. In November 1983, following a spell in the London Clinic, it was to Claridge's that he withdrew to convalesce rather than his own house in Chapel Street.

On 9 March 1982 Victor's second daughter, Isabella Frederica, his fifth and last child, was born. She was baptized in the private chapel at the Palace in Monaco. Victor was by now sixty-six, and had just three years to live, dying in Monte Carlo on 10 March 1985, a day after Lady Isabella's third birthday. He had become such an Establishment outcast that *The Times* could not be bothered to write its own obituary, and it was left to Michael Wynne-Parker, Principal Secretary and Receiver General of the Monarchist League, to pen a forty-four line personal memoir. He described Victor as 'essentially a private man' and forbore to mention that he had promoted himself to the rank of His Excellency the Ambassador-at-Large of the Monarchist League. Needless to say, on the occasion of this prestigious appointment the 6th Marquess of Bristol was not received in audience by the Queen.

12

---·•·•·---

'HE'S GOT TO GO'

When she was nineteen, up at Oxford and desperate for a holiday job, Lady Selina Hastings, a daughter of the 15th Earl of
Huntingdon and later to become the author of distinguished
biographies of Nancy Mitford and Evelyn Waugh, found herself
escorting a little boy of nine to Italy, to be reunited with his
father and stepmother. He was Frederick William John
Augustus Hervey, Earl Jermyn, who was semi-educated by a
succession of governesses (Lady Selina's tour of duty only
lasted three months), before joining his father's old preparatory
school, Heatherdown, at Ascot. When John was thirteen,
instead of going to Eton, on the recommendation of the headmaster of Heatherdown, James Edwards, he moved on to Harrow, entering the school in January 1968 as a boarder in Druries
House and leaving at the end of the summer term of 1972.
Thanks to a recent change in the law, on 16 September that year
he came of age, and to celebrate the event, and to safeguard
against death duties, he received a life interest in land worth £4
million. It was said to amount to 'between 7,000 and 8,000 of
some of the richest acres in East Anglia.'

Despite an assurance of private wealth, John as a young man took paid jobs, working for a short time in an estate agent's office and then in a Rolls-Royce garage, where he lost no time blotting his copybook, being fined for stealing 'No Waiting' signs from the street outside. This was no more than a youthful jape, and far less reprehensible than his father's had been. But his ideas of practical jokes soon got out of hand, in the unfortunate way that Hervey jokes so often did – throwing furniture out of someone's windows at Cambridge and shooting open the obstinate door of a fridge with a shotgun.

John's childhood had seen his parents divorce when he was four. He acquired two stepmothers and a stepfather, three half-brothers and two half-sisters, but like his father he was in reality an only child. His greatest curse was to inherit a great deal of money and, like his father, to have been born with a capacity for making even more, for without almost limitless wealth he would never have been able to feed to the extent he did the drug habit that killed him.

A contemporary, the Marquess of Blandford, heir to the Marlborough dukedom and, like John, destined for a lifetime of drug-taking, wrote in 1999 that while at Harrow John had 'modelled himself on Oscar Wilde', wearing 'ties with huge knots and a gold pin, which made people look at him.' Lord Blandford thought that John was complicated, 'a reserved character hiding behind a flamboyant personality.' He has claimed that by the age of seventeen John was drinking half a bottle of vodka a day, 'and exuded an air of debauchery'.[1]

No one will ever know precisely why John Bristol became so disastrously addicted to drugs, but it is reasonable to make an informed guess. Until he was seven he was his father's only son, and even after the birth of his half-brother Nicholas he would have felt an instinctive obligation to produce an heir to the titles and estate. Unfortunately he was homosexual, managing to put off marriage until he was twenty-nine. It is always possible that he told his father of his sexual disposition and was shunned as a result; it is even more likely that his father guessed, and had Victor known that John was gay he would, in the opinion of Lady Juliet Tadgell, have been 'antagonistic and disappointed'.[2] Although Victor did not find children easy, his relations with John when he was a boy were good, and John's childhood was by no means as bleak as has sometimes been suggested. In his mother's second husband, Edward Lambton, he found an affectionate father-figure, and he became fond of his stepmother, Juliet Bristol. But by the time John was in his early twenties, relations with his father were strained; just as most fathers need to feel they have produced a son after their own heart, so most boys need a father they can look up to, and Victor must have dreaded the day when John would discover the details of his own shady past.

Matters were not assisted in later life by open antagonism between John and his second stepmother, Victor's third wife, and we may safely assume that by 1984, the year John unwisely became engaged to a young divorcee, Francesca Jones, there was little love lost between Victor and John. The following announcement appeared in *The Times*: 'The Marquess and Marchioness of Bristol will not be able to attend the marriage of Earl Jermyn to Francesca, daughter of Mr & Mrs Douglas Fisher, on 14 September owing to a prior engagement in London.' To have cut his son's wedding, which took place at St Mary's, Ickworth, would have been bad enough; publicly to announce his absence, and on such feeble and clearly untruthful grounds, was unforgivable.

At least Victor did not leave John, thirty when he succeeded as 7th Marquess of Bristol, short of money; quite the reverse,

even though for six years after Victor's death his widow fought
a legal battle contesting the will – a battle, she told Nigel Dempster of the *Daily Mail*, that had been 'unnecessary, totally con-
suming and a complete waste of time and a lot of money'.
Yvonne, Lady Bristol also told Dempster: 'Before my husband
died he said of John, "That boy has been a permanent thorn in
my side all my life. I beg you not to have anything to do with
him. But he is godfather to my son Frederick and I still feel
families are very important."'[3] It was a strange slip for both
Lord and Lady Bristol to have made; it was Victor's second son,
Nicholas, not John, who stood as godfather to Frederick.

Often diplomatically referred to in the press as a confirmed
bachelor, John's homosexual affairs had been common knowledge among his friends, one of whom, in conversation with the
author, has described him as 'very camp, the campest queen I
have ever known, very funny and naughty, but appallingly rude
to waiters. It was not so much his title that he threw around as
the weight of his money.' Lord Blandford has recalled John
'hanging out with loads of gay men in New York'.[4] And at the
age of about twenty-four, John was living in Paris with another
man. It was from a flat in Paris that for some years John control-
led his profitable network of business interests; he had companies in Holland, the Isle of Man, even the Virgin Islands.
Francesca was only twenty and had already made one hasty marriage of convenience. She was extremely attractive, and together
they made a handsome couple. But the marriage was only to last
three years. Unlike his father, John had no idea how to treat
women; indeed, he seems to have held them in contempt. A story
retailed in *The Times Magazine* in 1994 by Adam Nicolson was
never denied; apparently an American woman guest who was
staying at Ickworth took a rubber dingy on to the lake to fish, so
John went indoors to fetch an airgun, with which he proceeded

to puncture the boat. Nicolson's informant told him, 'The more she screamed the more he laughed.'

For a young wife to give emotional support to a homosexual, or bisexual, husband is one thing; to expect her to bear the strain of a homosexual drug abuser is quite another. Who wants to be left in a Bentley hanging over the edge of a cliff?[5] In 1986, two years into the marriage and a year after the Jermyns had become Marquess and Marchioness of Bristol, John rented a bungalow at Porto Ercole in Tuscany for £3,500 a week, in order to entertain half a dozen friends. One of these, a heroin addict called Andrew Pierce, was discovered dead in mysterious circumstances.

By now there was no shortage of former friends who felt it prudent to distance themselves from John. On 10 June 1988 John was in court in Jersey accused of possessing and importing cocaine, having been arrested when he landed at St Helier airport in his private helicopter. Four months later he was jailed for a year. The Royal Court rejected a plea for him to be put on probation or even given a suspended jail sentence to enable him to continue treatment at a drug addiction centre on the mainland. By this time his fortune was estimated at £19 million, and he was believed to be spending £25,000 a year on cocaine. When arrested, presumably on a tip-off, he was found with more than 13 grammes of cocaine, with a street value in Jersey of £1,625. There was no suggestion, however, that John Bristol intended selling his precious drugs; they were intended solely for his own use.

So, like father like son; John, 7th Marquess of Bristol had followed Victor, 6th Marquess, to prison. He served only seven months of his sentence, working as a prison chef, a job that would have called for few culinary skills, and boasted that while inside he had completed business agreements worth £4 million. He also palled up with a car thief whom he later hired as his chauffeur. Within two months of his release he was in trouble with the National Trust. They were threatening legal action because at Ickworth one of John's Irish wolfhounds had attacked a visitor from Chesterfield who was walking her collie. Such threats were water off a duck's back as far as the Marquess of Bristol was concerned; a year later the Bury St Edmunds magistrates ordered him to keep his wretched wolfhound, Basil, reputed to weigh 12 stone, under proper control after it had attacked a man who was walking *his* dog in the grounds. Basil was also alleged – although this may have been a slight exaggeration – to have consumed forty-seven cats. July 1989 saw John again following in his father's footsteps when he was remanded on bail at Bury St Edmunds accused of driving under the influence of 'drink or drugs'. That appears to have been a holding charge, for when John appeared before the local magistrates on 12 September (and it must have been quite difficult to convene a bench on which no JP was personally acquainted with the defendant) it was to answer a charge of possessing heroin and cocaine worth £320. He pleaded guilty and was fined £3,000, the chairman of the bench urging him to continue treatment for addiction at the Charter Clinic off Harley Street, 'because,' he said, 'you know as well as we do it is a matter of life and death.'

Such well-intentioned advice was wasted breath. In January 1990 John appeared before magistrates in Lowestoft, having refused to give a blood sample to police who suspected him of driving under the influence of drugs. He was fined a modest £100 and banned from driving for three years. He could of course well afford to be driven, and he was still able to indulge his love of handling fast cars on the Ickworth estate. Three months later he was being sued by a firm of solicitors in Jersey who alleged that he owed them £6,842. By this time he had thought of a way of getting round his driving ban; he flew to Australia, where he purchased an E-type Jaguar and installed himself in a mansion in Sydney, costing £1,500 a week to rent. He had also conjured up a not very subtle scheme for getting round the Australian immigration laws, which strongly disapproved of convicted criminals being allowed to enter the country; he travelled under the name of Jermyn.

'He's got to go,' the president of Victoria's Returned Services League was reported as saying. 'He's a criminal and an addict and we don't want him here.'[6] John had what he thought was an apt riposte to this unfriendly welcome. 'Considering half your country comes from criminal stock anyway, I find it extraordinary that you feel so strongly about criminals now.' He had overlooked the fact that Australia had decided they had already imported all the criminals they needed. 'We breed enough of our own without importing them,' the opposition spokesman for immigration retorted.

Officially, John was in Australia to reinvest the proceeds from the sale of a 57,000-acre stud farm in Queensland. Since 1979 he had been, on and off, a tax exile, with business interests in France, the United States and Jersey that had enabled him to multiply his fortune at least three times. 'Aussie Knives Out For Posh Pom With a Prison Record' were the sort of overseas headlines his behaviour was now encouraging, while back home, the marquess having been deported from Australia, *The Times* was reporting on 4 March 1991, 'Village Split as Marquess Takes a Swing at Business.' The word 'swing' was by way of a mild pun; it seems that 'The colourful Marquess of Bristol, whose eccentric habits have long been an object of curiosity among his fellow villagers in deepest Suffolk, has stirred fresh controversy with a plan to spend half his £20 million fortune building a vast

[221]

leisure complex on his 4,000-acre estate.' John's brainwave was to build an eighty-bedroom hotel with conference facilities, shops and an eighteen-hole golf course, never mind that the plan would have meant the principal tenant farmer losing his Grade II listed home, his land and his livelihood. Fortunately it all fell through.

When in October 1991 the *Daily Mail* sent a feature writer to Ickworth to interview John Bristol, they dispensed with formalities, headlining the piece 'The Rake's Progress,' the interview having been prompted by a drugs raid on the house by police with sniffer dogs twelve days before. John and a friend called James Whitby had duly been carted off to the police station in Bury St Edmunds, and Whitby was charged. During the course of the *Mail* interview John recalled that when his father moved to Monaco he had stripped the east wing of many of its valuable possessions – so many that he had been compelled to raise the money to buy them back. 'One weekend,' he said, 'I came down here, opened the front door and there was absolutely nothing in the house at all, apart from a pair of pictures on the stairs. He had taken the lot.'

John was overlooking the fact that the furniture belonged to his father, although one might certainly have expected that a wealthy man moving overseas would have negotiated with his son. For all his wayward behaviour, there is no doubt that John loved Ickworth, and did spend an enormous amount of money and time restoring the interior. He blamed poor relations with his father on the circumstances of his third marriage, telling the *Mail*, 'He married, shall we say, an under-secretary.' This catty remark was followed by further unpleasant innuendos for which, on 15 November, the *Daily Mail* felt obliged to print a retraction and apology for any embarrassment caused to Yvonne, Marchioness of Bristol.

The *Daily Mail* reported that John currently had unpaid bills amounting to £34,000 for furnishings, and if this was true either he had a cash-flow problem despite his wealth or a reckless disregard for the cash-flow problems of other people. He was crazy enough to buy a yacht on hire purchase from the King of the Belgians for £350,000. Much of his income went on professional spongers, for – again like his father – he relished the company of disreputable people. As he became more and more addicted to drugs, and his behaviour became more and more erratic and destructive, so friends of his own social status were to desert him, and he became ever more dependent for company on social climbers and male prostitutes.

Optimistically, on 11 February 1992 the local magistrates adjourned four charges against John for six weeks when told by his counsel he was halfway through a course of detoxification at a London clinic. He was back in court on 24 March accused of possessing and intending to supply heroin and cocaine with a street value of about £800, and had the case adjourned for a fortnight. The litany of offences seemed to be gathering a fatal momentum. On 29 June Snaresbrook Crown Court in east London heard that John kept cocaine and heroin in the false bottom of a can of furniture polish and could not go more than two hours without a fix, stopping even on car journeys to snort cocaine and heroin off the dashboard.

John's complicated life had become more complicated still when he went into partnership with someone called Bruce Smith. They planned to open a motor museum at Ickworth for classic cars, but fell out when John threatened Smith with a writ for £134,000, whereupon Smith warned John he would tell the police about his current drug activities. Prosecuting counsel told the court that Smith became aware that the Marquess suffered from mood swings and dramatic personality changes, from lethargy and depression to hyperactivity. 'The two men often drove long distances to vehicle auctions,' he said. 'During the course of such journeys such was the degree of addiction of the defendant it was necessary to stop every couple of hours or so, and the defendant, pulling into a service station or café, would go off to a lavatory, and on his return, from being subdued and lethargic, he would be excitable and alert.'

The judge dismissed Smith's evidence as 'sickening hypocrisy', and John heard his own character described by his QC, George Carman, as that of a 'sad, emotionally deprived figure'. He was cleared of supplying cocaine and heroin, having pleaded guilty to possessing the drugs. The judge deferred sentence for five months so that John could again undergo treatment. The scene then transferred to St Edmunds Crown Court where, on 28 October, it was alleged that someone called Nicholas Ashley, acting out of 'a totally misguided sense of loyalty,' had offered a £10,000 bribe to Bruce Smith to 'fudge' his evidence against John, as he 'did not want Lord Bristol to go to prison'. Ashley admitted attempting to pervert the course of justice, and was jailed for three months.

Back at Snaresbrook Crown Court, on 6 December, 'looking gaunt and pale,' John Bristol was sentenced to ten months in prison. He had, the judge told him, thrown away his last chance. Ignoring the advice of doctors he had discharged himself from the clinic and gone on a 'drug binge' to the south of France. According to a reporter from *The Times*, 'he showed no reaction when he was sentenced and walked stiffly from the dock.' Mr Carman had told the judge that his client had dissipated his inheritance, having spent £7 million on drugs in the past ten years, and was hoping to raise another £2 million by selling what remained of his Ickworth estate, thus helping to ease 'profound' tax problems. His

plan was 'to live abroad, when he can, in more modest circumstances,' Mr Carman said.

In his judicial lecture, the judge told John, 'I gave you a
chance in July and in my judgment you have thrown it away ...
I am satisfied you have no real motivation to be cured of your
addiction ... you have never seriously intended to try to give
up.'

No one read about this turn of events with more surprise
than the National Trust, for the impression had been given that
the £2 million would come from a sale of land to them. 'It was
all news to us,' a spokesman said. 'We own the house and its
contents [the contents in the Rotunda] and Lord Bristol is our
tenant. Supposedly he is going to sell us the rest of the estate for
£2 million. But we haven't even been approached, so we are
very surprised by all this talk of buying. I'm not even sure we
would want it.'

Far from wanting more of Lord Bristol's acres, what the
National Trust decided they wanted was forfeiture of his lease
on the east wing – to have him out, in other words, claiming
persistent breaches of the terms of the lease. The list of John's
offences included injury to visitors (today there are some 95,000
a year) by his dogs, reckless driving in the park and, needless to
say, possession of drugs on the premises. Lord Chorley, chairman of the Trust, said the decision to evict John had been taken
'with great reluctance and only after the most careful consideration'. As for the 2,200 acres of farmland still belonging to John,
these were sold at auction by his trustees in 1994.

John's time in prison cannot have been too unpleasant; he
was interned at Downside Open Prison in Surrey, from where
he was collected by a chauffeur after serving just five months of
his ten-month sentence. Within forty-eight hours of his release
he had been arrested again, in Eaton Square, on suspicion of

possessing cocaine. When he was charged on 6 July it was for possession of Class A drugs and obstructing police officers into the bargain. It was yet another tip-off that had alerted plain-clothes detectives from the South East Regional Crime Squad to pounce outside his Chelsea home. Heroin to the tune of 0.88 grammes was found in John's jacket pocket when he was searched at Belgravia police station.

One bright light on the horizon was a softening of attitude by the National Trust, which said it had always been the wish of the Trust that a representative of the family should live at Ickworth, and that 'amicable and constructive discussions' between the Trust and John's trustees had resulted in the draw-ing up of a fresh agreement 'which will ensure that the prob-lems in the past will not reoccur'.[7] Even better news resulted from John's appearance for sentencing at Horseferry Road mag-istrates' court on 13 September; amazingly, he was put on pro-bation for two years. It was small wonder that people were saying there was one law for the rich and one for the poor.[8] Not only was time running out for John, now turned middle-aged, 'ostracized from the society he was born into,' according to his latest defence counsel, and looking almost moronically haggard (he left St Mary's Hospital, Paddington in the spring of 1995 reportedly weighing less than seven stone and unable to walk without the aid of a stick); stories about his exploits and life-style were gathering a life of their own. On 10 January 1996, the year his mother Pauline Lambton died, *The Times* calmly asserted he had inherited 'a £35 million fortune on his 21st birthday,' a vastly inflated sum mysteriously reduced three years later to £1 million, and Ickworth had become the most beautiful mansion in England, which it most certainly is not.[9]

From the sunny Bahamas John himself was pondering his fu-ture, such as it was, and seemed to be coming to the conclusion that he would save quite a lot of expense if he moved out of the east wing of Ickworth and into a smaller house on the estate. By March he had made up his mind. He would sell the contents of his private apartments at Ickworth (372 lots offered on the first day of a two-day sale raised almost £800,000) 'in case a Labour government was returned to power'. He claimed to have spent £350,000 a year maintaining the east wing. At his age – he was 41 – he should have 'a lot less financial hassle', but he would miss the shooting. Having just completed his period on probation he told reporters whom he escorted round Ickworth, 'I have never felt as well as I do at this moment.' He intended building a house in the Bahamas. A 'tremendous burden' was about to be lifted from his shoulders by his pending departure from the east wing. To pay for the new house in the West Indies he intended selling nine meaningless lordships of the manor, hoping thereby to raise perhaps £50,000 or £60,000 from gullible snobs.

John Bristol was not the only member of his generation of the family to face emotional, even mental, problems. At his preparatory school, Heatherdown and then at Eton, Lord Nicholas Hervey had seemed, according to his mother, a very normal, healthy child. He entered Martin Whiteley's house in September 1974, and in point of fact his record at Eton would indicate that he was an industrious boy with plenty of initiative. He was commended for good effort in Michaelmas 1976, in Lent and Summer 1977, and again in Lent 1979. In Michaelmas 1978 Nicholas took part in his House Debate, and during his last two halves he was in the House Library (ie, a prefect). Poor eyesight seems to have debarred him from playing ball games, but he did row in a Baby House IV. He founded and was president of the Burlington Society, a fine arts society with an emphasis on modern art, and appropriately enough, in view of his family's

[227]

connections with land and parliament, he was a member of both the Agricultural and Political Societies. Nicholas left Eton at Christmas 1979 with A-Levels in French, Spanish and economics. He moved on to Yale, where he studied economics and took a degree in the History of Art. As he was heir presumptive to his half-brother John, and might one day quite reasonably be expected to inherit land at Ickworth, it also made sense for him to study agriculture at Cirencester. His behaviour, however, now began to seem erratic. For example, he failed to pay money he owed to the Monarchist League and eventually allowed his membership and vice-chancellorship to lapse. A family friend found him charming but 'a very strange boy' who seemed emotionally detached, unable to form permanent relationships, despite the fact that as a boy his relations with his father had been very good. He and John had also been very fond of one another; Lady Juliet Tadgell believes that John was as fond of her son as he was of anyone. But a story that for Nicholas's 21st birthday in 1982 John splashed out on a Maserati is not true; it was Lady Juliet who gave Nicholas (who appropriately enough already possessed a Bristol) a Volkswagen. She has recalled that Nicholas was 'very loyal to family traditions'.[10] In a letter in *The Times* of 4 May 1978 he gently rebuked a feature writer for suggesting that his 'great-great-great-great-great-grandfather Lord Hervey' had 'spelt "Hervey" "Harvey" as in the sherry, whereas technically it is spelt "Hervey". Us Herveys are few and far between now,' he wrote, 'whereas the Harveys are many!'

By the time Lord Nicholas was twenty-two he had been diagnosed as schizophrenic. When he was thirty he underwent treatment in a clinic, but 'from the time he was institutionalized,' says Lady Juliet, 'he was never himself again.' He showed no inclination to marry and lived alone in a flat in Pavilion Street, Knightsbridge. It was here that in January 1998 he hanged himself. John's heir presumptive was now his seven-teen-year-old half-brother Lord Frederick Hervey, a schoolboy in Branch's House at Eton.[11]

Three months after this tragedy John, by now a very sick man indeed, surrendered his lease on the east wing of Ickworth and took up residence in Horringer Hall. For years his sole purpose in life had become the all-absorbing business of taking doses of heroin, which, other heroin users have explained, would have given some shape and meaning to an otherwise shapeless and purposeless life. The more dependent on drugs John had be-come, the more boring he appeared to other people, much like an alcoholic; but for him heroin would have anaesthetized his self-critical faculties and – if only temporarily – reinforced his self-esteem. A relatively early end to this cycle of illusion and disillusion was inevitable as a potentially brilliant business brain degenerated beyond recall.

John Bristol's death occurred on 10 January 1999 as a result of 'multi-organ failure attributable to chronic drug abuse'. Although he had done his best to disgrace his heritage he died, at the age of forty-four, on property owned by his family for nearly 600 years. He will almost certainly prove to have been the last Hervey ever to do so. At the age of nineteen, while read-ing French and business studies at Edinburgh, John's half-brother Lord Frederick Hervey awoke to find himself 8th Marquess of Bristol. Asked what his relations had been with his immediate predecessor, he replied, 'They were only ever benefi-cial. He told me to have nothing to do with drugs.'[12] Although the new Lord Bristol can do nothing to eradicate any Hervey genes he may have inherited from his father, the 6th Marquess, at least he is only half a Hervey – and no reader of the often bizarre tale of his paternal family will do other than wish him well.

[229]

NOTES AND REFERENCES

PRELUDE

1. Pronounced 'Harvy'.
2. The *Independent*, 12 January 1999.
3. *Knole and the Sackvilles* (Heinemann, 1922).
4. Quoted *Eddy: The Life of Edward Sackville-West* by Michael De-la-Noy (Arcadia Books, 1999).

1. THE MOST MAGNIFICENT ENTRY (pp. 5–21)

1. Gilbert Burnet (1643–1715), Bishop of Salisbury.
2. Robert Halsband, *Lord Hervey: Eighteenth Century Courtier* (Oxford University Press, 1973).
3. Not Sir 'Charles' Carr, Halsband, ibid.
4. *England in the Eighteenth Century* ed. Roy Porter (The Folio Society, 1998).
5. Halsband, op cit.
6. *Queen Anne* (Routledge & Kegan Paul, 1980).
7. It is odd that two distinguished modern historians contradict Lord Hervey's diary entry for the arrival of the king – and disagree with one another. In *The First Four Georges* (Batsford, 1956) J H Plumb says it was 29 September; in *George III* (Constable, 1972) John Brooke opts for 30 September. Hervey was undoubtedly correct.
8. Halsband, op cit.
9. When dismissed from office with a curt note, Lord Bolingbroke admitted it had shocked him 'for at least two minutes.'
10. Not her 'three' daughters; Plumb, *The First Four Georges*, op cit. Princess Caroline was not born until 1715.
11. Extensive accounts of the exceedingly complex lives of the 1st and 2nd earls of Bristol of the first creation may be found in the *Dictionary of National Biography*.

2. MAMA'S TEARS AND FEARS (pp. 23–9)

1. Halsband, op cit.
2. On their arrival in England all the members of the royal family adjusted their birthdays to the Julian calendar, which was 11 days behind the Gregorian calendar, in use in all countries on the Continent save Russia and Turkey. The Julian calendar was abolished on 31 December 1751.
3. Not 1699, Halsband, op cit.
4. The Prince and Princess of Wales had taken possession of Richmond Lodge, just to the south of the present Kew Gardens, in 1718 as a summer retreat from Leicester House after being banned from Windsor Castle, Kensington Palace, Hampton Court and St James's Palace by George 1 in November the year before. Richmond Lodge was formerly the home of the exiled Jacobite duke of Ormonde, who had leased it from William III. When the Prince of Wales obtained the property from the Commissioners for the Confiscated Estates Court for £6,000 it was described as 'a pleasant residence for a country gentleman,' and it was at Richmond that the future George II joined the newly established hunting fraternity.
5. No Maids of Honour have been appointed since the death in 1936 of George V.
6. *Samuel Johnson* (Chatto & Windus, 1978).
7. In *Samuel Johnson*, ibid, Jackson Bate tells us Henry Hervey delivered his sermon 'in full regalia' to 'an appreciative audience.' A sermon is more usually preached to a congregation, and Hervey would merely have worn a surplice.
8. *The Life of Samuel Johnson* by James Boswell (London, 1791).
9. *Caroline the Illustrious* (Longmans, Green, 1904).
10. *Horace Walpole* (Faber & Faber, 1940).

3. A SHARP AND BLOODY DUEL (pp. 41–66)

1. *Lord Hervey's Memoirs* ed. Romney Sedgwick (Batsford, revised edition 1963).
2. Geraldine Norman, The *Independent*, 13 February 1992.
3. Stella Tillyard, *Aristocrats* (Chatto & Windus, 1994).
4. *A Traitor's Kiss: The Life of Richard Brinsley Sheridan* (Granta Books, 1997).
5. Op cit.
6. Halsband, op cit.

4. KEEPER OF THE PRIVY SEAL (pp. 67–80)

1. In his *Memoirs* Hervey erroneously refers, while writing about this incident, to the 'Act of Succession.'
2. *Caroline the Illustrious*, op cit.

---

5. MANY MOST BEAUTIFUL NUNS (pp. 81–97)

1. Amanda Foreman, *Georgiana: Duchess of Devonshire* (HarperCollins, 1998).
2. *The Dictionary of National Biography.*
3. 16 April 1776.
4. *The Dictionary of National Biography.*
5. Letter to Sir Horace Mann, 24 April 1776.
6. *Journal.*

6. LE COMTE DE BRISTOL, EVÊQUE DE DERRY (pp. 99–114)

1. *Memoirs of James Caufield, Earl of Charlemont,* vol 1.
2. Today the see of Derry is united with Raphoe, and Cloyne no longer exists.
3. *The Mitred Earl: An Eighteenth-Century Eccentric* (Faber and Faber, 1974).
4. Fothergill, ibid.
5. In *Georgiana*, op cit, Lady Erne is incorrectly referred to as Lady Mary Erne. She was never even Lady Mary Hervey, her father not succeeding to his earldom until three years after her marriage to Lord Erne.

7. A STUPENDOUS MONUMENT OF FOLLY (pp. 115–33)
1. Op cit.

8: GEORGIANA'S LOVELY FRIEND (pp. 135–51)

1. Cavendish, Elizabeth, Duchess of Devonshire.
2. Not 'the same age', *Georgiana*, op cit.
3. Amanda Foreman, *Georgiana*, ibid.

9. A DUCHESS AT LAST (pp. 153–67)

1. *The Journals and Letters of Fanny Burney* (Oxford University Press, 1972–84), ed Joyce Hemlow and Althea Douglas.
2. Not 1787 as stated in the *Dictionary of National Biography.*
3. Antony Dales, *Fashionable Brighton* (Country Life, 1947).

10. MAYFAIR PLAYBOY NO. 1 (pp. 169–91)

1. Not in 1820, *Debrett's*, 1995.
2. At one time the archdeaconry of Sudbury was in the diocese of Norwich. It was incorporated in the new diocese of St Edmundsbury & Ipswich in 1914.
3. Joyce Coombs, *George Anthony Denison: The Firebrand* (The Church Literature Association, 1984).
4. *Queen Alexandra* by Georgina Battiscombe (Constable, 1969).
5. In conversation with the author.
6. Mrs Penelope Hatfield in a letter to the author, 20 September 1999.

7. The *Sunday Dispatch*, 9 July 1939.
8. *The Times Magazine*, 19 February 1994.
9. Letter from the Curator, the Sandhurst Collection to the author, 23 February 2000.
10. There is no such location as Seamore Place in London today.

11. IN A LEAGUE OF HIS OWN (pp. 193–213)

1. In conversation with the author.
2. In conversation with the author. On the death of her second husband Somerset de Chair in 1995 the former Lady Juliet Fitzwilliam married Dr Christopher Tadgell.
3. In conversation with the author.
4. In conversation with the author.
5. A second attempt on the life of Archbishop Makarios was made in 1973.
6. Letter of 3 September 1993 from Professor Vincent Powell-Smith to the secretary-general of the Monarchist League.
7. In conversation with the author.
8. Lady Bristol to the author.
9. The author received a letter from Yvonne, Marchioness of Bristol addressed from 15 Chapel Street, Belgravia in April 2000.

12. 'HE'S GOT TO GO' (pp. 215–29)

1. The *Sunday Times*, 17 January.
2. In conversation with the author.
3. The *Daily Mail*, 16 December 1991.
4. Ibid, The *Sunday Times*.
5. The *Independent*, 12 January 1999.
6. The *Sunday Times*, 8 April 1990.
7. Links between the Hervey family and Ickworth were effectively severed for good when in 1998 the 7th marquess of Bristol and his trustees surrendered his freshly negotiated lease on the east wing, thus leaving the National Trust free to make whatever use they wanted of that area of Ickworth House. Although on inheriting the title in 1999 the 8th marquess expressed a desire to retain at least some connection with Ickworth this became an impracticality when the National Trust decided to make arrangements to lease the east wing for conversion into an hotel.
8. The *Sunday Times*, 12 December 1993.
9. John Bristol's stepfather Edward Lambton had died in 1985.
10. Lady Juliet Tadgell in conversation with the author.
11. The 7th marquess of Bristol had a third half-brother, George Lambton, his mother's son by her second husband.
12. Asked by the author.

INDEX